SLAVES IN PARIS

SLAVES IN PARIS

Hidden Lives and Fugitive Histories

MIRANDA SPIELER

Cambridge, Massachusetts
London, England
2025

Copyright © 2025 by the President and Fellows of Harvard College

All rights reserved

Printed in the United States of America

First printing

Library of Congress Cataloging-in-Publication Data

Names: Spieler, Miranda Frances, 1971– author.

Title: Slaves in Paris : hidden lives and fugitive histories / Miranda Spieler.

Description: Cambridge, Massachusetts : Harvard University Press, 2025. | Includes bibliographical references and index.

Identifiers: LCCN 2024045259 (print) | LCCN 2024045260 (ebook) | ISBN 9780674986541 (cloth) | ISBN 9780674300781 (epub) | ISBN 9780674300798 (pdf)

Subjects: LCSH: Enslaved persons—France—Paris—History—19th century. | Slavery—France—Paris—History—19th century. | Slave trade—France—History—19th century. | Enslaved persons—France—Colonies—History—19th century. | Enslaved persons—Emancipation—France—Paris—History—18th century. | Black people—Legal status, laws, etc.—France—History—18th century. | Fugitive slaves—Legal status, laws, etc.—France—History—18th century.

Classification: LCC HT1179.P37 S65 2025 (print) | LCC HT1179.P37 (ebook) | DDC 306.3/62094436109034—dc23/eng/20241209

LC record available at https://lccn.loc.gov/2024045259

LC ebook record available at https://lccn.loc.gov/2024045260

For my mother, Phyllis Friedberg

CONTENTS

	INTRODUCTION	1
1	JEAN	17
2	PAULINE	48
3	LUCIDOR	77
4	JULIEN	103
5	OURIKA	130
	CONCLUSION	164
	Notes	171
	Acknowledgments	229
	Index	233

SLAVES IN PARIS

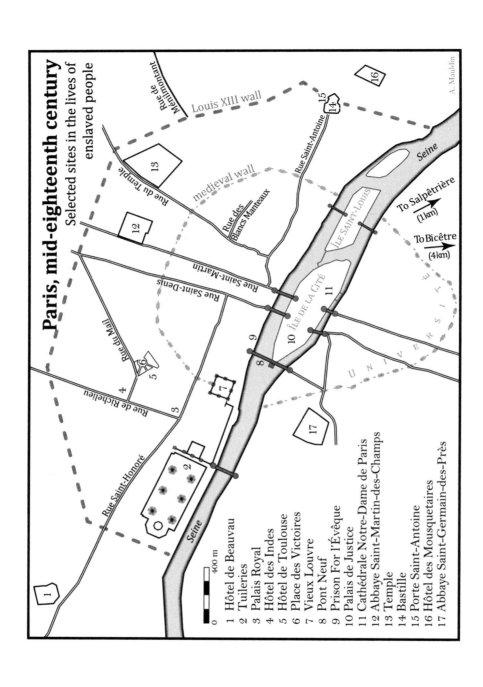

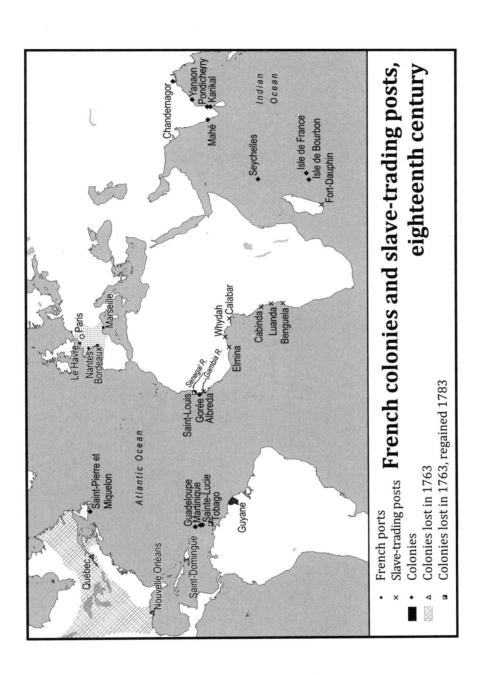

INTRODUCTION

AT MIDNIGHT ON MAY 16, 1753, police agents ransacked rooms near the Abbey Saint-Germain-des-Près in search of teenage slaves named Victor Balthazar and Antoine Lafleur. The pair had just fled Nantes, France's leading slave port, and were known to be making for the capital. The merchants who claimed to own the boys sent descriptions to the Paris police. Balthazar, five feet four inches, broad shouldered with slender calves, was last seen wearing a black curly wig and three-cornered hat. Lafleur, five feet tall, newly recovered from smallpox, could be recognized by his disfigurement. The police captured the boys in a master carpenter's basement. Balthazar and Lafleur wound up in the waterlogged dungeon called For l'Évêque, on the right bank of the Seine.[1] Two weeks later, the Widow Desbrières & Son, a small Parisian banking house, approached the police. On behalf of the boys' masters, the bank arranged for the escort of Balthazar and Lafleur back to Nantes.[2]

This is a book about people in the eighteenth century who tried to get out of slavery in Paris, fell back into slavery while living there, or exited slavery to discover that freedom in Paris remained elusive. Some came as fugitives. Some were living in Paris with their masters at the time they fled. Some put their faith in lawyers, believing that the city's courts would free them. Others pictured themselves as already free—able to live and work unafraid, out in the open—only to learn, on being arrested, that the Crown thought otherwise. At some point in their lives, all of these people imagined Paris as a place where they would be sheltered by an ancient and inflexible law expressed in the phrase *there are no slaves in France.*[3] Many were encouraged to picture Paris as a refuge from slave colonies and slave-trading ports in domestic France—Nantes, but also Bordeaux, Le Havre, La Rochelle,

Saint-Malo. They were eventually disabused of their belief in the freedom legend. Some managed to exit slavery anyway. Yet becoming free, when it happened, depended on friends and circumstance. It was not something that the city could or would bestow. You needed to know that Paris would not protect you.

The idea for this book began with the chance discovery of police files containing stories of slave flight, urban slave hunts, and scenes of capture. Many of those stories unfold in places that are now major tourist destinations—the headquarters of the French Indies Company, for instance, is now the National Library of France. The dungeons where slaves and many others got locked up were demolished long ago. But many of the places in which they lived and to which they fled remain.

This book's five chapters move between the colonial empire and domestic France to depict the many encumbrances people experienced when attempting to become free in the capital. In police files, the intensity of slaves' hope for a new life in the capital is plain from what they did to get there. Take, for instance, the flight in March 1753 of a different Balthazar, nicknamed Favory, who walked from Rennes to Paris. According to his master, a sea captain, he was "eighteen although you would think that he was older because of his height, 5´6, and his vigorous air, and I must warn you, Monsieur, that he is armed with two pocket pistols and a saber." The guns and sword were not the trappings of an outlaw. They were the traveling kit of an intrepid youngster on a 200-mile journey who may have walked alone. Balthazar, though a fugitive, was not running to Paris to hide. He carried a letter of introduction from an unknown source "for a domestic named Babaut who serves the Comtesse d'Auroy, residing with the Marquis de Gouffier behind Saint-Sulpice." The length of Balthazar's journey, like the letter, suggests that he walked with encouragement, believing as others did that Paris would make him free.[4]

Few non-Europeans, enslaved or free, lived in eighteenth-century France. When, in the 1770s, Crown officials discussed expelling people of African and Indian descent, they pictured 4,000 to 5,000 people in a country of 30 million. Of this minuscule fraction of the population, many lived in Paris, where they worked unpaid as domestics in a variety of household roles: as cooks, maîtres d'hôtel, lady's maids, nannies, valets (with wig and hair-styling skills), doormen, postillions, ornamental pages in houses of the great.[5] A reader might perhaps question the importance of a study concerned with so small a group. But the value of a person's life does not lie in its typicality. That person's story does not matter in proportion to how many other people wound up in the same predicament.

Nearly everyone of African or Indian descent in eighteenth-century Paris came there as someone's property. Slaves, however few in number, were not invisible. They were conspicuous within certain social groups and in certain neighborhoods. They circulated among the most powerful people in the country. They lived in the wealthiest parishes. The concentration of brown and black people in those neighborhoods helps to account for the otherwise baffling hysteria of Crown officials about the dangerous ubiquity of "negroes, mulattoes, and other people of color."[6] Nonwhite people lived near the ministers.

The files about slaves that inspired this book all come from a well-known depository of police sources called the Archives of the Bastille. Until 1789 this archive included the files of everyone arrested by special writs of the king in the *généralité de Paris*—a large zone reaching well beyond city limits. When insurrectionary Parisians seized the Bastille fortress, they liberated the dungeon's archive by shredding, burning, and tossing its papers from the ramparts. In the days after the dungeon's capture, people removed those documents by the cartful. Given the scale of that plunder, it seems miraculous that more than 600,000 pieces of paper survived from the original collection. In 1810, workers piled the Bastille papers into an obscure mezzanine of a Parisian library, the Bibliothèque de l'Arsénal. The documents, dubbed "the archive of despotism" in 1789, moldered in this forgotten crypt for thirty years until a kitchen renovation led to their rediscovery.[7]

Special warrants in the Archives of the Bastille were known to officials as *ordres du roi* (orders of the king; royal writs). The public called them *lettres de cachet*. A cachet was a stamp or engraved bit of metal or stone that people wore on watch chains, or as rings, and applied to wax when sealing a letter. The colloquial name for these writs was an allusion to the royal insignia that sealed and authenticated them (or was imagined to). It is expressive of the developing character of the French state that eighteenth-century versions of this writ usually had no seal and bore the signature of handwriting dummies employed by the Crown. A few high officials kept a stock of prefabricated writs, which they signed at the bottom of the page, below the fake Louis signature. There was always a second signature to indicate where the order really came from.[8]

4   SLAVES IN PARIS

Thanks to brilliant work done a generation ago by the historian Arlette Farge and the philosopher Michel Foucault, we know about the widespread use of these extrajudicial writs in eighteenth-century Paris. In response to the complaints of townsmen, the lieutenant-general of police issued these writs on his own authority to round up neighborhood nuisances, disobedient servants, abusive husbands, putatively crazy relatives, and spendthrift children. In the decades before the French Revolution, these writs became a weapon of the Paris police against private forms of misconduct that had nothing to do with the written law.[9]

Lettres de cachet against slaves were written on the same paper, with the same ink, as other royal writs of arrest. Warrants against slaves also came from the same officials, targeted people in the same neighborhoods, and locked people up in the same prisons. Writs ordering the arrest of slaves slaves further resembled other lettres de cachet in punishing behavior the city's laws did not criminalize. Nonetheless, both masters and their allies at court understood the roundup of slaves by lettres de cachet to be different. They pictured these arrests as a conscientious mechanism of legal enforcement. When used against slaves, lettres de cachet preserved the property of masters and reinforced slave owners' authority.

IN THIS STUDY I build on the work of historians who began, in the 1990s, to unearth the history of people of color in Old Regime France. My book owes much to those early works and could not have been written without them. Nonetheless, this study differs from previous works in method, choice of sources, and basic argument. The most essential difference lies in my depiction of the capital as an imperial city where freedom was often fragile, perilously uncertain, and reversible.[10]

In *"There Are No Slaves In France,"* a now-classic work, Sue Peabody contends that enslaved people systematically became free within the jurisdiction of the Parlement of Paris (the country's most powerful court) for the whole of the eighteenth century. Her book chronicles the rise of the freedom maxim during the final decades of the Old Regime alongside, and in resistance to, racist practices that developed simultaneously. Her book ends with an account of late eighteenth-century laws, which excluded "blacks, mulattoes, and other free people of color" from entering the kingdom (1777), required the registration of all nonwhites in Paris (1777), and forbade mixed marriages (1778). Notwithstanding those laws, however, Peabody suggests, a "liberal notion of the individual," coupled with Christian morality, triumphed over racism. Relying on legal archives, she finds that "the Parlement of Paris and the Admiralty Court of France refused to confiscate slaves and instead freed them unconditionally."[11]

Many tales of liberation in Peabody's book were not the judicial triumphs she suggests. Such was the case of four domestics, led by an African housekeeper called Corinne, in 1755–1756. Notwithstanding the success of their suits, chronicled by Peabody, all four women were snatched from their mistress's house, and from nearby hiding places, and whisked to a prison in the port of Le Havre. They remained there for more than a year until being forcibly returned to Saint-Domingue.[12] The same thing probably befell a man called Jacques Médor, who, according to Peabody, "successfully achieved his freedom, as did all slaves who sued through the Paris Admiralty Court." Do we know this? His master, Goupil de Fontenay, was a slave-trading agent in Senegal who came to France when the British captured the colony. When Médor sued for liberty, Goupil obtained a lettre de cachet from the navy ordering his arrest. The hunt for Médor began after the Admiralty pronounced him (provisionally) free.[13]

Even people who did manage to become free, despite tenacious opposition from masters, endured prolonged detention in a Parisian dungeon following arrest by lettre de cachet. So it was for Boucaux (1738), the first man to win his freedom in Paris on the grounds that *there are no slaves in France.* During his freedom suit, Boucaux moldered in various dungeons, eventually quitting the Grand Châtelet prison with the stipulation, by order of the king, that he never again set foot in Paris.[14] The extrajudicial nature of this writ and its content (exile from Paris) do not support Peabody's claim about the efficacy of the freedom principle, or her belief in the protective power of Parisian courts. What of the famed freedom case of 1758–1759 involving a South Asian teenager called Francisque? When the boy fled, fearing resale in the Americas, his master obtained a lettre de cachet for his arrest in Paris. Francisque landed in the prison of Bicêtre. In late February 1758, he was transferred to another dungeon: the Conciergerie. Notwithstanding a court order in March 1758 for the boy's release, his new jailer kept him locked up anyway and only capitulated (in May) when threatened with prison himself. After three or four months of captivity, Francisque went free—but not

6 SLAVES IN PARIS

because of the maxim *there are no slaves in France*. Omer Joly de Fleury, avocat-general of the Paris Parlement, insisted that the boy be freed on racial and physiognomic grounds. His legal defense of Francisque hinged on his non-resemblance to "the negroes of Africa" whose faces "particularly destined them for slavery." Joly de Fleury also claimed that legislation about slaves in France applied only to "slaves from America." While defending Francisque's right to liberty, Joly de Fleury insisted that the freedom maxim did not apply to slaves of African descent.[15]

People who claimed to be free before getting to Paris, and others who thought the city's courts had freed them, became targets of slave hunts. The navy issued lettres de cachet at the demand of slave owners—or, rather, of people claiming to be slave owners. In July 1763 a veteran named Jean-Baptiste, born in Guadeloupe, told the court he had been captured as a free man while fighting to defend Martinique. He later escaped from England "through cunning, along with ten Frenchmen." Three years after the Admiralty confirmed Jean-Baptiste's freedom, a merchant in Martinique, Sieur de la Prise-Héligon, claimed him as a slave. Héligon asked the navy to arrange for Jean-Baptiste's forcible return to the colony. In November 1766 Jean-Baptiste was arrested in Paris, imprisoned in the Abbey Saint-Germain, and whisked to Le Havre.[16] Earlier that same year, a police inspector and plainclothes "men in black" dragged Ambroise Lucas, a Martinican doorman, from an elegant townhouse on Paris's Rue de Seine. He languished in the Abbey Saint-Germain for four months until embarking for Saint-Domingue as the slave of a new master. At the time of his kidnapping, Ambroise Lucas had papers. The Admiralty granted him liberty at a preliminary hearing on the grounds that "all slaves arriving in France are free."[17]

Slaves in Paris who petitioned the Admiralty became free so long as their masters assented to their manumission, encouraged it, or were otherwise unable to object. Petitioners included favorite domestics who kept the same jobs after obtaining formal liberty. Such was the case of Luce, a lady's maid and doyenne of the Parisian black community, who became free yet remained in the household of the Vicomtesse de Castellane, a Creole from Saint-Domingue, who later bequeathed her an annuity.[18] Yet, as we have seen for Jacques Médor and Ambroise Lucas, apparently uncontested petitions, resulting in provisional judgments of freedom, did not hold up when one's master disagreed.

The arrest of freedom-seeking plaintiffs at the demand of masters was routine, as lawyers and administrators acknowledged. In 1777 Antoine de Sartine, minister of the navy and a former lieutenant-general of police in Paris, described the use of royal writs against slaves as a seasoned practice. "The old king [Louis XV] always prevented those judgments or interfered with their effect by causing orders (of the king) to be dispatched to the secretary of state charged with the department of the navy so as to arrest and return to the colonies negroes who fled or demanded their liberty." Though the Paris Parlement—the only French court to do so—had refused to enact laws relating to slaves on domestic soil, Sartine explained, the king wished to avoid "depriving masters of a property that is recognized by the state itself, and by the laws governing your majesty's colonies."[19]

Bouncing judicial records against other sources reveals that the Crown ordered the arrest of slaves before, during, and after their freedom suits. At least 31 of the 125 lettres de cachet I have found were intended to thwart legal proceedings or issued in defiance of freedom judgments. In their study of lettres de cachet, Farge and Foucault note the spottiness of records after 1770 in the Archives of the Bastille.[20] Given the archive problem, and the randomness with which I discovered most slave arrests, it seems reasonable to suppose that there were more instances of judicial interference, and more lettres de cachet generally.[21]

One finds clues about slave arrests inside the same documents that scholars have used to depict Paris as a haven of liberty. The records of the Paris Court of Admiralty mention the extrajudicial capture and imprisonment of enslaved plaintiffs. Those clues have, alas, been ignored, treated as "confusion," or cited as evidence of a defunct practice, overtaken by the freedom maxim.[22] Admiralty documents about the ruin of a black veteran (1777–1778) show what sort of horrors lie strewn through what historians have read as an archive of freedom. In 1778 a former musician in the French Guards called Gratia registered with the Admiralty in Paris. That same year a colonist from Saint-Domingue denounced the imposture of his slave Andronique, who was said to be impersonating a free man under the name Gratia in the capital. The alleged owner of Andronique mentioned a stomach brand (COURCEL) by which to identify the fugitive. He wanted Andronique sent back to Saint-Domingue and put in the hands of a slave retailer. The last piece of this story is a letter by Gratia, written in phonetic French. In July 1778 he appealed for help while locked up in a prison in Le Havre. Gratia

8 **SLAVES IN PARIS**

said that naval officials in the port considered his freedom papers—issued in Paris—to be invalid. He had been living in France for twenty years. Gratia requested a copy of "a freedom paper signed by the Maréchal de Bellisle" (former minister of war). This was probably a military discharge paper. Yet service in the armed forces did not trump the proprietary claims of masters, nor could soldiering erase the stigmata on this man's torso. Given his imprisonment at the time of writing this letter, it seems likely, following the general pattern, that Gratia was returned as a slave to Saint-Domingue.[23]

The archives of the Admiralty serve as the foundation for all previous works about people of color in Paris. Those sources do not accurately depict the lives of black and brown people in the city. Nor can they tell us how many slaves, former slaves, or freeborn people of color lived there.[24] In this book, the main figure in Chapter 1, Jean, does not appear in the records of the Admiralty, nor do several other people I mention in that chapter, who all became the objects of slave hunts. The main characters of Chapters 2 and 3 appear in those records in distorted ways. André Lucidor, the protagonist of Chapter 3, entered that archive, for the first time, thirty years after arriving in the capital as a slave. Secondary characters in Chapter 3 are entirely missing from Admiralty sources, including the ex-drummer Louis Lircot, who taught dueling in the army, and the maimed bugler François Bourval, who died in the Hôtel des Invalides, a refuge for injured soldiers. Julien Baudelle, of Chapter 4, is missing from surviving Admiralty records, port records, and the Archives of the Bastille. Because of the 1777 decree banning "negroes, mulattoes, and other people of color" from entering France, his owner—who was also his aunt—gave him a false name and passed him off to port authorities as a white orphan. None of the black people discussed in Chapter 5 appears in the archives of the Admiralty, including the title figure, a Senegalese girl named Ourika. On the periphery of Chapter 5 is Joseph Theleman, whom I discovered while trawling through police case files. In 1774, when Theleman reported the theft of his magnificent silver-trimmed scarlet servant uniform, a police commissioner described him as "the negro of the Chevalier de Boufflers."[25] Another background figure from Chapter 5, the teenage Crispin Loff, is not in Admiralty or surviving police archives. I learned of his arrest and deportation while reading the personal papers of Armand Kersaint, a noted revolutionary. The Kersaint archive includes a scrap of paper mentioning payment to a policeman for Crispin's arrest and a letter from Kersaint's plantation manager about his forced removal to Martinique.[26]

The story of Pauline, in Chapter 2, reveals just how much judicial records conceal and distort about the struggle for freedom in Paris. According to Pauline's police file, she was imprisoned as a prostitute at her master's demand (after she swore at him); she went into hiding for months during a police hunt—coinciding with her freedom trial; and she exited slavery when a libertine society bachelor bought her from her master. She soon absconded from Paris, stowing away on a ship bound for Mauritius. Her life looks quite different in the records of the Paris Court of Admiralty, of course. There, on fleeing her master's house, she is rescued by Parisian justice. In Admiralty documents, she triumphs without discomfort or incident. By viewing Pauline's life through those sources, it becomes easy to picture her remaining in Paris for the rest of her life, at home in the city that freed her.[27]

The invalidity of the freedom principle opens the question of what it was really like in Paris for people who vainly sought liberty there or for others who exited bondage only to stumble on unforeseen impediments to free life in the city. Setting aside the freedom legend also makes room for a new narrative of the capital. If Paris was not a judicial asylum for enslaved people, how should we instead describe the city in legal terms? The biographical structure of this book allows a case-by-case approach to these questions. In general, however, the city was a site of dangerous allurement and precarious liberation for slaves. It was also a place of resistance, complicity, fugitive solidarity, and quite a few benevolent rescue efforts by inhabitants and sojourners in the capital. Paris was a theater of contested legal meaning, institutional conflict, and unwritten rules. The very lack of consensus about slave status, and about how one became free there, patterned the lives of just about all people of color in the city.

As for whether colonial law applied to the capital, and how far it applied there, the Crown never varied in its stance on this question. From the mid-eighteenth century to the Revolution, royal administrators did not explicitly sanction or enable the violent punishments that befell slaves in the colonies either at the whims of their owners or as stipulated by colonial law. By contrast, the Crown proved unswerving in its efforts to give force to the law that defined colonial property. Officials in the navy and police did everything to ensure, in defiance of the city's courts, that a slave in the colonies remained a slave in Paris. After being arrested, imprisoned, and forcibly removed overseas, an enslaved person became subject to forms of violence that were impossible in the capital.

It is impossible to understand Paris as a fractious world of flight, capture, concealment, and legal contestation without paying close attention to the people who claimed to own slaves or freed them. There is a staggering imbalance, well known to historians of plantation societies, between the number of sources about individual masters and those about individual enslaved people. To learn about a specific slave owner, the researcher can often find shelves of archive boxes; for details about a specific slave, we are lucky, inside that vast archive, to find jottings on a small slip of paper, or a haberdasher's receipt (as in the case of Crispin, the vanished Martinican, in the Kersaint archive). Indirectly, however, the archives of the master class are rich sources of information about the material, spatial, and social context of the lives of slaves in Paris. We could not understand master-slave relations in Paris or see the city as a hierarchical, disputatious space of life without studying its elites.[28]

Slaves and masters in Paris need to be understood in light of where they used to live and who they were there. Enslaved people who appear in this book came to the capital from West Africa, the French Antilles, and the Mascarene Islands of Mauritius and Réunion, near Madagascar. Some were orphans of the slave trade and child survivors of the Middle Passage. Place-related memories and connections to the wider world were essential to their experiences of the city.[29] Decoding their stories has required a lot of imaginative (and real) back-and-forth between former French colonies and Paris, the city where I live. I use Paris-based notarial documents and sources relating to the navy, Admiralty, police, army, and ecclesiastical legal jurisdictions. I draw on local archives in Réunion, Martinique, and Mauritius. I rely on colonial documents, housed in Aix-en-Provence, relating to Senegal, Martinique, French Guiana, and Saint-Domingue. I have also incorporated family papers conserved in Paris and elsewhere in France.

OF THE MANY QUIET perversities of archival research, the most glaring occurs when a historian goes looking for a vulnerable person whose physical safety or very life depended on remaining invisible to the authorities—on not being in those documents. Ideally, the historian's reward after a few hours of diligence in the police archives will be a report about the fugitive. The most valuable arrest report will describe the manner of a person's capture, specify the location, and indicate the owner or main tenant of that building. It will name other people in the room. It will give the hour of the raid—usually at night. Through the immediacy of such details, hunted people become newly present and palpable to the historian at the very moment they vanished from the lives of friends and relatives. There is a disturbing convergence between the inspector who conducts the raid and the historian who is, after all, tracking the same suspect.

In police archives, silence can mean safety. For fugitives, being spotted and mentioned is the problem. Silence has a different meaning in the archives of slave societies. Saidiya Hartman asks, "How does one recuperate lives entangled with and impossible to differentiate from the terrible utterances that condemned them to death, the account books that identified them as units of value, the invoices that claimed them as property?" To remedy the "silence of the archive" she proposes to reconstruct enslaved lives by "narrating counter-histories of slavery" while respecting "the limits of what cannot be known."[30] The silence of which she writes is haunting because of the sheer abundance of written records about slaves. The conceptual architecture of those sources, like their vocabulary, comes from the master class. In reading those documents, we topple into a world of buying, selling, gifting, inheriting, bickering over, and attaching exchange value to humans. People become voiceless in the archive of slavery because of their legal status as killable nonpersons and their economic function as salable tools. As nonpersons, they could not make wills, testify, own anything, marry freely, have surnames or (usually) claim lineages the law would acknowledge. If unbaptized, they remained nameless to their enslavers. The kind of slave names one finds in testaments and sale documents are often utilitarian designations akin to object tags. The people beneath these names called themselves and each other something else.

The documentary record of French colonial slavery is particularly voiceless for several reasons. First, France lacked a powerful abolitionist movement. In consequence, there are no autobiographies by former slaves in the French language from the seventeenth, eighteenth, or nineteenth century.[31] Second, the French style of colonial rule ensured that there

12 SLAVES IN PARIS

would be few nonmilitary institutions in the overseas empire. A branch of the French military—the navy—governed nearly all French colonies during the Old Regime, to predictable effect: there were no incorporated towns or provincial assemblies; there was neither an independent judiciary nor a powerful clergy to counterbalance the navy's bureaucracy. For the historian, this dearth of colonial institutions, together with the lack of Francophone slave narratives, means there are comparatively few places to look for knowledge about enslaved people who lived in French colonies.[32]

Because of the dehumanizing content and noisy silence of colonial documents, slaves who lived on European soil matter more than their numbers would suggest. Masters and officials controlled the narrative about slaves in the overseas empire. In Paris, by contrast, enslaved people moved around a town with a flourishing press, a high level of literacy, extensive spying networks, nosy neighbors, and an array of overlapping legal authorities. Their mobility in the city helped to produce written counternarratives, in which Parisians challenged the claims and authority of slave owners (with patchy success). Slaves and freed people also figure in correspondence, memoirs, and financial deeds that link them to well-known figures in the Enlightenment.

I have adopted a biographical approach to the history of slaves in Paris. Nonetheless, much remains unknown and is probably unknowable about the people who stand at the center of this study. I spent years sifting for clues. I have since glued those pieces into shapes that are, despite my best efforts, still marred by seams and holes. Traditional biographies explore people's interior lives and depend on sources like letters and journals—textual emanations of the self.[33] For a host of obvious reasons, we lack documents of this sort by enslaved people. I have chosen not to fill those gaps. I do not speculate about my subjects' thoughts and feelings. Wary of ventriloquism, I leave the task of imagining who they really were to my readers.

In *D'Alembert's Dream* (1769), a dialogue by Denis Diderot, the titular philosopher urges friends to "drop your idea of essences" and babbles about "a whole province populated by the fragments of one individual."[34] Places of this sort are the precinct of scholars who do archival work. All historians to some degree inhabit the crumbled worlds they study and grow accustomed to seeing the world in pieces. When researching the lives of enslaved people, even on metropolitan soil, the problem goes beyond fragmentation.

INTRODUCTION   13

In Diderot's text, all those scattered shards of a single man would—if we could gather and merge them—add up to a whole being. By contrast, the documentary record of enslaved people's lives can, at best, yield a shattered version of reality—a picture of the human subject that is irremediably broken and full of missing parts.

Finding the recovery of speech and affect all but impossible, I have sought to understand the lives of slaves in Paris by another method. I look at their actions and at things they touched, places they visited, and people they knew. I examine the institutions and laws they bumped up against. Forgoing the allure of inwardness out of necessity, I embrace contiguity.

Exploring the contiguous worlds of silent and elusive subjects is a pragmatic way of coping with gaps in the historical record. From a structural point of view, this descriptive method can be understood as a variant of the rhetorical trope called metonymy. In poetry and prose, writers use metonymy to intensify a particular image by refusing to speak its name. In d'Alembert and Diderot's *Encyclopédie* (1751–1772), the entry for metonymy quotes a line from Ovid's *Metamorphosis:* "Mount Pelion has no shadow." Here, shadow, "which is the effect of trees, is taken here for the trees themselves." (Mount Pelion has no shadow because there are no trees to cast them.) Metonymy works through the suppression of a word and its replacement by an adjacent one. As with Ovid's missing tree, metonymy is about unnaming. It intermingles silence and allusive suggestion.

Scholars who write about slaves confront lacunae in the historical record that are most emphatically not of their own choosing. The involuntary nature of those gaps, and the problem of filling them, brings to mind a famous essay by the linguist Roman Jakobson about aphasia. Jakobson describes metonymy as arising from the damaged linguistic practices of people who cannot call up the right word. Aphasics (of certain kinds) replace irretrievable words with associated ones, such as "spyglass for microscope or fire for gaslight."[35]

The words of this book's five protagonists rarely crop up in historical documents. As a consequence of social injustice, this pathology of the written record cannot be fixed. It can be managed, somewhat, by locating people carefully in space and reconstructing their material, social, legal, and institutional surroundings.[36] Slaves who lived in Paris, or fled there, moved between dissonant spaces of experience that are striking (to us, if not to them) for their varied mixture. They served and also ran away from bankers,

14 SLAVES IN PARIS

nobles, colonial sojourners, sugar millionaires. They went in and out of the army. They got locked up with deserters and vagabonds. They quarreled with neighbors. They hid in the apartments of seamstresses, innkeepers, street-walkers, and artisans. They moved between mansions, garrets, taverns, fairs, convents, barracks, dungeons, and palaces. Each space they moved through, sometimes as fugitives, offers a new context for understanding who they were. Each place they went in Paris also supplies an opportunity for re-thinking the city in light of their experience.

SLAVES IN PARIS are guides who reveal hidden worlds of connected-ness. Nearly all Parisian households that included an enslaved or formerly enslaved domestic had links to overseas colonies or the slave trade. Those links came to the surface whenever I tried to account for the presence of a slave in a Parisian home. Somewhere else in that house were inventories, wills, military service records, love letters to people with colonial appoint-ments, Indies Company deeds, sale and marriage contracts listing slaves on colonial estates. Those households thereby became recognizable points in a complex network of bankers and slave traders, ministers, colonial heiresses, soldiers, sea captains, and bureaucrats spread across the world.

Following slaves into, around, and out of Paris makes the city's ties to the colonial empire newly visible. Those itinerant experiences reveal the transformation of Paris into a new kind of city. Did it become an imperial capital? The word *empire,* in French or English, refers to sovereign dominion and hence does not in itself have anything to do with slavery or overseas territory. No one in the eighteenth century referred to French colonial pos-sessions, in a collective sense, as the French Empire. Moreover, as a center of national power, consumerist luxury, and Enlightenment culture, Paris bore no resemblance to provincial Atlantic ports specializing in slaving and colonial commerce. It was unlike any single colonial city. But it was wired to all these places and became more so as the century wore on. Global power radiated from the capital. The French Company of the Indies had its head-quarters there. The navy's Bureau of Colonies, which governed most of the overseas empire, remained in Paris until 1762, when it moved thirty kilo-meters away to a larger building at Versailles. Paris was the center of banking in the kingdom. Major investors in the slave trade lived there. The upper tier of the nobility, who monopolized the highest military appointments, moved between Paris, Versailles, and overseas postings, as did the plantation heiresses they married. Lawyers moved back and forth between Paris and French slave colonies, especially Saint-Domingue. Families with colonial connections, who had hitherto lived elsewhere in France, moved to the capital in the eighteenth century to spend, marry, and contend for influence.[37]

Changes to eighteenth-century Paris need to be pictured in light of France's unusual imperial story. France came late to the Atlantic slave trade. Sugar plantations developed later in French colonies than in Brazil or in the British and Dutch West Indies. The French colonial empire also followed a different development pattern. French plantations underwent explosive growth during a narrow band of time (ca. 1720–1790), and the French slave trade grew apace.[38] The astonishingly rapid growth of French plantation societies—especially Saint-Domingue—during the final decades of the Old Regime changed the relationship between the kingdom and the world. By the mid-century, the re-export of French colonial products—sugar, but also coffee and indigo—accounted for half of all French exports.[39]

A breakneck speed of colonial development, a ballooning slave trade, and constant imperial war changed metropolitan France. Scholarly interest in the relationship between overseas slave societies and domestic France has flowered in recent years, inspiring rich studies of French Atlantic ports, including Nantes, Bordeaux, La Rochelle, and Le Havre. The remaking of France by chattel slavery remains, however, a largely provincial tale, relegated to the coastal margins of the country and outside the acknowledged center of political power.[40] To the degree that historians trace connections between Paris and the colonial empire, they do so by approaching the city as a site for the production of new kinds of global knowledge.[41] Even the late Marcel Dorigny, a leading scholar of French slavery, wrote about the colonial dimension of Old Regime Paris without reference to the presence in the city of slaves, slave owners, slave-trading merchants, and slave ship investors.[42]

Through the accretion of transoceanic capital, power, and knowledge, eighteenth-century Paris did, over time, become an imperial capital. That development did not, however, require residents of the city to embrace a common understanding of what the French Empire meant (or even to use the word *empire*).[43] The anthropologist Fredrik Barth emphasizes the way disparate individual stories meet to form what becomes a shared social

reality. That reality is not a holistic organism but a chaotic assemblage—
"a multiplicity of partial and interfering patterns, asserting themselves to
vary in degrees in various fields and localities." What becomes a common
culture takes shape "at variance with the intentions of the individual actors."[44] Imperial Paris took shape as Barth describes—by agglomeration
and confluence. It was a mutually constituted social montage. Energized by
the slave trade and sugar, it developed out of the convergence of disparate
life paths and their entanglement.

Paris became an imperial capital through the travels of soldiers, naval
officers, lawyers, and colonial bureaucrats; through the enmeshing of personal and institutional ties to Africa, the Americas, and the Mascarenes;
through the transactions of financiers; and through the experiences of people
of color from Africa and the colonies who held an ambiguous status, and
moved between slavery and freedom—in both directions—while they sojourned there.[45]

Chapter 1

JEAN

IN MAY 1752 the minister of the navy, Antoine de Rouillé, wrote to the governor of Saint-Domingue about the new problem of slaves in France. Slaves were "multiplying every day, more and more, in almost all the towns of the kingdom."[1] The minister's disquiet followed a controversy that centered on an African man, age 22, whom I shall call Jean, though he also appears under other names (Charles-Auguste and Adonis) in the police archives. He was enslaved to Guy Coustard, a sugar planter in Saint-Domingue. Jean had the Coustard family's monogram (CO) branded on his left breast.

An Admiralty document from La Rochelle dated June 30, 1751, describes Jean as a *mina* slave. The late Gwendolyn Midlo Hall, a renowned historian of ethnicity in French Louisiana, believed that the term *mina* in eighteenth-century sources referred to Gbe-speaking people who immigrated from the Gold Coast to Little Popo (Aneho in modern-day Togo). The Africanist Robin Law, disputing her account, suggests that *mina* originally designated slaves from the Costa da Mina (Coast of the Mine), a broad area spanning modern-day Ivory Coast and Ghana, and later came to include diasporic groups from that region who moved east of the Volta River to places including Little Popo and Allada (modern-day Benin).[2]

Documents about Jean's brief sojourn in France come from two slender files at the Bastille Archives, which contain letters to the lieutenant-general of police from the minister of the navy and from Jean's would-be benefactor, the Dowager Princess of Nassau-Siegen, born Charlotte de Mailly de Nesle, who tried and failed to protect Jean from Coustard.[3] Her staff and Coustard lodged in the same hotel, near the Luxembourg Palace. Through her servants, she learned of Jean's physical abuse and despair.

From Mailly de Nesle we learn that Jean arrived in Paris during the spring of 1751 and fled from the city twice. On both occasions he tried to escape by joining the army. In March 1752 the French constabulary arrested him in Sedan, a frontier garrison town, and escorted him back to Paris in chains. He wound up in the dungeon of For l'Évêque, a former ecclesiastical prison. Many of the other inmates at that time were soldiers. Unlike Jean, who had hoped to become free by joining the army, those men were draftees, who had sought freedom from the army through desertion. On April 8, someone other than Coustard claimed Jean from prison. Port records in La Rochelle note that a slave named Jean sailed for Saint-Domingue in July.[4]

The capture and imprisonment of Jean resulted from an order of the king, popularly known as a lettre de cachet. Masters paid a fee to police for these roundups and paid for the maintenance of their slaves in prison. In March 1752, Jean-Jacques Coustard, an elderly Parisian judge, lobbied the Crown to arrest Jean by royal writ. The judge did not own slaves himself and had probably never set foot in the colonies. He came from a clan of Angevine drapers who bought their way into the Paris legal establishment in the seventeenth century. The Paris Coustards abandoned trade for the law, to become a judging dynasty, just as a more intrepid, piratical sprig of the family settled in Saint-Domingue.[5] The judge and Guy Coustard, Jean's master, were cousins, not brothers. The capture of Jean resulted from the maneuvering of Crown officials to oblige both a sugar magnate and a member of the city's judicial elite.[6]

Jean's failed bid for liberty offers a glimpse of how elusive freedom became for many slaves in Paris after the mid-eighteenth century. His removal from the army and deportation back to Saint-Domingue resulted from new policing practices that crystallized around the time of his brief stay in France. Despite fleeing Paris, Jean became one of the first victims of an emerging system, based in France's capital, by which slave owners, or their proxies, caused freedom-seeking domestics to disappear. Jean's story also reveals the remarkable abuse that some enslaved domestics continued

JEAN   19

to experience at the hand of colonial masters during sojourns in France, which made flight a life-saving necessity.

ACCORDING TO Charlotte de Mailly de Nesle, Jean traveled from La Rochelle to Paris on a post horse in spring 1751, which meant he galloped there, stopping at relay stations to switch horses. Traveling northeast from the coast, he crossed a distance of more than 300 miles. Coustard did not give him money for food. Jean survived the trip on scraps he received as alms from innkeepers. Lacking "tall boots, short boots, or even gaiters," he reached the city with sores all over his legs and wounds on his body.[7]

Jean was part of a story about opulent migration. Until the 1750s, planters and other colonists tended, on return to France, to cluster around port cities—especially Nantes, but also Le Havre, La Rochelle, and Bordeaux. Paris became a new destination for sugar moguls and their families at the mid-century. A spike in the slave trade in the years after 1720 enabled the flourishing of French slave plantations during the two decades that preceded the War of the Austrian Succession (1740–1748). The daughters of magnates from Saint-Domingue began to intermarry with the peerage. They took up residence in the capital as travel to and from the colonies resumed.

Léogane was one of the first places that French people colonized on the island of Hispaniola. When early settlers arrived, they found Indian and Spanish ruins. Early colonists of Saint-Domingue pictured themselves as new occupants of a glorious ancient kingdom. They called Louis XIV the king of France, Navarre, "and Léogane."[8] The Coustard family began there. The allure of Léogane for the first generation of French planters derived from the fertility of the earth and the nearness of the sea. The plain of Léogane, where early plantations clustered, was encircled by mountains and criss-crossed by rivers that emptied into the bay. After the rapid depletion of this once-fertile soil, the Coustards and other great fortunes of the island would migrate to the nearby plain of Cul de Sac. Early colonists saw that region, too, as lying within the ancient kingdom of Léogane.[9]

Guy Coustard's trip to Paris overlapped with the wedding of two other young planters from Léogane in the capital. The 1751 marriage of Jean-Baptiste Merger and Marie-Françoise Boisgautier Desperrières makes it

20 SLAVES IN PARIS

possible to picture not only the clustering of planters in the capital but also their ascent to the pinnacle of Parisian society. Signers of the Merger-Desperrières marriage contract included Georges-Julie, the Vicomte de Talleyrand-Périgord, and his wife, Catherine Olive de la Salle, who were "maternal uncle and aunt" of the groom. Cousins of the bride included Louis-Paul, the Marquis de Brancas, and his wife, Marie-Anne Renée Jacqueline Grandhomme de Gizieux; the Maréchal Philippe-Henri de Ségur, future minister of war, and his wife, Louise-Anne-Madeleine de Vernon de Beauval, were also cousins of the bride. All three young noblemen were newly wedded to heiresses from western Saint-Domingue, beginning with Talleyrand-Périgord (1746), followed by Brancas (1747) and Ségur (1749).[10]

In the published memoirs of Louis-Philippe de Ségur, son of the Maréchal and his Creole wife, the family slave plantation appears in the book's second sentence. "She had a property that yielded 120,000 livres in annuities, which procured to my father the capacity to live at court and in the army in a manner befitting his birth, rank, the services of his father and his own."[11] The thousands of slaves who belonged to celebrants at the Merger-Desperrières wedding were enablers of high society. Invisible in the streets of the capital, slaves toiling elsewhere still marked the city and hence need to be accorded a kind of presence in eighteenth-century Paris. It was they who staged the commingling of nobles and Creoles at the Merger wedding and made the Merger-Desperrières house on Paris's Rue de Richelieu into a beacon for socialites. According to the playboy Jean-Nicolas Dufort de Cheverny, who presented ambassadors at court, "We saw the best people there," including the Ségurs. "I consecrated all my evenings to this charming society" he wrote.[12] The Mergers lived next door to another plantation owner, called Madame le Gentil, née Fournier de Varennes, whose son married into the family of Louis-Philippe Rigaud de Vaudreuil, naval commander at Rochefort, whose brothers were Pierre, governor of Louisiana (1742–1753) and later Canada (1755–1760); and Joseph, the Marquis de Vaudreuil, lieutenant du roi and governor of Saint Domingue (1753–1757). The Marquis moved back and forth between the colony and Paris because of his "horribly dilapidated health."[13] His wife, née Guyot de Lamirande, a Creole from Saint-Domingue, was in Paris in September 1751 and probably attended the Merger wedding.

There is no doorway to mark the place where you pass from Paris, an informal haven of liberty, into Paris, a place with close ties to transatlantic slavery. That was a transformational process, not a matter of stepping from one place into another, and it would be easy to quibble over the pace and signs of change. It might still be useful, for the sake of clarity, to picture a threshold. The Merger wedding might serve as one. We might also picture this new Paris in spatial terms with the Rue de Richelieu, where the Merger family resided, as its center.

In Louis-Sébastien Mercier's comedy, *L'habitant de la Guadeloupe* (1782), the main character lives "on the Rue de Richelieu, in a magnificent mansion."[14] This was a well-known neighborhood for planters, slave traders, and financiers with links to the colonial empire. The celebrated art patron and financier Pierre Crozat, who worked conjointly with his brother Antoine (a founder of the Guinea Company), lived in a mansion on the Rue de Richelieu.[15] The French Company of the Indies had its headquarters—the Hôtel de la Compagnie des Indes—in the block-sized Hôtel Tubeuf, on the Rue des Petits Champs, abutting the Rue de Richelieu.[16] (The word *hôtel* in eighteenth-century France was usually a term for magnificent urban residences.) Its directors lived inside the company's vast compound and nearby. The financier Pâris de Montmartel owned a townhouse next to the Compagnie des Indes. He and the Nantes slave trader Antoine Walsh bankrolled the Angola Company—as did several other Parisian bankers, including Michau de Montaran, a royal commissioner at the Company of the Indies.[17] Gabriel Michel, a director at the Company of the Indies, who was also a Nantes slave trader (he armed forty-two slave voyages), lived in the company's headquarters at the time of the Merger wedding. A few weeks earlier, steps from the Indies Company, Michel paid an installment to the Marquise de Vaudreuil for the purchase of several plantations in Saint-Domingue, which he acquired jointly with slave traders Antoine Walsh and Nicolas Luker. The area around the Rue de Richelieu was not just a swath of earth where people with distant colonial connections liked to gather. It was a place for transacting and speculating in slaves and sugar.[18]

The rising importance of the slave trade, and of colonial slave plantations, to Parisian social and economic life led the city's elites to adopt a new attitude toward people of African and South Asian descent, whom they increasingly viewed as potentially saleable belongings. Resplendent sojourners from Saint-Domingue played a role in diffusing new racial concepts in Paris, but their influence should not be overstated. Ideas of race did not waft into the capital as a foreign essence. By 1750, slave plantations and the slave trade out

22   SLAVES IN PARIS

of East and West Africa had become economically vital to Parisian institutions, including the Company of the Indies, which enjoyed direct support from the Crown and strong ties to Parisian high finance. There was nothing distantly managerial about the activities of Paris-based officials in the Africa trade. Consider this document from 1750, written one year before Jean arrived in Paris. Signed by all directors of the Company of the Indies, it sets forth a new scale of value for slave sales in Senegal.

RÉGULATION DES NOIRS, NÉGRESSES, NÉGRILLONS ET NÉGRITTES

21. Every negro between 14 and 40 will be reputed as one Indian piece so long as he has none of the defects indicated below.
22. One *négrillon* (boy) of 14 equals one Indian piece.
23. Four *négrillons* (boys) or *négrittes* (girls) from the age of 8 to 13 equal three Indian pieces.
24. Six *négrillons* (boys) or *négrittes* (girls) from the age of 4 to the age of 8 equal three Indian pieces.
25. Four *négrillons* (boys) or *négrittes* (girls) who are 4 years of age or younger equal one Indian piece so long as they are not nursing.
26. One negress who is between 14 and 35 years of age equals one Indian piece.
27. One negress who is age 13 and 14 equals one Indian piece.
28. Men between 40 and 50 years of age, and women between 35 and 40 years of age, equal one half Indian piece and cannot compose more than 3 percent of the cargo.
29. All nursing children will follow their mothers and not be counted.
30. All negroes, negresses, *négrillons* (boys), and *négrittes* (girls) will be considered valid Indian pieces so long as they are not epileptic, maimed, blind, or suffering from formal disease.
31. Some missing teeth, and negroes with enlarged testicles who do not have hernias, cannot be refused by captains and surgeons, or excepted from the above regulation.
32. Negroes with one bad eye who are not over 30 years, others of the same age who are missing one or two fingers, how-

ever robust their bodies, will only be counted as one-half an Indian piece.

33. A negro who is lacking two toes will be estimated as two-thirds of a piece; a negress in the same case will be evaluated similarly; and *négrillons* (boys) and *négrittes* (girls) by the same proportion.[19]

To pin down the novelty of this document requires that we identify what is not new. At direct points of sale among slave buyers in Africa or the Americas, this meticulously commodified view of the human body was familiar. It was normal for company agents to haggle over people with missing toes and enlarged testicles. There is also nothing new about the term *pièce d'Inde* (Indian piece), from the Portuguese *peça das Indias,* which originally referred to the value of a piece of cloth exchanged for slaves in Africa by fifteenth-century traders. French merchants began to employ this term in the early eighteenth century.[20]

What seems new is this bald enactment by Paris-based officials of a common system of meaning that binds together the capital and trading posts in Senegal in which Africans about 30 years old are whole units, Africans about 40 years old are half-units, and nursing babies, the blind, and ailing people literally have no value. This is not merely a blunt statement of adhesion to the language of the slave captain by the city's most eminent merchants; it is the other way around. It is Paris scripting the dialogue at the point of sale.

Police sources about slaves in Paris might seem worlds away from plantation inventories, or Indies Company contracts, yet they convey the same matter-of-fact view of black people as property. These stakeouts and arrests could not have occurred otherwise. Urban slave hunts, far from chafing against local values, reaffirmed them. The property that officials in Paris were willing to defend changed in step with the kind of property that Parisians believed in. By the mid-century, policemen accepted that property could take the form of people.

Slave hunts brought the ideology of the slave owner into the streets of Paris, raising the question of what neighbors thought. At least for bystanders, the arrest of slaves looked just like regular police raids. The question is not how neighbors reacted to the spectacle of capture so much as how they understood the status of their neighbors' domestics, whether they reported

24 SLAVES IN PARIS

fugitives to the police, and whether they hid people. It is impossible to venture a single answer to this question. Police files offer many clues to friendship, love, and complicity between Parisians and enslaved people. There were, nonetheless, some residents of the city who described their neighbors' domestics in the crudest possible terms. In 1751, la Dame Mallecot, the wife of an administrator in Cayenne, sought help from the police with the removal of Esther, an African (Igbo) domestic. Mallecot plotted the woman's arrest, sent Esther to the home of an elderly neighbor, and left town. The neighbor's son complained to the lieutenant-general of police. "I beg you sir to order that Mallecot come for her negress, whom I will return. It is her property, she will do with it what she wants." Esther was "a deposit" (un dépôt) for his neighbor to reclaim.[21]

There did not need to be a slave master in the picture. Police agents presumed black and brown people to be stolen goods even when no one reported them missing. The arrest of a man called Mustapha in 1755 offers a revealing instance of this. Mustapha, newly arrived from Marseille, was doubly jinxed. The police had doubts about the fancy napkins Mustapha was hawking on a bridge, and they were just as suspicious about the provenance of Mustapha himself. He deepened their concern by refusing to answer questions (although he was believed to know French) and spent four weeks in For l'Évêque. "We did not find anything in his pockets indicating to whom he belonged."[22]

It was common to describe ordinary domestics as belonging to their masters. (Failure to reveal the name of a master did not typically result in a month's detention, however.) Servants in the public eye, such as doormen, pages, and footmen, wore special uniforms, called livery (livrée), whose hue and special markings assigned them a rank in a particular master's household. Domestics found the proprietary significance of those uniforms demeaning.[23] Nonetheless, livery conveyed a message of social inclusion that becomes manifest when we compare liveried servants to enslaved retainers. Servants in livery were supposed to be treated with the dignity due to the person whose regalia they wore. Ambroise Lucas, the kidnapped doorman who cropped up in the introduction to this book, was wearing livery when police dragged him over the threshold of his employer's house on the Rue de Seine. The year was 1766 and his master was the young Pierre-Augustin Caron de Beaumarchais (1732–1799), who had recently returned to Paris after slave-trade negotiations in Madrid on behalf of the French Company of the Indies. During Lucas's

1.1 Anonymous portrait of slave dressed in court livery in slave collar and a pearl earring (late eighteenth century).
Oil painting, 54.9 × 46 cm. The Image of the Black in Western Art Research Project and Photo Archive, W. E. B. Du Bois Institute for African and African American Research, Harvard University.

kidnapping, Beaumarchais threw himself in fury on his servant's ravishers, for which he soon repented. He later gained renown as the author of *The Barber of Seville* (1777) and *The Marriage of Figaro* (1781–1784).

Lucas worked as a free man for Beaumarchais and wore the uniform of his household. In a letter of apology to the police, Beaumarchais explained that he "took their enterprise for a scandalous insult because the man had my costume (*habit*) on his body."[24] Enslaved retainers did not usually wear

26 SLAVES IN PARIS

livery. In art of this period, they appear in distinct, invariably opulent costume. Tufted turbans were the norm. Paintings of enslaved retainers at court and among the high nobility also show them in silver slave collars, worn with sultan costumes and soldier suits.[25] These metal neckbands probably had clasps. Whatever the rest of the costume—martial, oriental, or even a real livery jacket—a silver collar expressed a different relationship between master and servant than existed for other members of the household. It was a dehumanizing symbol of total subservience. The newly ennobled Beaumarchais thought his livery was worth fighting for. He might not have felt the same scorch of indignity over the abduction of a man in a slave collar.[26]

When a Bengali-born slave called Louis-Camille Crispin, age 12 or 13, petitioned the Admiralty for freedom in 1775, he showed his collar "closed by a chain, on which were written these words: *I belong to Monsieur the Vicomte de Besse, Mestre de Camp of the Dragoons.*"[27] Crispin knew how to read and understood the indignity. A legal brief for the viscount described the collar as "a mere ornament with which the Vicomte de Besse chose to decorate [Crispin] to enhance the brilliance of his complexion."[28] Removable or not, with or without an inscription, the silver collar defined its wearer as a thing.

DURING THE REIGN of Louis XIV, royal officials began to theorize policing as a vast, tentacular cleansing project by an all-knowing state. As Michel Foucault observes, the rise of new policing ideas would change the structure of government as people began to reimagine its purpose. Policing became a boom topic for publishers and Crown officials, especially after the death of Louis XIV in 1715. The end of Louis's long reign heightened the reforming zeal of police enthusiasts, to inspire dictionaries, treatises, proclamations, and experiments in repression and surveillance. In Paris, the word *police* encompassed just about everything. It meant ridding the city of moral filth, actual filth, crime and delinquency, crooked houses, illegal workers, badly lighted streets, family embarrassments, and riotous effervescence among the laboring poor. In the service of this billowing project, the lieutenant-general of police in Paris could issue his own royal writs for the arrest of undesirables, who entered dungeons without passing through the courts.

The practical ability of municipal authorities in Paris to police evolved over time. The invention of inspectors in 1708, with an amplified role after

1740, altered the relationship between police and city dwellers. Through their webs of spies and informants, twenty police inspectors maintained an unrelenting, round-the-clock surveillance of lodging houses and rented rooms frequented by *étrangers* (strangers).[29] The French word *étranger,* imbued with a sense of danger and suspicion, referred to outsiders in general, including people from elsewhere in France.

Changes to the policing of Paris responded to dearth, social unrest, and an increase in human mobility. Migration expanded both the city, as a physical space, and its population. The new brutal efficacy of police inspectors around the mid-century also came on the heels of war—the War of the Austrian Succession—and should be read in light of that conflict. As Arlette Farge notes, resistance to troop levies, together with mass desertion, spurred social upheaval in Paris. This may help to account for the menacing force of police in Paris after the war in confrontations with strangers and crowds.[30]

Once agents of the Paris police put themselves in the service of slave owners, it became perilous for fugitives to hide in the city. Jean needed to escape from Paris and not into it. Enslaved domestics who accompanied masters to Paris in the 1740s tended to disappear after a couple of weeks. Admiralty records provide numerous examples of flight by teenage Africans between 1742 and 1747. The police did not catch these people and there is no evidence they tried to. (They may have been focusing on deserters.) On the rare, documented occasions before 1750 when masters sought help from the police to recover enslaved domestics, nothing happened.[31] In 1742 Anne-Marie-Josephe de Sorel, from Léogane, reported the flight of her slave Pierrot to the Admiralty. To find the boy, she summoned "Sir Genesty, exempt, and she charged him with conducting searches for the said negro, which he assures her of having done for several days and nights" to no effect. In August 1749 a Parisian solicitor reported the flight of his slave Jeanne, who remained at large despite "investigations and house searches that her master caused to be done"—which suggests another failed police hunt.[32]

Masters in the 1750s who appealed to the police framed their demands by emphasizing the moral threat posed by escapees. At the time, the police and most of French society viewed the whole serving class as degenerate scoundrels.[33] Through their depiction of runaways as urban contaminants, masters recast slave hunts as normal policing. In 1751 the Portuguese bishop of Noronha, governor of Sao Tomé, reported the flight of Figueret, "about

4 foot 3, black, dressed in black, in a curly wig gathered at the back, age 16 or 17, from Goa in the Indies."[34] Figueret was known to be spending his days at the Saint-Germain fair. Noronha explained that the boy "who belonged to him, has been extremely deranged for five or six months, since arriving in Paris, and it being important to oversee his conduct, to prevent him from committing some disorder, he would be very grateful for him to be put in the prison of For l'Évêque until he departs Paris for the Orient."[35] When informing the police about the flight of his slave, Louis Aubin, the Chevalier de Nolivos noted "how much pleasure (his arrest) would give me, because, independent of the real loss caused by this domestic, he swindled me."[36] Masters in the 1750s emphasized the resemblance between runaways and other delinquents. They did so to enable the extrajudicial arrest of people they regarded as valuable assets. And yet it would be folly to dismiss references to theft and licentious derangement as mere fictions. Many slaves in Paris were adolescent boys. They tended to be inmates of households marked by extraordinary wealth. They lived at the center of European consumer society. Social life in the city, even for people of modest means (the café, the tavern, the cabaret), required money. Though richly upholstered by their masters in livery or exotic costume, domestic slaves earned nothing. To obtain money required them to engage in illegal traffic. Petty crime became a necessity, even a form of tradecraft. They pilfered trinkets, probably sold sex, and sold their uniforms.

The writing paper of a haberdashery called La Tête Noire offers a clue to the city's market in secondhand trim. Raymond, the owner, touted his shop for "fashion[ing] fine and artificial (gold) braid for regiments, livery braid for domestics," and for "buy[ing] second-hand fine braid for reasonable prices."[37] Enslaved domestics, in common with servants at the bottom of the household pecking order, sold their fancy clothes to dealers. The teenage Polidor, a fugitive from Rouen, "has been seen in Paris wearing a jacket of gray toile and a wool cap, doubtless because he sold his outfit and turban either for money, or as a disguise."[38] Police documents about Louis-Pierre Hazard, a Martinican teenager, include an interrogation about whether "he sold his Hussard costume, trimmed in silver braid, which his mistress had made for his use." Answer: he "gave the fabric to Charlotte the kitchen maid, and sold the braid in two parts, first on the Rue Saint-Honoré near Saint-Roch for twelve francs and second at the Place des Trois Maries . . . for nine pounds and a few cents."[39] Such stories furnish a context for Mailly de Nesle's account of Jean's circumstances in Paris. She wrote of his "being completely naked," which required her to "clothe and equip him with everything." It was axiomatic in eighteenth-century Paris that a man who had no wages and no food also had no clothes. You sold your buttons and epaulettes to eat and drink, or flee.

Thus far, I have underscored the need to distinguish urban slave hunts from the pursuit of alleged scoundrels, spendthrifts, family embarrassments, and other victims of royal writs. In turn, the arrest of slaves by lettres de cachet in Paris should not be mistaken for a satellite form of colonial slave hunt. In places like Saint-Domingue, militiamen hunted for maroons in forests and hilltop redoubts. The people they captured (usually men) then faced judgment by the Superior Council according to the French slave code, known as the Code Noir. Colonial statutes defined the flight of slaves as a crime to be punished by death or mutilation. Sentences to hard labor tended to replace death in the eighteenth century.[40] None of these punishments, nor the Code Noir itself, applied in metropolitan France, and especially not in the capital.

Masters pictured their runaway slaves in Paris as criminals. Because colonists understood legality in terms of colonial slave law, they viewed orders of the king demanding the arrest of their slaves in Paris as instruments of legal enforcement. From the perspective of officials in domestic France, however, colonial slave law, the Code Noir, could not justify the arrest of runaway slaves in Paris. The invalidity of the Code Noir in France's capital held symbolic importance to Parisian lawyers and judges. In 1716 the Paris Parlement refused to enact royal decrees setting forth rules about slaves who sojourned in France. It is intriguing, however, that Parisian judges strayed from standard procedure by opting not to explain themselves in writing. They did not publish what was called a *remontrance*—a speech of protest, addressed to the king. The muteness of judges in these instances would seem unique in the history of this court.[41] The refusal of the Paris Parlement to register the act of 1716 did not express opposition to the slave trade or to colonial slavery. Had there been such opposition, judges would not have enacted, that same year, the Declaration of the King concerning Guinea (1716), which fixed the bounties, payable to French slave traders by the Crown, for transporting children 12 years old or younger from Africa to the colonies.[42]

The Paris Parlement did not need to reject a second slave-related act, the Declaration of 1738. By special arrangement with Parlement, the king did

1.2 Receipt from Parisian haberdasher's shop, La Tête Noire (1786) from seized property archive.

Carton T 1297. Archives Nationales.

not bother sending this law for approval by that court.[43] Why did judges care? In refusing their assent to these laws, judges hoped to draw an uncrossable line between colonial slave law and the laws of domestic France. Both the 1716 Edict and the 1738 Declaration mentioned the Code Noir, the 1685 slave code. Parisian judges rightly considered royal acts relating to slaves in France as amendments to the Code Noir. The attorney-general of Paris in 1758, Omer Joly de Fleury, even used the term *Code Noir* when describing formalities for registering slaves in France. "By the edicts and declarations duly examined by the courts that form what is called the Code Noir, the king permitted not only the purchases of negroes in the colonies but also the continuance of their enslavement, even in the heart of the realm, by observing certain formalities."[44]

In refusing to register laws relating to slaves in France, judges hoped to prevent colonial slave law from being insinuated into domestic law. They failed in their object. That process began years earlier. Parisian courts heard cases about colonial property relating to the status and sale of slaves. In 1705, the Parisian civil court at Châtelet declared slaves to be movable goods (rather than real estate).[45] To address the thorny problem of minors who inherited sugar estates, the 1721 Declaration of the King "[forbade] minors who are emancipated from selling their negroes," which Parlement duly registered on February 14, 1722.[46] By the end of the century, the number of African captives disembarking in Saint-Domingue would approach 40,000 per year and the assets of Parisians increasingly came to include property in both France and the West Indies.

Although Parlement never enacted (or received) the 1738 Declaration concerning slaves, "the intention of His Majesty is that this declaration be executed according to all of its provisions" in Paris.[47] So said Jean-Frédéric Phélypeaux, Comte de Maurepas, who then served as minister of the navy and as head of the royal household. Until 1738, colonial masters were supposed to register slaves before embarking for France and again at their port of arrival. The 1738 Declaration introduced mandatory slave registration in Paris.

The Palais de Justice on Paris's Île de la Cité was an immense compound that housed both the Parlement and the Court of Admiralty.[48] In 1739 the Paris Court of Admiralty created new registers to record the names of slaves residing in the city. The 1738 decree took effect in Paris under the noses of

32 SLAVES IN PARIS

the very judges who had refused to enact it, in the same building where Parlement met. Lawyers sometimes registered slaves on behalf of masters, a quick errand for men who had business in the same building.

The use of lettres de cachet to enable slave roundups became necessary because the Paris Parlement did not register royal decrees of 1716 and 1738 relating to slaves on metropolitan soil. In consequence of their refusal, there was no statute in Paris that recognized the existence of flesh-and-blood slaves in the capital. How to arrest slaves for fleeing where slavery does not exist? Lettres de cachet were the answer. This elaborate legal context explains, partly, how lettres de cachet, when used against slaves, differed from identical-seeming royal writs that targeted a large number of other urban undesirables. These lettres de cachet also differed from other writs in their consequences. Royal orders for the arrest of slaves enabled forms of violence that did not befall other people who wound up in Parisian dungeons.

Imprisonment in a Parisian dungeon might be the end punishment, or the just the beginning. Slaves arrested by royal writ experienced harm that varied in form and magnitude. In April 1761 the chemist, engineer, and administrator Philibert Trudaine de Montigny (1733–1777)—intendant of finances, director of the national engineering school, the École des Ponts et Chaussées—sought help from the police with Télémaque, aged 15. With a view to stemming "a derangement, with fearful consequences," he asked that the boy be locked up in the Bicêtre prison. He hoped that "a rigorous correction might recall him to his duty." Trudaine de Montigny immediately received a lettre de cachet for his slave together with a personal note and an order for the slave's liberation from prison with the date left blank so that he might extract the boy from Bicêtre whenever he wished. The instructions regarding Télémaque also indicate that Trudaine de Montigny's father, Daniel-Charles Trudaine (1703–1769)—the country's director of finance and the founder of the École des Ponts et Chaussées—had sought the same favor from the police. "Several years ago, Monsieur de Marville [lieutenant-general of police, 1740–1747] accorded the same favor to Monsieur Trudaine for a child of the same age in whom he took an interest." In this case, rigorous correction probably meant a couple of weeks in a dungeon to frighten Télémaque.[49] For other slaves, however, arrest and imprisonment enabled their eventual transfer to Atlantic ports—usually Le Havre—and deportation to the colonies at the demand of masters or the Crown. Once overseas, they could be resold or punished according to the customs of a different country.

Of the 600,000 inhabitants of eighteenth-century Paris, historians estimate that at least 43,000 were domestic servants.[50] The brutal punishment of domestics in the capital could provoke neighbors to report the incident to the police.[51] Nonetheless, few in the eighteenth-century capital would have categorically opposed beating servants. People caned their nominally free retainers throughout the kingdom. Nonetheless, slaves endured forms of cruelty at the hand of colonial masters during their sojourns in France that exceeded what regular servants experienced. When a Rouen merchant sought the arrest of his slave Polidor in Paris, he described the boy as small for his age and marked "with scars on the back and backside."[52] In 1745 Marville learned that a slave in Paris from Saint-Domingue had just shot himself in the head because of unrelenting abuse. As the man lay dying, his master Couti, a planter in Le Cap (Saint-Domingue), tried to prevent him from being "baptized and administered [final rites]."[53]

Guy Coustard crossed a line in an already violent culture. Charlotte de Mailly de Nesle, the Princess of Nassau-Siegen, reported that he starved Jean and covered him with wounds. She also warned the police of the "barbaric pleasure [Coustard] tastes in killing men of this type."[54] We will never know whether Coustard really did kill fourteen slaves on his own plantation, as Mailly de Nesle told the police; or whether he threatened Jean to "make him perish like his fourteen comrades."[55] There is no way to check her allegations against Coustard and no reason to dismiss them. According to the intendant of Saint-Domingue in 1751, "the murder of slaves is so frequent." The main cause of slave flight in the colony was "abuse and lack of food."[56]

Coustard's tantrums were notorious. In 1748 he spent a month in prison after insulting Simon-Pierre Maillart, the intendant of the colony, "in a manner so indecent as to shock all the listeners." (The governor did not repeat what Coustard said to Maillart.)[57] To believe local reports, the problem went beyond obscene discourtesy. Officials in 1759 accused him of plotting to kill Louis Guyot de Mongeot, a native of Paris who owned a plantation and managed estates for absent property owners. The two men quarreled over water access. Their dispute went to law and ended badly for Coustard.[58] Of the subsequent murder plot, the minister observed: "From the

34 SLAVES IN PARIS

details you furnish about the various excesses to which this inhabitant is disposed—especially that of conceiving and causing to be executed by his own son the assassination of Sieur Guyot—his majesty approved the decision you took to send this inhabitant to France."[59] In 1759 the minister of the navy banned Coustard by lettre de cachet from returning to the colony. It was, however, a time of global war. Ships had ceased to move between France and the West Indies. Coustard could not have traveled back to the colony anyway. Guyot died in the hospital in 1760. Coustard left Paris for Saint-Domingue after the war.

IN MAY 1751, servants led Jean to a recruiting officer for the regiment of the Duc de Penthièvre, Admiral of France. Jean's friends had reason to think he would be safe in the army. An order of the king of December 1739, which became a guide to future policy, stated that Jean-François, a slave enrolled in the royal riflemen as a bugler, would remain with his regiment because his master had failed to comply with "formalities prescribed by the ordinances." According to the 1738 Declaration, the Crown was supposed to confiscate slaves whose masters did not register them with the Admiralty. Such was the case of Jean-François. The king ordered "that the said Jean-François continue to serve for the rest of his days." He could never leave the army. The body of Jean-François belonged to the state.[60]

Jean's situation resembled that of the bugler. Guy Coustard did not register Jean on arrival. After Jean's escape, someone else registered Jean with the Admiralty of La Rochelle. Guy Coustard was absent—allegedly convalescing in bed. The point of registering Jean belatedly was to secure Coustard's property claim. In the event of Jean's capture, registration might prevent his confiscation by the Crown.[61]

It is likely that people of African descent in Paris guided Jean to the recruiter for the Penthièvre regiment. At least nine black men joined that regiment between April and August 1751. Of these nine men, five were African, two came from Saint-Domingue, one from Mauritius, and one from Cayenne. All nine men had earlier served together in a regiment of light cavalry, the Saxe Volunteers, created by Maurice, Comte de Saxe,

VUE DU CHATEAU ROYAL DE CHAMBORT DU COTÉ DE LA PORTE ROYALLE
Appartenant aujourd'huit a S.A.S. Monseigneur le Mareschal Comte de Saxe

1.3 The Château de Chambord, residence of Maurice, the Maréchal de Saxe.
Jacques Rigaud (1680–1754). Etching, 21.4 × 46.9 cm. Bibliothèque Nationale de France (Paris).

marshal general of France, bastard son of the king of Poland. Maurice led France to victory in battles in the Austrian Netherlands—modern-day Belgium—during the War of the Austrian Succession. At the count's death in 1750, the Saxe Volunteers dispersed.[62]

In 1743 Louis XV rewarded the count's bravura with princely sums, the Chambord palace in the Loire Valley, access to the royal furniture storehouse, and a new regiment of cavalrymen. Maurice, who brimmed with schemes, intended his regiment to be unusual from the beginning. After the end of the War of the Austrian Succession, he sought a new role on the world stage. He wanted to become the king of Madagascar—or Tobago. According to his eulogist, Antoine-Léonard Thomas (1732–1785), the scheme that drew particular mirth among his friends involved his becoming the king of the Jews.[63] A Lutheran in a Catholic land, Maurice had a savior-like enthusiasm for renegades and castaways. He also approached the government of men as a science akin to opera staging. Somehow, whimsy and theatricality fed his military genius. In accord with these visionary tendencies, the posthumous handbook by Maurice de Saxe, entitled *Reveries,* is packed with surprisingly earthy tips about all details of war, including battle comfort (grease your feet and do not wear

36 SLAVES IN PARIS

socks).[64] At first Maurice had imagined filling his regiment with crack Hungarian, Polish, Ottoman, and Tatar horsemen. The recruitment of black men began in 1745.

A spate of royal writs for the arrest of enslaved fugitives, issued by the Crown in the 1740s, makes it possible to glimpse who joined the Saxe Volunteers and what sort of obstacles Maurice encountered when seeking black men for his regiment. Most lettres de cachet from the 1740s ordering the arrest of slaves remained unfulfilled in their object. Out of seventeen slaves mentioned in orders of the king in navy records between 1740 and 1750, most were at large at the end of the war. The missing men are likely to have become soldiers. Fleeing to the army was what one did as a slave in wartime. At the demand of slave owners, Crown officials tried to prevent slaves from enlisting to the considerable disadvantage of recruiters for Maurice's regiment. Some would-be soldiers were imprisoned. Take, for instance, the case of Pierre Lorient, who disappeared from Paris in January 1745. One month later he was in the army. The Comte de Maurepas, minister of the navy, declared his enlistment null.[65] That April, Maurepas learned that a 9-year-old domestic from Léogane had just enrolled in a cavalry regiment (presumably Maurice's) and was "hiding in the Hôtel des Invalides" in Paris.[66] In January 1747, Jean-Baptiste Noël, a domestic sojourning in Paris, enlisted in Maurice's cavalry regiment. His master, the Earl of Westmeath, an Irish peer, soon obtained an order to lock him in the Bicêtre dungeon.[67] One month later, in February 1747, a fugitive called Télémaque enlisted in the Saxe Volunteers and wound up in the same prison. (He could not have been the same Télémaque, mentioned in early pages of this chapter, who was imprisoned in 1761 at the age of 15 for unruly conduct.)[68] In Bordeaux, recruiters for Maurice enlisted two enslaved youngsters in 1747 whose masters, Quin and Noyer, did not register them with the Admiralty. The recruits included Phaeton Sicca, a 9-year-old from Angola, and Scipion, aged 16, from Saint-Domingue. Both boys enlisted for life, like the bugler in 1739. Maurepas did not want them in the army. He confiscated them for the Crown, ordering that they be sold in the colonies for the king's profit.[69]

In 1752 a royal writ for the arrest of Jean led to his expulsion from a regiment at Sedan. He returned to Paris on foot, walking more than 150 miles in chains while escorted by mounted constables. By contrast, Maurepas did not succeed in extracting soldiers from the Saxe Volunteers.

On February 14, 1749, he demanded the return of Jean-Louis, a fugitive carpenter, who fled from Nantes and joined the regiment on the eve of his forcible removal to the colonies. Maurepas promised to send a royal writ for his arrest.[70] According to the regimental roll, a cooper from Léogane named Jean-Louis, age 22, 5 foot 3, joined the Saxe Volunteers on April 5, 1748. He was discharged on February 1, 1749—two weeks before Maurepas sent his letter. It seems likely that he got wind of the manhunt and left to avoid capture.[71]

Maurice de Saxe and Maurepas also clashed over the recruitment of black men from British ships. During the war, people of African descent entered French ports aboard seized enemy vessels. Some of these people were legally free when French corsairs captured them. Their original status did not matter. Slaves and free men from enemy ships were spoils of war. Legally, both had the status of naval prize. According to Maurepas, "At the beginning of the war, we distinguished between the negroes who were free and the negroes who were enslaved aboard seized English vessels, and we sent the former to be exchanged (as prisoners). But the English did not wish to recognize this distinction on seized French vessels and we were obliged to make objections on this subject." According to Maurepas, the French followed the English in treating all black people as war booty.[72]

Maurepas claimed that a fundamental law of the kingdom—*there are no slaves in France*—forbade the auction of these captives on domestic soil. Seized black people had to be sold in the colonies. As with other naval prize, profits from the sale would be split between the Crown, the Admiralty, and privateers. Of the *Pelling,* an English ship, Maurepas observed, "All the negroes . . . belong to the captors of the vessel but they can only dispose of them by sending them to one of our islands to be sold. And if the captors do not wish to do this, you will do me the favor of informing me."[73] Ultimately, the fate of black men from the *Pelling* did not lie with Maurepas. Of the eight black sailors taken from that ship, "three found a way of escaping in a boat they built." Another seems to have finagled his freedom by becoming Catholic.[74] The presence of black British escapees in wartime France may account for the enlistment of William Godwin, age 21, from Jamaica, in the Saxony Volunteers.[75]

In 1747 Maurice de Saxe offered to buy a dozen black men for his regiment who were languishing as unsold war booty in the prisons of Bayonne. Maurepas refused. The minister schooled him in the hallowed law of the

38 SLAVES IN PARIS

kingdom. There were no slaves in France. Selling men was illegal. Two months later, privateers in Bayonne renounced their claim to these captives. Maurepas did not inform the Maréchal de Saxe. He issued a lettre de cachet ordering that they "be transported to his Majesty's colonies in America to be employed in public works."[76]

After flouting recruitment efforts by Maurice, while pretending to do otherwise, Maurepas donated a few people who nearly reached the gates of Chambord on their own. In 1747 eight men were arrested in Orléans, twenty miles from the sumptuous compound of Maurice and his regiment. They had traveled more than 200 miles, perhaps on foot, from the port of La Rochelle. One man was returned to his master. For the others, Maurepas issued lettres de cachet ordering their confiscation by the king. As Crown property, Cyrus, Auguste, Cupidon, Laurent, Cyrus, Philippe, and Jonquille would serve "for the rest of their lives" in the Saxe Volunteers.[77] Maurepas had the men remitted from prison to the Chambord master of the hunt.[78]

From these navy documents, it seems that the hundred or so men of African and Indian descent who joined the Saxe Volunteers included slaves on the lam from French masters, fugitive captives from British ships, and fugitives whom Maurepas confiscated from white slave owners who lacked influence at court. The composition of this regiment helps to explain a proposal, or *Mémoire,* that Maurice sent to Maurepas in 1747. The Maréchal de Saxe proposed that all fugitive slaves in the Americas, known as maroons, be amnestied in exchange for surrendering, moving to France, and pledging lifelong service in his regiment. Had Maurice wished to rattle Maurepas's cage for the fun of it, he could not have devised a more ingenious scenario. Maurepas rebuked the proposal.

> It is, in effect, only by the terror of punishment that we can contain slaves, whose numbers prodigiously exceed those of whites settled on each island and this example of impunity would increase marronnage. But what would scare the colonies even more is the danger that some of these maroons, after mastering the use of arms while in the service of France, and being habituated to this, would find a means of returning to the islands, where they could become all the more redoubtable through their knowledge of the woods and mountains where they were maroons. I cannot let you ignore any longer

that the establishment of your troop of negroes has caused much anguish among inhabitants of the islands. To calm them, I have tried to make them understand that they can count on your efforts to prevent the desertion of negroes whom you do not cause to be killed in the service of the king.[79]

The decade-long insurrection in Jamaica, known as the First Maroon War (1729–1738), convinced Maurepas that "troops of negroes" should not be trained and armed in Europe.[80] Maurepas's opposition to the count's regiment did not arise merely from spite. Maurepas pictured those troops as future enemies of state whose military prowess would enable a black seizure of power in the Americas. He was not the only person to harbor that fear. Maurepas claimed that colonists took the same view, as would the next minister of the navy. Maurepas fell from power in April 1749. Maurice de Saxe suddenly died on November 20, 1750. Three weeks later, Antoine de Rouillé, who succeeded Maurepas at the navy, banned travel to the colonies by unauthorized black people, whether they claimed to be enslaved or free. "The intention of the king, monsieur, is that ships bound for the colonies shall embark no slave unless presented by someone who is known to us, and no one calling himself free, unless the individual carries proof of individual permission granted by his majesty."[81]

Jean's several attempts to join the French army need to be understood in light of enlistment attempts by slaves during the War of the Austrian Succession. During the 1740s, in spite of a constant need for new recruits, the Crown obliged slave owners in France by trying to prevent slaves from becoming soldiers. That effort stemmed, in part, from the Crown's informal but staunch commitment to defending colonial property in domestic France. There were, however, other motives behind this policy. Maurepas did not want men of African descent to remain in the country. He spared no opportunity to dispatch unregistered slaves overseas for auction or use in public works. He also feared that black soldiers would combine their mastery of Western warfare with maroon knowledge—a mastery of hills and forests—to enable the overthrow of colonial society.

The brief history of the Saxe Volunteers helps to explain why, in the immediate aftermath of the War of the Austrian Succession, and in spite of government efforts to hunt down slaves in earlier years, black people in

40   SLAVES IN PARIS

Paris pictured the army as a refuge and encouraged Jean to enlist. The earlier struggle between Maurice de Saxe and Maurepas also underscores a second, essential feature of Jean's failed struggle for liberty in France. As in the case of runaway slaves during the 1740s, the lettre de cachet for Jean's arrest came from the minister of the navy. From the War of the Austrian Succession to the end of the Old Regime, the navy was the main source of royal writs ordering the arrest of slaves in Paris.

The navy was responsible for ships of the line and their military personnel while governing nearly every French overseas territory. In the performance of their expansive duties, ministers of the navy (like ministers of war) made constant use of lettres de cachet for matters small and large. Signed by the king, these were sovereign commands that no one dared protest, which could make anything happen (including but not only imprisonment), without anyone needing to explain why. The navy's everyday reliance on royal writs increased considerably in wartime—in 1740–1748, 1756–1762, and 1778–1781—and spilled into peacetime, as officials coped with the chaotic aftermath of global conflict.

Lettres de cachet that came from the navy had a strength superior to orders by the lieutenant-general of police for the arrest of urban riffraff. The navy could countermand decisions by courts—typically the Paris Court of Admiralty, but also the Parlement of Paris. The power of these writs to subvert French justice became evident a few years after the Jean affair, in 1755, when the Paris police rounded up four enslaved women who all had freedom suits pending before the Admiralty. They worked as domestics for two Parisian families (the Bouchauds and the Silvecannes) who owned plantations in Saint-Domingue.[82] In August 1755 all four women were imprisoned in the port of Le Havre to keep them away from Parisian legal authorities.[83] The minister of the navy, Machault d'Arnouville, reproached Parisian lawyers for "ill-placed warmth" in assisting the women and justified the arrest of slaves by lettre de cachet on legal grounds. He explained that Parlement had not registered edicts of 1716 and 1738 because it "refused to recognize negro slavery" (which was not the same as condemning it). To soften that refusal, it was "agreed that affairs of this sort, being very rare in its region of authority, could be handled easily either by individual orders of the king or by evocation of the case [to the royal council]. And it is thus that such matters, which are very rare, have been handled since then without the slightest difficulty." Machault also noted that Guillaume Poncet de la Grave, prosecutor at the Paris Court of Admiralty, "reminded him of the practice that had always been employed in cases where masters failed to register their slaves, as stipulated by the edict of 1716 and the declaration of 1738."[84] The customary practice, according to Poncet de la Grave, was the lettre de cachet.[85] The Crown then and thereafter would defend slave owners against the Parisian judicial system. The lesson of the women's arrest was a stark one. When enslaved people defied their masters in Paris and sued for freedom, they were supposed to disappear.

The role of the navy in orchestrating the arrest of slaves by lettres de cachet shaped the language of race that became commonplace in police documents. One of two files about Jean in the Archives of the Bastille contains a single, three-sentence text—marked COLONIES in the left-hand upper corner. This letter by Antoine-Louis Rouillé de Jouy, minister of the navy, accompanied the writ for Jean's arrest (which is missing from the file). "Monsieur Coustard honorary councilor in the Great Chamber of the Paris Parlement has asked, Monsieur, for an order of the king to enable the arrest of an enslaved *nègre* belonging to Monsieur Coustard, inhabitant of Saint-Domingue. I enclose it here and am informing Monsieur Coustard. Make sure that everything is done at his expense. I am, sir, your humble and obedient servant."[86]

Racial epithets do not have universal definitions. They are performative utterances. They do a particular kind of work. Notwithstanding the ubiquity of the term *nègre* in colonial documents, this word had a particular meaning in the context of slave hunts organized by the navy.[87] The fact that Jean had dark skin and was born in Africa is actually beside the point. Skin color and birthplace had little to do with eighteenth-century uses of the term *nègre* in slave-related police files. The context-specific meaning of this epithet becomes evident by reading Jean's case against other files relating to slave capture from the Bastille Archives. In other files, a variety of contradictory racial terms crop up in different documents about the same person. Take the 1765 file of Pèdre, a domestic who became enslaved to French merchants in the port city of Masulipatnam. In 1760 an Indies Company official presented Pèdre to the clerk of the Paris Admiralty as "a nègre of the Moorish nation." Five years later, during his freedom suit, Admiralty documents list Pèdre as belonging to "the mulatto nation." To police inspector Muron, who hunted him, he was "the so-called Pèdre mulatto slave belonging to Mister Guerre." To a char-

42 SLAVES IN PARIS

itable merchant, François Larauza, he was "Pèdre of the Indian nation." To the minister of the navy, when orchestrating the man's deportation, he was always "a nègre called Pèdre or *this nègre*."[88]

The hunts for Jean and Pèdre did not originate as racist attacks. Their masters wanted them arrested because they were valuable property, not because of their skin color. Race shaped these stories, nonetheless. In naval dispatches, the epithet *nègre* had a meaning that cannot be translated into English. This term denoted an innate vulgarity of being, which the Crown had only to name to make real, which made people worthy of abandonment to administrative power. The word signified a form of embodied repugnancy that could be affixed to people by royal fiat to defend the dubious ownership claims of masters. Giorgio Agamben uses the terms *bare life* to describe the predicament of people whom the sovereign moves outside the legal order into a special domain of authority where people dangle as specimen-like remainders between life and death, stripped of whatever worldly identity or rights they had enjoyed. The epithet *nègre,* when used in slave arrest, was a lever of power that marked people for bare life and naturalized that transformation.

MOST DOCUMENTS RELATING to Jean's bid for liberty come from the same source: Charlotte de Mailly de Nesle, Dowager Princess of Nassau-Siegen. Mailly de Nesle learned of Jean's predicament through her servants, who resided in the same Left Bank hotel as Coustard and Jean. Her staff and the innkeeper's wife, Madame Armandy, gossiped about Jean's mistreatment and tried to helped him. They knew he had no bed or bedding and slept near Coustard, on the tile floor. They heard rumors about Coustard's murderous past. Mailly de Nesle, however, did not respond to her servants' gruesome revelations by helping Jean to become free. Instead she foiled his first escape attempt. She paid off the army recruiter (which explains why Jean is missing from the Penthièvre regimental roll) and whisked him to her castle in Burgundy. She paid for him to be doctored, clothed, baptized, and catechized. Baptism—ritual renaming—counted for more than an expression of piety in this case. It was an act of appropriation. "Charles-Auguste-Thomas nicknamed Adonis has belonged to her for nine months by the most legitimate and sacred rights." After these costly attentions, Mailly de

Nesle would later insist, like someone adopting a stray dog, that he belonged to her. She told the police that she had "acquired proprietorship of this negro" in the course of a year, during which she paid "for his food and expenses and administered spiritual and temporal assistance," which cost about 2,000 livres.[89]

The dowager princess had once been notorious. Her husband, Emmanuel-Ignace, Prince of Nassau, got her locked in the Bastille—maybe for adultery, maybe because she tried to move out. In April 1715 he called the police to prevent "the furtive removal of furniture" from his house by his own wife.[90] He instigated criminal proceedings against her for furniture theft. They had been married for four years and had lost two infant sons. Arrested on May 4, 1715, she spent three months in solitary confinement.[91] The king personally ordered that she "have no contact with anyone, inside or outside" the Bastille, except the prince. After her release, she lightened her loathing for Emmanuel-Ignace with all-night illegal card games.[92] On the eve of his death in 1729, the prince disavowed Maximilian, their only child, as a bastard.[93] During the War of the Austrian Succession, the dowager princess rebuffed a posse of forty mounted police, who surrounded her castle, by shooting at them with an artillery cannon.[94] She was also a pugnacious and unrelenting litigant.[95] The bastardy case dragged on for thirty years. Her son Maximilian died in 1748. In 1756, almost three decades after her husband's death, a French court acknowledged her grandson's right to his name and title.[96]

Her missteps as a protectress did not cost Jean his liberty. As we have seen, several institutions on domestic French soil conspired to retain Jean in bondage while removing him from the country. Nonetheless, Mailly de Nesle's lobbying attempts did little to sway the Crown in Jean's favor. After his arrest, her first aim was sensible enough. She wanted to get Jean out of prison, fearing (plausibly, it seems) that Coustard would kill him. "I suffer more than I can say now that I know all that he suffers and the dangers to which he is exposed."[97] But liberation from the dungeon would not have meant liberty or regimental life.

Mailly de Nesle did not understand Jean's flight in France as a struggle for liberty. Individual freedom had no moral or juridical meaning in the feudal world she knew. Nor did she know what chattel slavery meant. Her failure to grasp the rudiments of Jean's struggle would strengthen the hand of Coustard and his allies.

44 SLAVES IN PARIS

Mailly de Nesle was a feudal lord. Her estates were in eastern France—in Burgundy and Champagne. In this part of the kingdom, the *mainmorte* (mortmain, inalienable possession), an oppressive form of land tenure, existed until the Revolution. At the death of her peasants (or serfs, as some were still called on her estates), she seized their belongings and land. Mailly de Nesle could seize the property of her serfs and that of their descendants even when they moved away to places where neither mortmain nor any form of serfdom existed. Through this right of chase, she owned people after a fashion and perpetually, through generations. Rural historians of France look to the land of Mailly de Nesle in Burgundy, at Île-sous-Montreal (now Île-sur-Surein), as a singularly extreme instance of vestigial serfdom in France. To retain those obnoxious privileges, she fended off her peasants' counterclaims before the Paris Parlement, and won.

For Mailly de Nesle, Jean had a soul, which Coustard refused to acknowledge. He refused Jean's request for baptism, saying that "he would sooner baptize his dog." In the Jean affair, serfdom collided with slavery. Spiritual care was a basic lordly obligation. Mailly de Nesle denounced Coustard in a language drawn from the feudal world, in which lord and serf were bound together by reciprocal obligations. The right to own people—she imagined—came with the obligation to supply them with physical and spiritual protection.[98]

Nonetheless, Mailly de Nesle's s claim to Jean differed from that of a lord over a serf. While there is no question that she understood Jean as a man with a soul, her feelings still invite comparison with the sensibility of other peeresses, like the Duchess of Kingston, who "had a black boy named Sambo as a pet."[99] The Duchess kept Sambo at her side so long as he remained a decorative and asexual miniature person. She sent him back to the colonies when he reached adolescence. By contrast, Jean was in his early twenties. Mailly de Nesle even seems to have called him Adonis—after the paragon of male beauty who died horribly, gored in the groin or flank by a boar, and metamorphosed into an anemone flower. Depictions of Adonis, such as that by Peter-Paul Rubens (1614), show him fleeing the embrace of Venus toward the hunt: or depict him prone and Christlike, bleeding and castrated yet eroticized, in pietà-like death postures.[100] Mailly de Nesle did not write about Jean as an intact person. If she felt sexual attraction, it was overlaid by a fixation on his brokenness and approaching death. She portrayed him as a damaged foundling, ravaged by wounds, even stigmata, who fell into her life to be owned and healed.

To Mailly de Nesle, Jean was unmistakably human and yet ownable like a nonhuman. Feudal law regarding lost-and-found things and animals shaped her ideas of proprietorship. She understood her ownership of Jean as she would have understood her claim to a falcon with a broken wing that dropped on her house, or a maimed spaniel in her wood. In French law of the Old Regime, with little variation between regions, lost animals became the property of a lord when they wandered onto his property. So did lost objects, typically after a span of forty days. Animate and inanimate things reverted to the lord by the legal instrument known as the *droit d'épave* (the right to take ownership of unclaimed salvage). Feudal law did not equip Mailly de Nesle to know what it meant for Coustard to own Jean. Colonial slave owners staked an absolute and inextinguishable claim to slaves they owned. The flight of slaves to the forest did not matter. Nor did the length of time they spent there.

By insisting that Jean belonged to her, Mailly de Nesle diminished his chance of becoming free. She could have used other arguments. Apart from Jean's belated registration in La Rochelle, Coustard does not seem to have received authorization from the colonial governor to travel with his slave, as required by law. He also did not register Jean in Paris. She might have challenged Coustard's title to Jean on legal grounds. She might have pushed for Jean to remain with his regiment by demanding his confiscation by the Crown. By insisting on the king's claim to his person as an unregistered slave and a soldier, Mailly de Nesle might have helped him. She could also have bought Jean from Coustard. Mailly de Nesle did none of these things. By pressing her claim to own Jean, she made his departure for Saint-Domingue a certainty.

A second slave hunt in Paris of 1752 helps to illustrate the problem of uncomprehending benevolence that shaped the Jean affair. On March 1, 1752, the Paris police captured Marie-Thérèse, whose file identifies her as a mulatto slave, 20 years of age, from Martinique. She had been serving her mistress, Marie-Catherine Elisabeth Giraud de Crézol, who lodged as a non-nun in the Abbey of Montmartre, atop the hill that is now the site of the Sacré-Coeur church. The arrest of Marie-Thérèse met with opposition from a lofty source: the Duc de Noailles.[101] He was an elderly warrior who

46   SLAVES IN PARIS

sat on the royal council. Rivals despised his cunning. They mocked his religious exaltation and ceremonial pomp. He was rumored to have attended Mass wearing a bishop's mantel, and to have said a prayer while draped in a pall. The Marquis d'Argenson wrote acidly of the duke in his memoirs. "He is known to be crazy and hypocritical by everyone, but it is fashionable to call him pious and witty."[102]

As with Mailly de Nesle in the Jean affair, the brutal corporal punishment of a slave in Paris inspired the Duc de Noailles to intervene. Noailles claimed that Marie-Thérèse had endured shocking abuse. Someone in his circle must have known the girl, or seen her at close range. Unmarried daughters of the nobility often lived at the Abbey of Montmartre. Perhaps he got the story from someone who boarded there. Or from his servants. According to the abbess of Montmartre, Marie-Thérèse was hiding in the apartment of a bathhouse owner on the Rue de Richelieu, near the Hôtel des Indes and the duke's townhouse. The hunt for Marie-Thérèse required police inspectors to comb central Paris, causing rumors to circulate about the fugitive girl.

At the time of this affair, members of the Noailles family either owned plantations or soon acquired them. Colonial records indicate that in 1754 the Duc de Noailles requested and received land in Saint-Domingue to create a plantation.[103] A cadastre of the Cul de Sac plain near Léogane from 1780 indicates two Noailles plantations near the town of Croix-des-Bouquets. In 1752 the Duc de Noailles knew the legal formalities that applied to slave owners in France. He knew the colonial procedure for freeing slaves by contract. He knew that mastership was about money. He knew that slaves were absolute property. It seems unlikely, given the concession request two years later, that the Duc de Noailles held anti-slavery views. His rescue of Marie-Thérèse looks more like a blast of ducal philanthropy. Ultimately, Marie-Thérèse owed her freedom to the suppleness of an old courtier who understood modern slavery and its paperwork.

The Duc de Noailles recognized, and knew how to exploit, the problem that Mailly de Nesle lacked the sense or education to see. Marie-Elisabeth Giraud de Crézol had never registered the girl as a slave with the Admiralty in Paris. Noailles sent legal proof of this oversight to Rouillé, minister of the navy, with a note demanding that he confiscate Marie-Thérèse, as the law required, or compel Giraud de Crézol to "separate herself from this girl for a price that you think appropriate." Crézol freed her slave before a Paris notary on May 2, 1752, without mentioning the duke or the price he paid for her freedom. Marie-Thérèse left prison three days later and became a servant in the duke's house.

In his *Enquiry concerning the Principles of Morals* (1751), the philosopher David Hume (1711–1767) argued that benevolence preserved great men from "our severest hatred" by turning power to the advantage of the weak. Social inequalities that would otherwise be intolerable became, through benevolence, instruments of social utility.[104] Hume, though a frequent traveler, did not picture benevolent action in the context of a cosmopolitan world. For benevolence to work as he imagined, people at the top and bottom of society would need to share a common culture—traditions, usages, laws, morals, notions of how power works—despite disparities of rank. Hume did not foresee a needy stranger with exotic problems that powerful helpers failed to decode and hence were powerless to fix. This, unfortunately, was the situation of Mailly de Nesle in the Jean affair. In her dealings with the Coustard family, the navy, and the police, she bumped up against a world of law and social practice of which she had no inkling. Her fruitless campaign illustrates a paradox of benevolence that also shaped the struggle of Marie-Thérèse. To lobby effectively on behalf of a slave required more than wealth and influence. Would-be benefactors needed to understand what it meant to own and be owned in the colonial world. Yet the people who were most likely to grasp the predicament of slaves tended to live among slave owners or own slaves themselves.

Chapter 2

PAULINE

IN SEPTEMBER 1763, Pauline left the Isle of Bourbon (now Réunion) for France as the slave of Jean-Baptiste-Charles Bouvet de Lozier, ex-governor of the island. Two other slaves of the governor, Pierre and L'Empereur, whom Pauline had known for years, also made the three-month voyage to Lorient, the Indies Company port. [1] The governor and his retinue were in Paris by January.[2] Until her arrest and spectacular escape, Pauline lived with her master, his unmarried siblings, her enslaved companions, and the rest of the staff on the Rue des Blancs Manteaux.[3] The street took its name (Street of White Coats) from a Benedictine monastery that has since disappeared. Pauline was around 37 when she fled nearly a year later, in December 1764.

Pauline was born on the island next to Bourbon, which was then called the Isle de France (modern Mauritius). Those two islands, together with nearby Rodrigues and a host of smaller volcanic remnants, comprise the Indian Ocean's Mascarene island group. Lacking a record of her birth, I do not know where her parents were born, what they did, or who claimed them and their children as property. In 1750 Pauline entered the household of Bouvet de Lozier when he arrived in the Mascarenes as a newlywed, accompanied by his pregnant wife.[4] Pauline served the governor's wife and tended to the children in their infancy; at age 2, both girls were sent to France in the care of aunts.[5] The governor's wife died in December 1757, probably of smallpox.[6] Afterward Pauline ceased to work in the governor's household.

She remained his slave while plying a trade (undisclosed), and banked her earnings with the governor.

In Paris, Bouvet de Lozier refused to give Pauline her money or her freedom. Instead, in November 1764 he asked the Paris police to "lock up a negress who belongs to me, with whom I am unhappy, until I can send her back to the Isle of Bourbon from where she came."[7] She was sent by lettre de cachet to the women's prison of Salpêtrière pending her deportation. A few weeks later the prison released her at Bouvet's request to enable her involuntary travel to Lorient, and from there to Bourbon. She absconded the night before her scheduled departure.

Pauline went underground for six months (December 1764–June 1765), which triggered a manhunt, to which we owe almost everything that can be known about her sojourn in the capital. Details about Pauline need to be wrung from police reports, complaints by Bouvet de Lozier, retorts by her allies, and Admiralty documents, mainly concerning her freedom suit, which occurred while she was in hiding.[8]

The Pauline affair dates from a transformative period in the French capital. The Seven Years War (1756–1763), a global defeat for France, made the colonial world palpable in the everyday life of the city as never before.[9] Because of the war, colonists and their enslaved domestics in Paris found their temporary stays prolonged by years. Meanwhile, the conquest of French territory in Canada, Africa, and India, and the loss of Antillean islands (Martinique and Guadeloupe) displaced colonial elites. Uprooted by defeat, they straggled into Paris; many were accompanied by one or two enslaved attendants. With the demobilization of troops and the return of prisoners of war, more people from the colonies converged on the city. Nonwhite people who wound up in Paris between 1756 and 1763 included soldiers and sailors as well as body servants.[10]

Newcomers in the capital, whatever their rank in the social hierarchy, carried habits of mind that bore the imprint of the places they left behind. In Paris, one effect of global conflict and imperial collapse was to blur the distinction between domestic and colonial society. The Seven Years War and its aftermath shaped Pauline's struggle. Bouvet's lengthy administrative career in the Mascarene Islands would affect his behavior in Paris and general worldview. Pauline's earlier life as an island-born elite slave and tradeswoman would define who she was and what she stood for in the city.

50   **SLAVES IN PARIS**

In 1762 a white colonist living in Paris noted "the daily insolence to which these newly freed people [*nouveaux libres*] give proof . . . under the lowered eyes of their former masters."[11] He urged the navy to disgorge all domestics of African or Indian descent from Paris into French Guiana. (Naval officials treated this plan as a serious policy brief.) Such remarks could not have been written had the "newly freed" people it described been secure in their status. With the return of peace, domestics in Paris confronted the prospect of deportation and resale overseas. Fearing for their safety, they sued for freedom and back wages. In formulaic petitions to the Admiralty, their lawyers invoked the maxim that "all slaves who enter France are free."[12] The court responded by granting everyone freedom and retroactive salaries—back to the date of their arrival in France. Masters turned to the navy and police for help. The end of the Seven Years War produced a wave of freedom trials. It also triggered police hunts for slaves in the city. In 1765 the navy issued at least thirteen lettres de cachet to thwart efforts by people to become free; of these, at least nine targeted domestics who had already been declared free by the Paris Court of Admiralty or who had cases awaiting judgment there.

When peace returned, the leading minister at Versailles, Etienne-Francais Choiseul-Stainville, drew up plans to sweep the country of non-white people, enslaved and free.[13] In July 1763 he urged intendants of Atlantic parts to hasten the departure of free people of color in anticipation of a new law. "The intention of the king is that blacks and mulattoes, without distinction, leave the kingdom."[14] Choiseul's plan failed, apparently owing to opposition from courtiers. His unattained hope of a racial purge still mattered to the fate of nonwhite people in Paris, however. Beginning in the 1760s, the fear of racial pollution gave new energy to slave hunts by order of the king.

As a legal story, Pauline's bid for freedom was unique in the history of the Paris Admiralty Court. Lawyers for both slave and master presented arguments that had never been heard before and would never recur. At a hearing in February 1765, the barrister Malézieux, who represented Bouvet, announced his client's intention to punish Pauline according to "the declaration of the king of 1685"—otherwise known as the Code Noir.[15] Bouvet wanted to deport her overseas and donate her to the Isle de Bourbon as a public slave. He also threatened to punish her for marronnage, or slave flight, once she returned to the colony. The crime? Running away from Bouvet in Paris. To the ex-governor, punitive articles of French slave law applied to events in Paris as much as anywhere, though the actual whipping (or worse) needed to happen abroad.

Apart from Bouvet's original complaint about Pauline's insolence, her police file contains few direct quotations. Pauline feels present in these documents, but not because of what she says. Her petition to the Admiralty of January 1765 was written in the first person and thus mimics direct speech (in common with all petitions by enslaved litigants), despite being the work of an attorney. Legal documents about this case do not show the real extent of her grievances against Bouvet, or reveal how she understood her rights in the capital. In spite of her silence, Pauline becomes palpable to the reader in these sources. She does so physically, through reports of flight, capture, and concealment, and because of the complicity she seemed to inspire in everyone around her.

Pauline's legal representative in court, the barrister Denis Durouzeau, did not even glance at the freedom maxim when arguing her case. The postwar spike in petitions by slaves and the formulaic inclusion of the phrase "all slaves who enter France are free" everywhere else makes the absence of this phrase all the more conspicuous. Durouzeau instead depicted Bouvet as a liar with the conscience of a highwayman. He accused the ex-governor of confiscating the person and property of a colonial businesswoman. According to Durouzeau, Bouvet stole 12,000 livres from Pauline. No document accounts for this immense sum, amounting to more than 135,000 modern euros. Bouvet later recognized a debt of 3,000 livres. Inside court, Pauline's lawyer refused to acknowledge that she had ever been a slave; instead, he presented her as a free merchant whom Bouvet robbed and illegally placed in his power. Outside court, however, Pauline's allies made a different complaint. A memorandum written on her behalf denounced Bouvet for preventing Pauline from using the money he stole from her to buy her freedom.[16]

Bouvet treated the Code Noir as though it were a transoceanic charter, applicable to all French sovereign territory. By contrast, Pauline's friends made claims that defied the letter of colonial law. The Code Noir forbade slaves to own property or purchase their liberty. Unlike slaves in ancient Rome, they did not have a right to save money under a master's trusteeship (known in Rome as a *peculium*).[17] Yet Pauline's allies appealed to principles that were just as embedded in the colonial world as Bouvet's legal claims. In demanding Pauline's money, in clamoring against Bouvet's refusal to allow her to buy her liberty, they gestured to notions of fairness that structured

52   SLAVES IN PARIS

customary arrangements between masters and slaves in all French colonies. Buying yourself out of slavery veered from the letter of the law, but it happened all the time—usually, but not always, without the sanction of the state. There were, nonetheless, rulings by colonial courts that authorized self-purchase.[18]

Pauline's struggle for liberty was just as singular as a police story. Of the slaves with Bastille files from the 1760s, Pauline seems to be the only one who successfully eluded a manhunt.[19] How to explain her improbable triumph over a police chief, the navy, her master, and Inspector Muron and his lumpen clique of actors, spies, and informants? Pauline's path to freedom hinged on the assistance she received both from black domestics and from nobles whose fortunes depended on slavery. The conduct of slave owners in this affair needs to be understood in light of the moral and legal principles that framed their world, which defined how they saw Pauline and what they made of Bouvet. Only then does it become clear why Parisians who lived on colonial fortunes took the side of a slave against her master.

PAULINE BELONGED to the first generation of Creole slaves to be born under French rule on the Isle de France. The Dutch, who named the island after Maurice, Prince of Nassau, abandoned their settlement in 1710, fleeing its many fugitive slaves as well as its pirates, cyclones, locusts, and exploding population of rats.[20] In 1721 the French regent gave the colony to the French Company of the Indies. The slave trade began in 1723.[21]

Pauline was 37 or 38 when she fled Bouvet's household, which means she was born in 1726 or 1727. Parish registers for this colony are scarce for the first decade of French rule. At the time of her unrecorded birth, most enslaved people on Isle de France and the neighboring Bourbon came from Madagascar; a smaller number came from India.[22] Nonetheless, in 1738, more than half of the 1,400 slaves owned by the French Indies Company came from its trading posts in Senegal.[23] Vaunted by officials for their navigational skills, West Africans were somewhat less likely than Malagasies to steal boats and make for home on company vessels.[24] As a young captain, Jean-Baptiste-Charles Bouvet de Lozier, Pauline's owner, helped bring West African slaves to the Mascarene Islands. In 1744 he sailed a curiously small number of captives from Senegal to the Indian Ocean. A local administrator for the company, Estoupan de la Brue, informed Paris of "remitting to Monsieur Lozier Bouvet, sea captain of the *Héron*, 20 negroes and 10 negresses, all young and without defects, the elite of our slave pens [*captiveries*], for which we herewith remit the bill."[25]

The Catholic Church was a weak institution in Isle de France, both during the early years, when the Indies Company ruled the colony (1721–1767), and during the later period of direct rule.[26] The first article of the 1685 Code Noir for the Antilles, which expelled Jews from the French colonial empire, was cut from the revised code that applied to the Mascarene Islands (1723). By omission, the Mascarenes code, like that for Louisiana (1724), gave tacit recognition to non-Catholic marriage and allowed slaves to hawk wares on the Sabbath.[27] In the revised text for both colonies, the company also had no obligation to promote Catholicism. The 1685 Code Noir, written for West Indian crown colonies, specified that masters would need to inform the government within eight days of a new slave's arrival; governors and intendants were supposed to oversee the baptism of newcomers and provide priests for the cure of slave souls. The first article of the Code Noir for the Mascarenes did not require this hasty notification of the government about newly arrived slaves. Instead, the text deferred baptism to "a suitable moment."

The colonial capital, Port Louis, was a stop for ships going to and from India. Nearly all sailors, called lascars, came from India.[28] Because of the importance of this colony as a transit stop, Islam and Hinduism became officially tolerated religions. The government in Isle de France could not suppress those faiths without losing the sailors. In 1742 the vicar of Port Louis watched French soldiers join in a nocturnal festival led by Indian seamen on supposed orders from the governor "so that they are not troubled in their ceremonies, which they perform in public, walking on a sort of platform or niche, before which they burn incense on the statue of Mohammed or some other idol." The parade happened to coincide that year with "the celebration of the Third Mystery . . . of the death and passion of Jesus Christ." When lascars died, they received Hindu and Muslim funerals. "They inhume their dead publicly with all the ceremonies, accompanied by all sorts of folly and superstition."[29] French soldiers probably caroused with lascars all the time, indoors as well as out. The taverns of Port Louis drew revelers of all description—sailors, deserters, dockworkers, shipbuilders, company slaves, and garrison troops who often bunked with the villagers.[30]

Pauline belonged to the heterodox world of Port Louis. She was an urban slave, insofar as the squalid rectangular thing-in-progress known as Port Louis could be called a town. Everyday life in this Indian Ocean port did not encourage Catholic piety. Nor did Catholicism matter much to the enslaved people in rural areas. The multitude of "barbarian tongues" that slaves spoke in the Mascarene Islands made it impossible for priests to catechize them. The multilinguistic character of these islands helped to sustain cultural practices from slaves' places of origin without freezing those cultures in time. The historians Meghan Vaughan and Pier Larson underscore the importance of diasporic languages and traditions to people born on Isle de France, ranging from Malagasy hair-braiding, talismans, and circumcision to Indian ear-piercing and West African sacrifice. Far from being scattered vestiges, these traditions remained conspicuous and dynamic features of everyday life.[31]

Apart from the India ships, life in this colonial port centered on the slave trade. The infrequency of baptism, and the rising number of slave ships, turned parish registers in Isle de France into a mortuary chronicle about the nameless heathen dead. Unbaptized people had no names. Priests used the adjective *anonyme* (anonymous) to describe them. Thus in 1746, "I the undersigned . . . inhumed the body of an anonymous negress, slave of Picault, naval officer of the company, who was blessed [*ondoyée*] and died today." (To be *ondoyé* was a short-cut to baptism for the dying.)[32] In 1760, "I the undersigned . . . gave a holy burial in the cemetery of this parish to the body of an anonymous child belonging to Bocage, hairstylist."[33] Indexes in the National Archives of Mauritius now gather these anonymous people under the letter A.

The wife of Governor Bouvet de Lozier was called Pauline David. Could it be a mere coincidence that Pauline the slave bore the same name as her mistress? Of the eighteenth-century Mascarenes, the historian Prosper Eve observes, "It became the custom to give to the baptized person the name of the godfather or godmother."[34] The rarity of baptism in the 1720s, and the predominance of Indian, Malagasy, and West African practices among slaves, make it uncertain that Pauline bore that name from birth. She might well have received the name Pauline at the time of her baptism as an adult, with Pauline Bouvet née David acting as her godmother. It is possible that the slave Pauline spent the first twenty years of her life as a non-Christian and was called something else.

During her years in the Bouvet household, she probably called herself Pauline, because she gave that name to other people. On April 15, 1753, a priest in Port Louis recorded the baptism of "Pauline, age 3 or 4, slave of Broens. The godfather was Jean and the godmother was Pauline, both slaves of Monsieur Bouvet, who said they could not sign."[35] The child was an orphan. In view of the missing mother (not *anonyme,* just unmentioned), she might have come from a newly arrived slave ship. The name of the toddler's owner, Broens, is a common Dutch name. He cannot be traced in French records and might be a sailor.

Pauline returned to the Isle de France after obtaining freedom in Paris. She sailed home aboard the *Comte d'Artois,* an Indies Company ship, which left France on October 27, 1765, and reached Port Louis in March 1766.[36] The ship's passenger list describes her as "the free negress of Monsieur Bouvet." She is also noted as one of twenty-seven stowaways who boarded the ship at Lorient. Three of the other clandestine travelers—Marc, Cupidon, and Jean-Baptiste—were slaves of the captain, Marc-Joseph Marion-Dufresne, a planter in Isle de France and a slave trader. Marion-Dufresne would gain posthumous renown as a martyred navigator. In 1772, while sojourning in New Zealand, he provoked the Maoris, who ate him. Fated to become the doomed epigone of James Cook, he died from the quintessential Enlightenment travel disaster.[37]

The passenger list of the *Comte d'Artois* is a threshold of sorts. It is the last document linking Pauline, by name, to the ex-governor. When she disembarked in Isle de France, Pauline assumed a different kind of clandestinity. As a freed woman with no last name, she vanished into a world of Paulines. A few might actually be her. Two Paulines had daughters named Geneviève, whom they bought and freed. The mothers of the Genevièves were married—one to Pierrot, the other to Jacques. Another Pauline married a white Parisian who worked for the police. They lived in a ramshackle house with a couple of slaves and their daughter called Pauline.[38]

PAULINE'S LEGAL SUIT against Bouvet centered on the money she had earned as a tradeswoman and banked with her master. No surviving

56   SLAVES IN PARIS

document names the trade that Pauline practiced. Under French slave law, she could not own property, earn money, or make contracts. Notarial documents for Bourbon and Isle de France that survive from these years do not mention Pauline, slave of Bouvet. The testament of Pauline Bouvet, the governor's wife, who died in 1757, is unfindable or never existed. We cannot know what she gave or promised to give to Pauline. There are no clear references to Pauline in the archives of Isle de France following her return to Port Louis as a stowaway.

One must draw inferences about Pauline's commercial life by looking at the lives of other people. The Code Noir of the Mascarenes (1723) forbade slaves from engaging in commerce for their own account.[39] In practice, however, agents of the French Indies Company, a global trading firm, did not wish to police the transactional life of slaves. The criminals who mattered to agents of the Company were fugitive slaves, not peddlers. The old tolerance toward entrepreneurial slaves vanished after the Indies Company went bankrupt, when the Mascarenes came under royal administration.[40] Inaugural acts by the new royal government aimed to keep slaves from making money on the side.

The business life of slaves in Port Louis became central to police reports after the fall of the Indies Company. Police blotters from the 1770s and 1780s offer a glimpse of widespread commercial practices that survived into the era of Crown rule. Slave commerce in its humblest form meant selling wares from plates and baskets laid on the ground. Vendors of this sort included Marie, an old black woman who sold curry and rice from a wood bowl, and Julie, a young Indian girl, who sat with a plate of salt at her master's door.[41]

Slave commerce was not just a matter of small-time hawking. There were slave pastry chefs who cooked in the dark by arrangement with their mistress. There were slave bakers who sold their bread for profit in shops. There were seamstresses, like Magdeleine, a Bengali woman, who sewed men's shirts. A police sweep revealed that thirty-six "blacks belonging to townsmen and planters" were hiding in the barracks and cooking for the troops. There were unlicensed bars where slaves sold their own hooch and probably swapped things. In 1780, police raided the speakeasy of Christine, an island-born freed woman who hosted parties every afternoon that drew large crowds, including slaves of the governor and the intendant.[42]

A plausible livelihood for Pauline, after the death of the governor's wife, was *couturière*—designing and making clothes. When elite women from the colonies visited Paris, the only skill they wanted enslaved girls to acquire was dressmaking. Hairstyling and cooking, for some reason, were men's jobs. Dressmaking was a reputed specialty of women of color in the Mascarenes. In a text about the Isle of Bourbon from 1710, Antoine Desforges-Boucher, an Indies Company official (later governor), recalls how much officers liked his new suit "for its cut and buttonholes" and agreed "that fashionable clothes were not better made in Paris."[43] Dressmaking was a trade for which Pauline had the ideal clientele.

How rich was the slave Pauline? It is impossible to know whether the 12,000 livres mentioned by Pauline's lawyer at the final hearing of her suit was an accurate account of the money owed her. To begin with, the French livre did not exist in coin. It was a "fictitious" currency according to Anne-Robert-Jacques Turgot, the famed economist and statesman. The ubiquitous yet always "immaterial" livre was the French monarchy's official unit of financial accounting, whose legal value corresponded to a fixed weight of precious metal, as decreed by the Crown. To make Pauline's story even more complicated, the livre had a different value inside France than in the overseas empire. Although colonial legislation for the Mascarenes often mentioned livres, the Spanish piastre was the main physical currency there and throughout much of the French overseas empire. The word *piastre* originated with Venetian traders in the Renaissance. For centuries the *piastre* was the only internationally recognized coin of Levantine trade. The abundance of Spanish piastres in the hands of the French Indies Company helped to expand eighteenth-century French slave trading in East Africa, where the brokers were Portuguese. Whatever Pauline had earned and Bouvet owed, the actual money changing hands was in piastres, bills of exchange, or mixed coinage.[44]

Estate inventories and colonial sale documents make it possible to situate the everyday value of Pauline's lost fortune. At her death in 1751, Marie-Geneviève Gruel, the sister of a slave-trading magnate, owned diamond earrings worth 1,200 livres and a diamond cross worth 2,000 livres. The four African parakeets in her Parisian dining room were valued at 120 livres, including the cages. As for the value of livres in the Mascarenes, Pauline's fortune is most easily measured using records of slave sale. In 1774 the purchase of five slaves by a man called Banks on the Isle of Bourbon, including Noel (age 40), Dauphin (15), Jean-Baptiste (14), Xavier (10), and Marie-Jeanne (18), cost 6,000 livres in colonial money. When Dauphine, a freed woman, bought her sister from the owner Maillot, the price was 2,000 livres in colonial money.[45]

Knowing the price of people was a necessity of life for people like Pauline. Free black women often bought family members out of slavery. Pauline had been banking her money with Bouvet de Lozier. So long as she remained in bondage, she could not buy anyone other than herself. Available documents do not reveal whether Pauline had siblings, parents, or children. Nonetheless, an island-born slave might plausibly have living family members, not to mention a lover or longtime companion. The sum of money she banked with Bouvet more than covered the cost of her own freedom, raising the question of who else she hoped to rescue.

ON NEW YEAR'S DAY OF 1739, while cruising Antarctic waters, the young Jean-Baptiste-Charles Bouvet de Lozier spotted a tiny uncharted island, which he mistook for an unknown continent. He named the place "Circumcision Bay," after the day (January 1) Jesus was supposed to have undergone that Hebraic ritual. Bouvet publicized the voyage. According to the geographer Aubert de la Rue, it was "the phantom island that spilled the most ink." Bouvet has since earned a permanent spot in the annals of misdiscovery and remains a notable figure, thanks to the obscurity of his achievement. He is the eponym for the most remote island in the world.[46]

After the island incident, Bouvet became an Indies Company captain. On March 12, 1750, he married Pauline David (age 30), the daughter of Antoine Lélio David, a director of the Indies Company from Marseille, who reigned over two hemispheres through a network of male relatives. His son Pierre-Félix-Barthélemy David, a former governor of Senegal and slave ship owner, was the governor of Isle de France in 1750. Two of Antoine Lélio David's four nephews, Pierre Estoupan de Saint-Jean and Blaise Estoupan de Saint-Jean, served in Senegal. The first was governor, the second a company director. Their brother Charles-Antoine Estoupan captained Indies Company ships (though apparently not slave ships), and Jean-Baptiste Estoupan de Laval ran the company warehouses in Lorient.[47]

After marrying Pauline David, Bouvet trampolined from being a merchant captain to the governorship of Bourbon. He left for the Mascarenes with his wife in April 1750, one month after the wedding. He returned in

PAULINE   59

1763, six years after she died. The Seven Years War delayed his return. Bouvet spent an unprecedented thirteen years governing first one island (Bourbon) and then the other (Isle de France). He seems to hold the all-time record for uninterrupted service by a colonial governor in the 300-hundred-year history of the French Empire. That accomplishment is also a cautionary tale. When he returned, Bouvet understood the punishment of slaves, and the law that applied to slaves, in relation to the islands he left behind.

In the Indies, Bouvet ruled over thousands of people. In Paris he could not control his own housekeeper. In common with other slave owners, he wanted to remove Pauline from Paris and deport her to a place where freedom became impossible. What set Bouvet apart was his ultimate purpose. Other masters sent their slaves out of Paris at considerable expense to preserve their property. Bouvet was willing to pay to destroy Pauline. To understand his vehemence requires that we reckon with the sort of colonies he governed for thirteen years and see how he governed them.

In the eighteenth century, it was surprisingly easy for slaves in the Mascarene Islands, especially Malagasy slaves, to make for the hills, join a village, steal a woman, and eke out a life on pilfered goods under the rule of a maroon king. The Code Noir, as modified for the Mascarene Islands, guaranteed legal impunity to settlers during maroon hunts. "We permit our subjects in the said country who have fugitive slaves in any place whatsoever to search for them by such persons and under such conditions as they see fit, or to do so themselves as they see fit" (art. 34).[48] Because of the ease of slave flight, the Isle de France of Pauline's youth became a place where white sportsmen diverted themselves by people-hunting. It is revealing that the Baron de Vaux, a planter in Isle de France, introduced the topic of runaway slaves in his posthumously published correspondence while discussing agricultural pests. Colonists considered the maroons "obnoxious animals, and hunt them down in the same manner." During the reign of Pauline David's brother as governor there, "We have a species of hunting which . . . is indeed of a cruel kind in appearance, but absolutely necessary in point of policy."[49]

What the baron withheld about the local sport were the severed heads and hands that hunters bagged or hoisted on pikes. Heads and hands served as trophies, proof of kill, which a hunter remitted to the neighborhood clerk, who issued a receipt. To take an example from the Isle de Bourbon: "I the undersigned clerk in the quarter certify that Sieur Henri Hoarau . . . killed

60   **SLAVES IN PARIS**

a negress named Soya, maroon for ten or twelve years, belonging to Sieur Noel Hoarau, whose right hand was taken as was once the custom."[50] (The new custom was the left hand.) Heads and hands were mounted at "the usual spot"—probably near the church. One cannot help but wonder whether slave auctions, which took place on the steps of the church after Mass, unfolded against a backdrop of severed body parts.

Bernardin de Saint-Pierre, otherwise known for his idyllic novel about Isle de France, *Paul et Virginie* (1788), offered quite a different view of the colony in the published account of his voyage to the island two decades earlier. On maroon hunting, he observed: "There are inhabitants who make [the hunt] into a pleasurable pastime . . . they are chased out and dispersed like wild beasts, and when they are too difficult to approach, men shoot at them, cut off their heads, and carry [the heads] triumphantly to town on the tip of a stick. This is what I see just about every week."[51]

According to both the original and the local versions of the Code Noir, recaptured fugitives were supposed to have their ears lopped off and their shoulder branded with a fleur-de-lis. Army deserters underwent similar mutilation during the reign of Louis XIV.[52] In addition, colonial law punished prolonged slave flight, known as grand marronnage, with the slitting of Achilles tendons (for absence longer than one month) and death (for absence longer than three months). In practice, the killing and disabling of runaway slaves who were fit enough to work declined throughout the colonial empire during the eighteenth century.[53] On Isle de France, for lack of a public executioner—so said officials—the state resorted to imprisonment, forced labor, and beatings with "branches following the custom at the end of the parish Mass."[54]

The forced labor, beheadings, and ritual violence that punctuated Mascarene Sabbaths do not fully represent the custom of the country in relation to slave flight. To understand what I take for the essence of Mascarene society in the eighteenth century requires turning our attention to the bounties paid to locals for maroon capture.

From the early eighteenth century forward, locals received cash rewards for the capture of fugitives called grand maroons—defined as people who were absent for more than a month. The fees rose sharply over time from a meager 30 livres in 1735 to 200 livres by the mid-century and upward still. Colonies everywhere suffered from a notorious shortage of coin.[55] In Isle de France and Bourbon under Company rule, the enslaved human body was an alternative unit of currency. In 1737 the Superior Council of the Island of Bourbon hired a contractor to refurbish government buildings in exchange for *un noir pièce d'Inde* (one male slave in peak shape) and *un moyen noir* (one male slave in average shape).[56] This sort of thing—two men tendered for municipal roof work—began early in the colony's history and predated the arrival of Bouvet. That local tradition provides a context for later novelties during the Bouvet period.

Bouvet's years in the Mascarenes were a breakthrough phase in the regional history of marronnage. As governor, he presided over the destruction of long-established maroon villages on Bourbon and Isle de France. To advance the campaign against forest people, Bouvet introduced a new incentive for settlers to kill and capture maroons. During his reign on the Isle de Bourbon, beginning in 1751, the reward for killing a runaway slave became a new slave from the company warehouse. Bouvet launched this incentive scheme in collaboration with François Saige, brother of the mayor of Bordeaux. The Superior Council embraced the policy and asked for approval by the Company. Louis-Charles Grant, Baron de Vaux, credits Bouvet with importing the reward scheme from Bourbon to Isle de France. "M. Bouvet determined to offer a slave, at the Company's price, for every freebooter killed, which the inhabitants approve, and the Company has confirmed."[57]

Bouvet's colonial past helps to explain his pursuit of Pauline, although no surviving source can account for his rancor. In 1763 he returned from an uninterrupted thirteen-year stint in the Mascarenes. After his scorched-earth campaign against forest fugitives, Bouvet could not countenance the flight of his own slave in Paris. His plan to punish Pauline echoed the didactic terror that defined his island reign. When justifying his conduct to metropolitan officials—the Admiralty, the navy, the police—Bouvet always referred to colonial law and the danger of slave flight. When Pauline proposed to buy herself out of slavery, he refused, citing the Code Noir. "The royal ordinance does not permit freedom in the colonies except in recognition of good service." The manumission of slaves was a bad idea, to be generally discouraged. "Free blacks are dangerous . . . during the whole thirteen years that [I] governed either the Isle of France or the Isle of Bourbon, [I] only gave freedom to two or three blacks, and these were in response to orders from the Company."[58]

Bouvet did not acknowledge Pauline's role in any legitimate form of commerce. He insinuated that her money was ill-gotten and hinted at

62 SLAVES IN PARIS

prostitution. He complained about her scurrilous conduct on the ship that took them to France, and about her revelry during his absence from Paris. While he took the waters, she received expensive treatment by a surgeon "with mercury." He meant syphilis. (According to the *Encyclopédie*, mercury was a specific against parasites, worms, and a range of skin infections.) He could not allow Pauline to buy her freedom: "Is it decent for a slave who is laden with prizes for her misconduct, who has been so lacking and offensive, to snatch the liberty she would have earned by performing her duty?"

No document explains how Pauline came by this money. Her allies claimed she had the backing of a famous—notorious—colonial notable. "Madame Dupleix gave her 1,000 livres to start this business."[59] The Madame Dupleix in question, Jeanne Albert (1706–1756), was the Indian-born wife of Joseph-François Dupleix, an Indies Company official who served as governor-general of French possessions in India until the French Crown disavowed his expansionist policy and ordered his return to France. Jeanne Albert (known in India as Joanna Begum) was a Tamil and Portuguese-speaking mixed-race woman whose pious bigotry bloomed into the razing of mosques and Hindu shrines. She was also notorious for encrusting herself with the jewels she received from visiting nabobs.[60] Jeanne Albert passed through the Mascarene Islands with Dupleix in 1754, after his disgrace; she died in Paris two years later.

Of Jeanne Albert's generosity toward Pauline, Bouvet observed: "It is possible that Madame Dupleix and some other people of distinction—general and particular officers of land and sea—who came through the house of Monsieur Bouvet *lui aient fait des liberalités*."[61] Narrowly, this just meant that visitors to Bouvet's house gave Pauline gifts. Less literally, the phrase suggests that Pauline sold sexual favors to men who passed through Bouvet's house. It is unlikely, however, that house guests of Governor Bouvet in Isle de France or Isle de Bourbon would bother paying for sex with his slave or that she would remit the sex money to the governor at regular intervals; or that the governor, as he claimed, would "put the sums on his books whenever she remitted them."

Bouvet lived in Paris but remained in the colonial world in a moral sense. In late November 1764, when he first sought help from the police, he intended to imprison Pauline in Paris as a preliminary to deporting her from

France to Bourbon. On December 3, 1764, Inspector Muron reported Bouvet's accusations against his slave to Antoine de Sartine, lieutenant-general of police:

> that she has always sought to associate with those of her kind most likely to suggest to her the spirit of independence of which she gives him and his sister the most marked signs every day; that his admonitions have become useless; that a few days ago . . . this girl was with the other servants and making a lot of noise so he told her to stop because she could be heard by the master and mistress to which she replied that she didn't care. . . . Mademoiselle Bouvet entered after having heard her, asking "Pauline, was it you who spoke thus," "Yes Madame" she said, "I don't give a f*** and if you are not satisfied, you can dismiss me"; that he does not wish to use his authority here nor to punish her as she would be punished on the Isle of Bourbon; that the example of this negress is dangerous for his other negroes and negresses, who are also slaves.[62]

Bouvet told Muron about a scene of loud talk below stairs while suppressing the topic of the servants' heated exchange, which he manifestly overheard. Instead, he quoted a saucy retort by Pauline ("you can dismiss me") that inadvertently gave the lie to Bouvet's story. This remark could only be uttered by a woman who believed that she was free—and hence could be dismissed, like any other employee. A woman who knew herself to be a slave would not imagine she could be fired for disobedience. Bouvet's complaint contained a second lie. According to an Admiralty declaration by Bouvet's brother, there were only three slaves living in this house: L'Empereur (age 26, Malagasy), Pierre (age 20, West African), and Pauline.[63] Yet here, if Muron's report is to be believed, Bouvet told the police that a large but unspecified number of household slaves, male and female, would be corrupted by Pauline's insolence should she remain there.

At the top of this document, an unknown hand in the police wrote, "Pauline, 3 December 1764, Hospital by the Sr. Muron, enslaved negress of Sr Bouvet, arrested at his request for libertinage."[64] Antoine de Sartine used libertinage as a pretext for Pauline's arrest out of convenience: in cases of libertinage, the lieutenant-general of police could issue lettres de cachet on his own authority.[65] For the eighteenth-century police, the word *libertinage* was an umbrella term for debauched and atheistic misconduct with the connotation of freedom misused; mainly, it described voluptuary deviance. For educated speakers of French in the eighteenth century, however, the word *libertin* (libertine) carried the dust of its Latin origin. In *L'Encyclopédie,* Boucher d'Argis defined *libertin* as a jurisprudential word that "is sometimes used in our language to designate freed slaves or their children."[66]

Pauline wound up at La Salpêtrière prison, which the authorities called "The Hospital." It was a derelict compound without pretense of treatment that enclosed mad women, streetwalkers, vagrants, destitute nursing mothers, abortionists, geriatric paupers, and criminals unfit for release after their sentences expired.[67] The duration of a woman's stay often depended on the willingness of someone on the outside—usually the man who locked her up—to pay for her upkeep. Pauline spent twelve days in Salpêtrière, a miraculously short stint in a place that is worth pausing over, as are the people who preceded her and those she left behind.

Salpêtrière was a city within a city, operated by fake nuns who took no vows, assumed fake names, and went by the title "Sister." The compound contained herds of pigs and cows, flocks of sheep, hundreds of artisans, an internal police force, a children's school, and an anatomy theater. There were horse-drawn carts for wheeling sick people out and new people in. Inside, bald women in gray frocks spun, wove, and sewed uniforms. Girls who entered for morals offenses typically remained for about two years. Plenty of people languished in oblivion. In 1765, when Pauline left this place, someone in the police composed a text entitled "Notes on women . . . to whom we are not able to accord liberty," which mentioned "Marguerite Stuart—Irish mute." She had been at Salpêtrière for ten years. The directress of the prison did ask for her release, noting that "she promise[d] to go back to her country." Someone in the police annotated this request: "We do not know the reason for her detention and she does not figure in the police registers."[68] She could not leave because they could not explain why she was there in the first place.

With a shaved head, Pauline left Salpêtrière on December 15, 1764, at the request of her master so she could travel the next day. Bouvet planned to whisk her by carriage to Lorient and embark her for the Mascarenes. Pauline fled on the eve of her departure in a prearranged escape and went into hiding.

A bird called the Widow of the Indies belonging to His Serene Highness the Duc de Penthièvre has flown away. . . . We promise a fair reward to whoever brings it back to Sieur Philidor, concierge of the Hôtel de Toulouse, Rue de la Vrillière (June 19, 1760).

PARISIAN READERS OF *ANNONCES, affiches, et avis divers,* a semi-weekly leaflet of classified ads, learned in June 1760 about the escape of an improbably coiffed bird from the aviary of Louis-Jean-Marie de Bourbon, Duc de Penthièvre, the Admiral of France.[69] The duke was a melancholy widower born into staggering wealth (who, despite his title, never set foot on a ship). His father was a bastard son of Louis XIV.[70] His bird was a Paradise-Whydah (sounds like "widow")—familiarly known as a Widow of Paradise. Whydahs are tuneful cousins of the cuckoo with parasitic brooding habits and striking plumage. They lay their eggs in other birds' nests. They sing other birds' songs. Their cascade of black feathers in mating season might have looked to the duke like high mourning (picture a trailing pointy opera cape).[71] Native to sub-Saharan Africa, they prefer savannahs and live on seeds.[72] These birds were named, originally, after the kingdom of Whydah, on the coast of modern-day Benin, which was a slave-trading hub in the eighteenth century, especially for French ships.[73]

After fleeing her master, Pauline went into hiding in the duke's residence, the Hôtel de Toulouse, which opened onto the Place des Victoires. Inspector Muron and his spies conducted a long stakeout of the building, ending with an aborted kidnapping of Pauline at the foot of the compound. The gargantuan podlike self-sufficiency of the Hôtel de Toulouse suited Pauline's life as a fugitive; it gave her the luxury of never leaving. The untouchable grandeur of its owner made the building difficult to raid. But Pauline did not become free because of the security and amenities of her hiding spot. She owed her rescue to domestics and to French people in high society who might just as well have turned her over to the police.

2.1 The Place des Victoires and its centerpiece, the statue of Louis XIV surrounded by slaves, by Martin Van Den Bogaert (known as Desjardin). Inaugurated in 1685, demolished in 1792.

Paul Grégoire (1755–1842), Place des Victoires (1786). Graphite drawing, 33.2 × 45cm. Bibliothèque Nationale de France (Paris).

Seen from the air, the neighborhood around the Hôtel de Toulouse was geometrical and surprisingly green (suitable for avian escapees). The mansions with walled gardens were interlocked, resembling wedge-shaped puzzle pieces around a circle with a gleaming hub. From the street, the Place des Victoires was plantless and strange. It centered on a gargantuan (42 foot tall) bronze statue of the Sun King—draped in ermine, covered in gold, crowned by victory, standing on a polycephalous dog, and surrounded by four comparatively diminutive (13-foot) bronze slaves in chains, rippling and unclad, who looked European and represented conquered armies.

The monument was a gift to Louis XIV from a sycophantic peer, the Duc de Feuillade. Courtiers mocked the donor, the statue, and the tycoons who thronged to its feet, arraying their spanking new mansions around the gold colossus. A famous quip about the statue by the Duc de Saint-Simon compared it to other royal statues in Paris: "Henri IV is with his people on the Pont Neuf, Louis XIII is with his nobles in the Place Royale, and Louis XIV is with his tax collectors in the Place des Victoires."[74] The first occupants of the Place des Victoires included Antoine Crozat, Samuel Bernard, and John Law—all investors with fortunes tied to the slave trade.[75]

In April 1765, Muron discovered that Pauline was living inside the Duc de Penthièvre's compound. As a clandestine lodger in the Hôtel de Toulouse, she became a fugitive among peers at the apex of the social world. She went underground among the most watched people in the kingdom. Apart from domestics, her helpers included grandees who shimmered among atheists and literary outlaws in Parisian salons. They were also major colonial proprietors and investors. From where she stood, slavery bankrolled the social edifice.

Pauline found her way to the Hôtel de Toulouse through Luce, also known as Luce Diancra or Diancourt. She was a freed slave from Saint-Domingue and the lady's maid of the Vicomtesse Marguerite-Renée de Castellane-Esparron (1722–1781). Pauline's circle of outspoken black friends, whom Bouvet denounced to Sartine in 1764, surely included her. Luce lived with her mistress in the Hôtel de Toulouse. Gaspard-Constantin-Boniface, Vicomte de Castellane (1706–1779), was first equerry to the duke and a lieutenant-colonel in his regiment.[76] His wife, née Fournier de Varennes, married into the Castellane family in 1745 at the age of 23. At the age of 16, while still a slave, Luce left Saint-Domingue and became her maid in Paris.[77]

Years later, in her 60s, Luce became a revolutionary. She appears on the 1789 list of "seventy-five American colonists who have gathered behind Monsieur de Joly, attorney, since August 29 to demand the rights of their category [i.e., free people of color]." Luce was one of eight women who signed this petition. She and other signatories wanted "to apply the Declaration of the Rights of Man and Citizen to their unfortunate class" and to protest "the despotism of whites and the outrageous rigor of the laws."[78]

When Pauline fled from her master, Luce was the doyenne of slaves and freed people in Paris. Pauline was not the first luckless black person to whom Luce, together with the viscountess, offered shelter and assistance. The first known incident of this, in 1759, involved a young man, Jean-Balthazar Celse, who claimed to be the Prince of Timor (and probably was). He said he lost

68   SLAVES IN PARIS

his liberty, worldly goods, and slaves after embarking from Timor for France on a diplomatic mission. Celse wrote of his arrival in Paris: "There I was, without money, knowing nobody; by the grace of God, I made the acquaintance of a black woman, to whom I explained who I was and asked if she could arrange for lodgings with someone she trusted. . . . I saw this black woman several times. She is attached to the Vicomtesse de Castellane, with whom she procured an introduction. I paid her several visits and told her of my origins." The viscountess arranged for Celse to meet an Indies Company official, who arranged for a berth on a ship bound for China. Celse never got on the ship.[79]

In 1762, three years before the Pauline affair, Luce and the viscountess offered shelter to Marie-François Laperle, who walked to Paris from Auvergne, arriving there alone at the age of 15. Laperle was questioned about her life many years later. In 1777 the prosecutor general of the Admiralty Court launched a personal campaign against racial pollution. He began by hunting down black streetwalkers. When asked about her past, Laperle said she had been told, on arriving in Paris, to present herself "to the woman called Luce, black woman, chambermaid to the Vicomtesse de Castellane, where she remained for one month, after which she was placed with the woman Hardy, dressmaker, Rue Nicaise, Hôtel de l'Agriculture."[80]

Police documents do not ascribe any role to the viscountess in concealing Pauline or helping her to attain freedom. Still, Castellane surely played a role in this affair. As a patroness, she knew how to maneuver around ministers and their underlings to protect the people she wished to. Pauline could not have resided for months inside the Hôtel de Toulouse without her protection.

Marguerite-Renée Fournier came from a family in Saint-Domingue whose plantations buoyed the fortunes of grandees, including Charles Vintimille du Luc—presumed son of Louis XV; Comte Louis-Marie de Narbonne Lara; Nicolas de Montholon; Emmanuel-Henri-Eugène Ferron de la Ferronaye; and Marguerite's own husband, the Vicomte de Castellane. When it came to a Fournier marriage in metropolitan France, the contracts tended to be signed by the king and queen. Her young cousins were royal pages; her old cousins ran the navy or served as officers on land, on sea, and in the colonial militia. Her family seems to have founded the Haitian parish of Limonade.[81]

The Castellane household is part of a bigger story, about the grafting of France's high nobility onto the fortunes of colonial tycoons. This tendency,

2.2 Restored interior of the Galerie dorée in the Hôtel de Toulouse, now the Bank of France (2018).
© Miranda Spieler.

ever more pronounced as time wore on, inspired the Marquis de Gouy d'Arsy to remark, in a 1789 petition to the king, "Sire, your court has become Creole by alliance."[82] The Castellane-Esparrons lived entirely on slave wealth. In 1773 the viscount wrote to his cousin, Madame de Saint-Vincent: "We are living on loans since the beginning of the year, having been deprived of almost all of our revenue in America due to extraordinary circumstances."[83]

To the extent that a mother is revealed through the education of her daughters, the country seat of the Castellane-Esparron family, the Château des Pressoirs, was a theater of precocious female attainment. The Duc de Penthièvre spent afternoons with the two Castellane girls, who were known to read "the best authors" and to undertake "even the study of dead languages." Noted for their "pronounced taste for dramatic literature," they put on Corneille plays, like *Rodogune,* before Fontainebleau neighbors including the king.[84]

The Fournier family owned thousands of slaves. For the viscountess, the collision between conscience and economic necessity produced an interest, as befitted a woman of feeling, in the particular misfortunes of individual enslaved people whom she encountered outside the colonies. The help she gave to Pauline is a noteworthy departure from the moral vulgarity displayed by other members of her family in Paris. In 1789 two Fourniers sent civic oaths to the municipal government of Paris and a few unusual gifts. "Sir Fournier and Sir [Fournier] de Bellevue declare to this august assembly, sitting in the Hôtel de Ville—dare we request a copy of this act?—that they offer their persons and their fortunes to contribute to the general good of the nation and the tranquility of the good citizens of Paris, and they equally make the offer of persons attached to them, including two domestics, a negro, a jockey and a coachman."[85]

The worldview of the Vicomtesse de Castellane resembled that of her neighbor and protégé Pierre-Victor Malouet (1740–1814), who became a voice for colonial reform in the 1770s.[86] While a rising bureaucrat in the navy, he served as deputy commissioner in Saint-Domingue, an office job equal in rank to that of a lieutenant aboard a ship. He married a local woman, Marie-Louise Behotte. Through his wife, Malouet became the owner of slave plantations. After returning to Paris, he lived near the Castellanes in the Place des Victoires. Malouet opposed the cruelty of masters while harping on the need for racial purity. He wanted to make slavery more humane while intending that it endure. Malouet was the voice of the slavery lobby in Paris during the early 1790s. The Revolution exposed the limits of what he meant by reform.[87]

The convergence of colonial wealth and Enlightenment society in the Castellane household was not unusual. As Antoine Lilti observes, the cost of holding semiweekly receptions was 40,000 to 60,000 livres (about 500,000 euros) per year. This does not include the cost of buying or renting a house with a special suite of public rooms for entertaining. Salons were the product of an elite subcategory of plutocrats who were either court nobles or bankers. Only 210 families in all of France had an annual income above 50,000 livres per year.[88] The identity of this social group makes it all the more striking that historians of enlightened sociability do not make more of the overlap between wealthy families who could afford salons and wealthy families who could afford slave plantations, married people who owned them, helped to run the Indies Company during its phase as a slave-trading outfit, and invested in slave ships.

Both the Vicomte de Castellane and his wife frequented the salon of Julie de Lespinasse, who described him as "a frank, excellent man, what we call a philosopher, and a bit of a rebel."[89] Julie de Lespinasse did not belong to a slave-owning milieu. Other women of equal renown did. Such was the case, for instance, of Madame d'Épinay (1726–1783) and her sister-in-law, Madame de Houdetot (1730–1813), who were both famous salon hostesses.[90] The former, née Louise-Florence-Petronille Tardieu d'Esclavelles, married Denis-Joseph Lalive, Marquis d'Épinay; Madame de Houdetot, née Elisabeth-Sophie-Françoise Lalive de Bellegarde, was the sister of the Marquis d'Épinay. Their father was the financier Louis-Denis Lalive de Bellegarde d'Épinay (1675–1751), a farmer general and onetime director of the Indies Company.[91] His other son, known as Lalive de Jully, married a daughter of the banker Laborde, who owned 1,400 slaves in Les Cayes (Saint-Domingue). The archive of that wealth, captured at sea, is now held in the Prize Papers of Britain's High Court of Admiralty.[92]

Lilti's illuminating study of salons includes a chart of sites where foreign dignitaries spent time during the years running up to the Revolution, 1774–1789.[93] Several hostesses mentioned there owed their fortunes to slave trading or sugar—including people who were active during Pauline's stint in Paris. The Duchesse de Choiseul, née Louise-Honorine Crozat, was the granddaughter of Antoine Crozat (1665–1740). Reputed to be the richest man in France, Crozat was one of the first in France to invest in slave trading.[94] Many members of the Choiseul family owned plantations in Saint-Domingue.[95] Antoinette-Eustachie Crozat du Châtel, the sister of the Duchesse de Choiseul, married the Duc de Gontaut. Her son, Armand-Louis de Gontaut Biron, Duc de Biron, was a star of the social world in the 1770s.[96] Biron's wife, Amélie de Boufflers, invested in slave ships belonging to Pierre-Félix-Barthélemy David, the brother-in-law of Bouvet de Lozier.[97] The Marquis de Brancas, another society host of the 1770s and 1780s, was a major slave owner in Saint-Domingue.[98]

Beyond Luce and the Vicomtesse, Pauline's other ally during her time on the lam was the playboy Charles-Victoire-François de Salaberry (1733–1794), who became a judge at the age of 16 after inheriting his father's post at the Cour des Comptes (Court of Auditors). Inverting the general trend among Parisian socialites, the Salaberry family had a stronger connection to colonial slavery at the beginning of the eighteenth century than at the time of Pauline's arrival in the capital. As first clerk of the navy, his grandfather Charles de Salaberry served on the board of the Company of Saint-Domingue (est. 1698), which developed sugar plantations in cooperation with the Guinea Company. The elder Salaberry also invested in colonial sugar on his own account. Through ministerial patronage, he further acquired a right to the property of colonists in Saint-Domingue who died without heirs; this property included land and slaves.[99]

The published memoirs of Jean-Nicolas Dufort de Cheverny, a childhood friend, credits Salaberry with two enthusiasms. Most importantly, Salaberry was a libertine. He "loved women above everything" and "knew how to delight, to please, to chase after the next woman with marvelous style and grace." Police records from the 1760s mention Salaberry as a client of upscale Parisian bordellos. Intermittently, he went whoring with men in the entourage of the society hostess Madame d'Épinay—including her husband, lover, and brother.[100] (Three months after Pauline's departure, on January 22, 1766, Salaberry married Anne-Marie Legendre de Lormoy, the daughter of a fellow judge in the Court of Auditors.) Salaberry's second weakness was Enlightenment philosophy. He "spent his whole life ill digesting the convoluted phrases of Diderot, Rousseau, and Voltaire."[101]

The magnanimity of people around Pauline opens the question of whether she toppled into a milieu of abolitionists. Owning slaves did not rule out opposition to slavery of some kind. Quite a few early members of the Society of the Friends of the Blacks, founded in 1788, were or had been slave owners.[102] Supporting Pauline, however, did not require anyone to attack slavery or even to question the ethics of buying and selling people. Her 1765 Admiralty suit aimed to recover the money she had earned, which Bouvet refused to relinquish, so that she could buy herself out of bondage. This was the rare freedom suit where a slave put a price on her own body and championed the inviolability of colonial property.

PAULINE   73

As for abolitionism, her friends had nowhere to talk about it. The sly rules of conversation that governed French salons made frank exchange about social injustice impossible and kept the topic of abolition off limits. In Parisian high society, then known as *le monde* (the world), feelings were possible but arguments were not. Antoine Lilti even claims that salon speech, which depended on aphorism and anecdote, made scientific inquiry impossible.[103] Too much detail just struck the wrong tone. Judith Shklar's perceptive discussion of the Lisbon Earthquake as it was understood by Rousseau and Voltaire offers a useful primer to the moral compass of *le monde.* For Voltaire, the mass death of Lisbonites in the earthquake was a misfortune; for Rousseau, the entombment of townspeople in collapsing urban slums made this an injustice. Voltaire, not Rousseau, exemplified the language of polite society. He stood for the world that saved Pauline.[104]

Pauline's suit against Bouvet needs to be read in light of the people who surrounded her when her case went to law. It is striking that Durouzeau, Pauline's barrister, never gestured to France as the soil of liberty, which had become a standard element of all such trials. The absence of any reference to this putatively ancient doctrine is a clue to the influence of the Castellane family and their milieu on the case. All colonial slave owners viewed the free-soil maxim as illegal. They understood the right to colonial property, including property in slaves, as transoceanic and ineffaceable. Living in Paris could not annul a planter's claim to his colonial estate. Nor could residing in the capital (or visiting it) affect his title to a slave.

The accusations against Bouvet by Pauline's protectors inside and outside the courtroom hinged on her master's contempt for customary practices, including the banking of earnings by slaves and their purchase of freedom by private arrangement. These practices were no less integral to the French world of slavery than was the Code Noir, though they defied written statute and (usually) thwarted the authority of the colonial state. It is no accident that Pauline's unusual case took shape while she lived clandestinely under the protection of Saint-Domingue sugar magnates; it was there, at the Hôtel de Toulouse, that Regnaud, her solicitor, and the barrister Durouzeau were obliged to meet her. Pauline supplied them with facts about her life, some of which later appeared in their legal arguments. But she was not the sole author of this suit, or even the main one. The milieu that hid Pauline shaped her legal voice and turned her case into an echo of themselves.

74   **SLAVES IN PARIS**

HOW, FINALLY, DID PAULINE elude the police? In June 1765, Inspector Muron launched an abduction scheme. In his account of the incident, he sent a spy into the Hôtel de Toulouse. The spy's job was to dangle wealth and freedom before Pauline. He (or she) had "several interviews" with the "so-called *Luce,* negress . . . friend of Pauline." Maybe the spy was an acquaintance. The inspector could easily have blackmailed someone they knew.

Muron sought to lure Pauline into a hired coach outside the duke's compound. His spy was supposed to convince Pauline that the coachman would take her to a notary, who would return her stolen money and grant her freedom. Instead the driver would take her to prison. Accompanied by her friend Luce and another black woman (unnamed), Pauline got into a four-wheeled rental carriage. The inspector watched from a cab nearby. Coaches glutted the neighborhood. The Place des Victoires was a rental station for horse-drawn carriages, pushcarts, and sedan chairs.[105]

When the women's carriage began to move, tailed by Muron, someone in the Hôtel de Toulouse yelled to Luce, who got out of the carriage and returned to the Castellane apartment. Muron later claimed that he "could have seized Pauline while she remained for a few moments in the carriage waiting for Luce." Tipped off about the scheme, Luce reappeared to warn Pauline, who exited the coach and accompanied her friend back into the building. What happened to the third black woman? She dematerializes in Muron's description as Pauline sits there, apparently alone. Muron did not name this third woman in his report, which seems unusual in the context of an elaborately researched kidnapping scheme by an inspector of police with spies everywhere. Maybe she was his agent.

According to Muron's report about the failed capture, he could not have spirited Pauline away in a carriage against her will in broad daylight without provoking a dangerous and embarrassing incident. He foresaw "an uproar at the door of the Hôtel de Toulouse" and worried about "stirring up the servants and the rabble [*populace*]. " He feared that Antoine de Sartine, the lieutenant-general of police, "would not approve of my conduct."[106] Was there a danger of uproar? Who counted as the rabble? The Place des Victoires was never just a neighborhood of financiers, navy men, and entrepreneurial government officeholders. During the 1760s, people in the neighborhood included habitués of the café de Toulouse, saddlers, blade smiths, mercers, purveyors of exotic spirits, fan makers, caterers, monks, virtuoso furniture makers, the contra tenor Pierre Jélyotte, and pupils at Madame Gracis's boarding school for girls.[107] Moreover, as Natacha Coquery observes, aristocratic mansions were continuous works-in-progress, maintained and refurbished by legions of specialized craftsmen who moved in and out.[108] For every artisan, a workshop, which meant journeymen, scampish apprentices, and porters.[109] 1765 was also a peak year for worker unrest and neighborhood brawls. From Muron's point of view, however, the most ignitable people in the Place des Victoires were the area's thousands of servants. The Hôtel de Toulouse contained enough people to fill a town. After halving his father's domestic staff, the Duc de Penthièvre still maintained a household of seventy-two workers, not including the fifty-eight people who tended the horses, dogs, and birds. Twenty-one people worked in the kitchens (and they still needed to outsource the bread and pastry). More than thirty people, including nobles, Admiralty staff, top servants, and an apothecary, had apartments in the compound with servants of their own.[110]

There were, perhaps, unstated reasons for Muron's reluctance to arrest Pauline. Maybe he noticed that Sartine had been dragging his heels in this affair. The lettre de cachet for Pauline's arrest from Versailles arrived on March 11, 1765. Its hasty dispatch was supposed to enable her capture before the final hearing of her freedom suit on March 18. Sartine did not rush to execute the warrant, as he did in other instances. Instead he wrote to Bouvet explaining that he was understaffed. He claimed that the inspector (Muron) who handled such matters was away. Nothing else in the file about Pauline mentions the absence from Paris of Muron. Moreover, he was not the only inspector who arrested slaves in the city.

The delay in transmitting the arrest warrant made it possible for the Admiralty Court to decide for Pauline and declare her a free woman. After the judgment, while Pauline remained in hiding, Salaberry visited Sartine at his residence on April 1 and sent him notes on the case. Still, Sartine did not send Muron the arrest warrant. When Muron, on April 3, requested the lettre de cachet on Bouvet's behalf, Sartine temporized. He sent Salaberry's notes to Bouvet with a request for comment. Only then did Sartine allow Muron to execute the order. What followed? Months of surveillance.

One cannot avoid the impression that Pauline avoided capture because Sartine, perhaps even Muron, did not wish to succeed in arresting her. This is all the more striking because the police conducted at least nine other successful slave hunts between May and September 1765—for Joseph Aza

76 **SLAVES IN PARIS**

(lettre de cachet of May 6), Pèdre (May 6), Charles-Dominique Lazy (May 17), Anne-Philippe Hector (June 7), Charles-Auguste (July 6), Hélène (July 23), Cézar (September 5), Papillon (September 8), and François (September 30).[111]

The power that saved Pauline was the same power that caused her friends, slaves in the neighborhood, to disappear. Sartine, who later became minister of the navy, was a creature of the Indies Company and of the Duc de Choiseul. He was married to the granddaughter of Charles Colabeau (or Colabau), who was syndic of the Indies Company from 1748 to 1764 and looked after Sartine when he first came to Paris as a young orphan from Spain. Colabeau invested in slave trading on his own account for the whole of his tenure at the company (as did other directors).[112] The slaves whom Muron hunted in 1765 often belonged to company employees.

The influence of colonial wealth in Paris and Versailles made it easy for masters to arrange for their slaves to be hunted down by the police. Pauline lucked into the protection of a slave-owning magnate who had more clout among the people who mattered than did her actual owner. The closeness of Antoine de Sartine to the Indies Company meant that he and the Vicomtesse de Castellane belonged to overlapping social sets, or the same one. Here is a description of maneuvering by the viscountess in the 1770s on behalf of her protégé Malouet, during Sartine's tenure as minister of the navy. "Happily for Malouet, one of his friends, who was also the friend of Monsieur de Sartine, the Vicomtesse de Castellane, lived nearby. She was Creole. She understood Malouet's ties to Saint-Domingue and the honorableness of his conduct and had little trouble persuading the minister. The deputy of the colony and the navy's chief of staff realized the project of Madame de Castellane."[113]

Chapter 3

LUCIDOR

ANDRÉ LUCIDOR came to France as an enslaved African orphan in the 1720s. The people who owned him came from a family of judges, art patrons, tax farmers, and money handlers for the state. Lucidor's owners did not keep him in their household for long. From the age of 15 he lived on his own. He began as a servant of soldiers. Later he became a dueling master. He married a French woman while still a slave, and had two daughters (who lived to adulthood). In 1750, when Lucidor obtained freedom papers from his master, the jurist Pierre-Philibert de Blancheton, he was already free in fact. Soon after becoming officially free, he bought a large house outside the city limits, where he died in 1771 at the age of 53.

Much of this book explores how the Paris police, the Crown, and slave owners connived in the abduction of slaves. The subversion of the free-soil doctrine is beyond the scope of this chapter. Here I explore the life of André Lucidor to understand what freedom meant—and did not mean—to people who managed to exit slavery in Paris. As we shall see, Lucidor spent the whole of his adulthood as an urban fugitive, despite enjoying de facto liberty from an early date, and obtaining freedom papers amicably from his master.

Lucidor was a dueling master, but he did not belong to the swordsmen's guild.[1] Because he did not belong to the guild, he plied this trade illegally, violating not only Parisian work laws but also edicts that restricted the bearing of arms to nobles, soldiers, and people enforcing the law.[2] Ancient laws prohibited servants from carrying weapons. On paper those rules en-

77

78 **SLAVES IN PARIS**

dured until the Revolution. In 1779, eight years after Lucidor's death, a royal ordinance with an explicitly racial character prohibited servants from usurping the costume and privileges of soldiers. It forbade "postilions, negroes, and all domestics" from wearing epaulettes or carrying "firearms, swords, hunting knives, sabers, canes, batons, long sticks."[3] Lucidor flouted the laws of the capital and kingdom by merely carry a sword, and by making unlicensed use of it as a self-appointed master of arms.[4]

According to the 1687 *Dictionary of the French Academy,* the word *liberté* meant "a sort of independence from the commands of other people." This definition of freedom also sums up the experience of an illegal laborer in eighteenth-century Paris. Before 1789 France was a place patterned by corporate affiliations and hierarchy. In the capital, and throughout Old Regime France, a person's status derived from his attachment to a corporate group, which conferred on its members an identity and certain legal capacities. Lawyers, Crown officials, and master tradesmen pictured these groups as an interconnected unity; they were bodies in a "Great Chain of Being" that added up to "the body of the Nation," as Stephen Kaplan has shown. For the monarchy, and for authorized tradesmen, to lack a corporate identity was to live in an "immense void." Isolated individuals who lacked some kind of corporate affiliation were "beings born to trouble the order of society."[5] The monarchy saw the unattached and self-directed individual as a deviant, whom the authorities defined in reference to what he was not. The active worker who did not belong to a tradesman's guild was *a man without quality.* The unemployed worker was a *man of no condition.* The man without a rank in an officially recognized hierarchy was a man *sans état* (without status). To the degree that a language of individual liberty coexisted with this corporatist worldview, it did so in subaltern workers' language of protest. When journeymen denounced their subordination to masters, while chafing at restrictions on their movement, they revolted against a system that "rendered them slaves" and "assimilated their fate and future to that of negroes in America."[6]

One-fourth of the workers in and around Paris lived beyond the power of the guilds.[7] André Lucidor's freedom to work in the city resulted from where he chose to live. Until the Revolution, medieval ecclesiastical institutions retained judicial power over pockets of the city despite attempts by the Crown to suppress those jurisdictions. These unusual neighborhoods— known as *lieux privilégiés* (privileged places)—were important to the everyday life of the Parisian working class. Within these bits of Paris, and in the neighborhood behind the Bastille—the Faubourg Saint-Antoine—artisans and other tradesmen lived outside the city's labor laws. People who could not work elsewhere without risking arrest thronged to these places. These privileged places were refuges for urban outcasts.[8] Lucidor and his family lived in one of those pockets: the Abbey Saint-Martin-des-Champs, on the Right Bank of the Seine. Extant portions of this once-vast abbey have since become the Musée national des arts et métiers (National Museum of Arts and Crafts). From the vantage point of authorized Parisian craftsmen, the original workers at the abbey were imposters who exploited the city's legal geography and hid behind impenetrable gates.

This chapter explores the biography of one man, who lived in a small Parisian neighborhood, yet whose life tells a global story. When we look at Paris through the prism of Lucidor's experiences, it becomes possible to see the tightening of bonds between the capital, the Atlantic ports, the slave trade, and overseas plantations. The hardening of racial attitudes—a sign of that connectedness—would disturb Lucidor's whole family, and probably shortened his life.

NO DIRECT SOURCES link Lucidor to any colony or allow us to know when he left Africa. Unlike other people of slave origin in Paris, he refused to talk about it. In 1762 all black and brown people, free and enslaved, were required to register—or be registered—with the Paris Court of Admiralty. According to the 1762 ordinance spelling out this requirement, "negroes and mulattoes" who worked for themselves needed to report "their names, nick-names, age and profession, place of birth, date of their arrival in France, by what ship, and whether they are baptized." In the case of domestics, free or enslaved, masters were supposed to provide "precise declarations about the negroes and mulattoes living with them, in what capacity and status, for how long, by what ship these negroes or mulattoes arrived in France, their age, name and nickname, if the said negroes or mulattoes are baptized, and from what colony or place they were exported."[9]

When Lucidor presented himself to the clerk of the Admiralty, he did not follow the script for self-employed people of color. He said nothing about his journey. He did not give his age. He did not explain how or when he

80   SLAVES IN PARIS

got to Paris. Details are missing from his statement that appear in every other statement in the register. To illustrate the significance of these gaps, let us look at the 1762 register in which Lucidor's story appears.[10] The whole page is atmospheric. It contains four statements, including that of Lucidor, which together offer a glimpse of imperial Paris near the close of the Seven Years War:

> On Monday May 24, 1762. Appeared Mister Jean-Joseph Amat, presently in Paris at the home of the Marquis Dupleix, Rue Neuve des Capucines, Madeleine Parish of the Ville L'Évêque, so as to satisfy the sentence of the General Admiralty of the Marble Table of the Palace in Paris of April 5 last, declares having taken with him from the Isle de France a negro named Le Douceur, native to Mozambique, Coast of Africa, about thirty years of age, baptized in Isle de France, on the Company of the Indies ship called *Le Bristol*, Captain Sureville the Elder, which departed on January 23, 1753, and disembarked at Port Lorient June 14 of the same year, to instruct him in the Catholic and Apostolic Roman Religion and have him master the profession of cook, of which statement the said declarant sir requested a copy . . . and signed.[11]

> On the same day. Appeared Mister André called Lucidor, negro, native of Azanda in Africa, who to satisfy the sentence of the General Admiralty . . . declares himself to be free by act passed before the notaries of this court on March 26, 1750, by Sieur Blancheton, Royal Counselor and Master of Requests Ordinary, in his hotel, at the bottom of which is the certificate of Monsieur le Prevôt des Marchands. The said negro lives presently in Paris, Abbey Saint-Martin, parish of Saint-Nicolas-des-Champs, where he demonstrates the use of arms, of which statement the said declarant negro requested a copy . . . and signed.

> Tuesday May 25, 1762. Appeared to the clerk the so-called Guillaume Quenaut free negro, native of Port au Paix, who to satisfy the sentence of the General Admiralty . . . declares himself to have arrived in 1718 on the vessel called *Port de Paix*, captain Auvray *père*, disembarking at Havre de Grace the same year, and to live presently

in the Rue Tiquetonne at the Grand Courrier, having the profession of master of arms, of which statement the said declarant requested a copy . . . and signed.

Wednesday May 26, 1762. Appeared Pierre Valette living at the home of the Countess of Butler, Rue de Bourbon, near the Rue de Belle Chasse, Faubourg Saint-Germain, who to satisfy the sentence of the General Admiralty . . . declares in the name of, and charged with the power of, Madame July Dutrouzet d'Héricourt, widow of Mr. Jean Butler, Esquire, Lord of Gonzaga, Earl of Butler, who took a negress named Babette Elizabeth called Pélagie, born on her plantation Morne Rouge, isle and coast of Saint-Domingue, Cap Français, who is a slave belonging to her as absolute property, aged approximately 25 years, baptized, who arrived in France four years earlier on the ship *L'Opinionâtre* commanded by Monsieur de Morieu in the Squadron of Vice Admiral Kersaint, disembarked at Brest in 1758, and arrived in Paris the same year, to serve as her lady's maid during her sojourn in France, of which statement the said declarant requested a copy . . . and signed.

Masters registering slaves were expected to indicate a traceable name, a point of origin, and account for their slaves' movements from the time of their purchase to their arrival in Paris. Those details helped slave owners lay claim to the people they said they owned. This is what we get from the Indies Company official named Amat about Le Douceur, who accompanied him from Mauritius to Paris in 1753. This is what we get from the Countess of Butler's errand boy about Babette, her lady's maid. Curiously, that is more or less what we get from Guillaume Quenaut, whose declaration follows that of Lucidor in the register. Quenaut provided a narrative with details that Lucidor omitted. He gave his colonial birthplace (Saint-Domingue). He named the ship and the captain who took him to France. He listed his ports of departure and arrival. According to his statement, he disembarked at Le Havre in 1718, the year of Lucidor's birth. If this date is correct, his arrival in France predated that of everyone else in this register.

Quenaut did not explain how or when he became free. By contrast, Lucidor waved an official-looking certificate granting him liberty, of which no copy survives, whose authenticity we cannot verify. The Admiralty Court

82 SLAVES IN PARIS

did not prescribe any formal way of proving one's liberty in 1762 and never created procedures for becoming free in Paris. Nonetheless, enslaved people and formerly enslaved people knew the value of legal papers and came with whatever scraps they could turn up. Quenaut had nothing.

Read against the statement by Quenaut, by Amat, and by the countess's errand boy, it becomes easy to spot the gaps in Lucidor's Admiralty declaration. What is missing? Life as a slave in the age of sail: ships, ports, people who chain you up and move you around. The missing details in Lucidor's story are those that would otherwise make it possible to glimpse the agony of his boyhood. We cannot know whether he chose to omit these details or could not remember them.

There are more curiosities. An earlier police document lists Lucidor as a native of *rada* whereas here he is a native of Azanda. Moreover, someone corrected the spelling of Lucidor's African ethnicity in the 1762 register, turning Aranda or Asanda into Azanda. Because Lucidor was literate and signed this document, he might have fixed the spelling himself.

In the first half of the eighteenth century, people whom the French called *rada, ardra,* and *arada* were sold to Europeans out of the Bight of Benin, which was then known as the Slave Coast. During the 1720s, local disputes over control of the slave trade destabilized kingdoms in this region. The inland martial kingdom of Dahomey capitalized on the fragility of local states to destroy Allada (1724) and Whydah (1727) in Armageddon-like wars.[12] There soon followed huge shipments of slaves, including many young people, to French islands. In 1726 the *Junon,* a 600-ton ship built in Hamburg for the French Indies Company, transported 643 captives, of whom 278 were children, from Whydah to Saint-Domingue. Seventy-four captives died during the crossing. In the slave trade, captives labeled as children tended to be under the age of 13 or less than 4 feet in height.[13]

What of the Azanda? There is not a single mention of the Azanda in French or British colonial records relating to African peoples, enslaved or free, during the lifetime of André Lucidor. During these years, according to most Africanists, the Azanda did not yet exist.[14] One solution to this puzzle would be to assume a spelling irregularity and consider Lucidor a member of the Asante or Ashanti people of modern-day Ghana. Even the term *Asante* was rare in French texts about African captives. It was unusual to come across Asante slaves, because they were usually the enslavers. As an inland people on the march, the Asante expanded their frontiers by waging continuous war, enslaving defeated enemies, and enslaving rebels in conquered lands. For Lucidor to call himself Asante (if that is what he intended) meant that he identified with a warrior kingdom of empire builders—a nation of masters, not slaves.[15]

There was no colonial property in the family of the people who owned André Lucidor. This was true of the Burgundian lawyer and collector, Pierre-Philibert de Blancheton, and of his wife, Catherine de Salins.[16] And yet the Salins family had ties to overseas networks that would account for the presence of at least one African in their household. Catherine de Salins was the daughter of a tax collector who spent the early part of his career in Nantes before moving to Paris.[17] Her mother belonged to the Prévost family, later known as the Prévost de la Croix. The scion of the family was a stockbroker of peasant origin.[18] His son, Jacques-Philippe Prévost de la Croix, who was Catherine de Salins's uncle, married into the Lestobec family of Breton notables. The Lestobecs had been mayors of Brest for centuries and port directors of the French Indies Company since the reign of Louis XIV.[19]

Lestobec family connections turned nearly all the Prévost boys into high-ranking naval administrators and Indies Company men. Their careers reveal how maritime commerce in the era of the slave trade wrought changes to French society in the form of a generational shift. The Prévost cousins of Catherine de Salins were all born around 1720. They were about the same age as Lucidor. During Lucidor's life, members of the Prévost family lived in Paris, Atlantic ports, the Antilles, and the East Indies.[20] By the year of his death, they had become a global imperial family with direct ties to transatlantic slavery.

The French Company of the Indies had a fleet of slave ships. During the epoch of chaos that followed the conquest of Allada by Dahomey (1724), those ships were at their peak of activity. Soon, however, private merchants took over most of the traffic in slaves from Africa to the New World.[21] Nantes merchants handled 60 percent of the French slave trade by the end of the 1720s.

Lucidor may have entered the Salins-Blancheton household as a gift, either by way of Hugues de Salins or through a member of the Prévost family. This is an inference we might draw from a letter Catherine de Salins wrote to the police in 1733. Lucidor was then 15 years old, in prison, and in disgrace. He had just been entrapped either for male prostitution or for cruising (the file is vague on this point).[22] At the time of his arrest, Lucidor

84 SLAVES IN PARIS

worked as the servant of an officer in the musketeers. Salins appealed to a family friend, Marc-René Rossignol, a high-ranking bureaucrat who worked directly under the lieutenant-general of police. She hoped he would help rid her of Lucidor.

> As it is a century since I have had the honor of speaking with you. I could not see you before my departure to beg you to ask Monsieur Hérault to permit an officer named Monsieur Bouchaud to take little Lucidor to the islands. He is perhaps still detained in the Châtelet Prison before being transferred to Bicêtre, where Monsieur Hérault has destined him to be sent for his lovely actions and gestures. I am persuaded that it will not be difficult to obtain this order . . . which is even to render him a service, by perhaps sparing him the ordeal [*supplice*] to which his disorder and misery would infallibly lead him, it being perhaps impossible to find a master after being noted at Châtelet, since he cannot lay claim to anyone. He served two musketeers during the six months since he left my house and he did not impress either of them, which is not a good sign for him. . . . If you could take your answer to me yourself at Chévry, I would take great pleasure in receiving it this way and Monsieur Blancheton also sends his compliments. Your very humble servant Salins Blancheton.[23]

From this letter, we learn that Lucidor left the Blancheton-Salins household six months earlier. After his arrest, Salins wanted to distance him even further. She proposed handing him over to "a ship officer" named Bouchaud. In his custody, "little Lucidor" would leave for an unspecified colonial destination (*les îles*). To justify the boy's removal, Salins noted that Lucidor could not "claim anyone" because of his sexual offense, and recalled that France sent criminals to the Americas all the time.

Masters who purchased their slaves considered them to be valuable assets. Slaves who came as presents, by contrast, got thrown away. Salins attached no value to Lucidor's person and made it clear that she would not take him back. Her effort to discard him suggests a link between Lucidor's predicament and that of other boys who came to Paris as gifts. Take the criminal duo of Capolin and Rama, lost boys of the 1760s. The Comte d'Estaing purchased Rama in Pondicherry in 1761 as a gift for the Marquis de Brancas. As for Capolin, the daughter of the governor of Martinique shrugged him off. Christophe Pajot de Villers, son of the postmaster general, took the boy "out of charity" in 1762 or 1763. Two years later Capolin was living in the streets of Paris "without fixed abode, sleeping where he finds himself." He belonged to the social category known to police as the night wanderers. The two boys were arrested in 1765 for attempting to sell valuables that Capolin pilfered from a drunkard. He claimed to have found the man asleep with his breeches undone on an outdoor bench.[24]

The story of André Lucidor's arrest for sodomy in 1733 is more than a squalid detail. His teenage police file provides clues to who he was and became. After his arrest, Lucidor spent two months in Bicêtre, a notorious adult dungeon. In the words of Louis-Sébastien Mercier, who chronicled eighteenth-century Parisian life, Bicêtre was "a terrible ulcer on the political body, a large, deep, oozing ulcer that we can only envisage by averting our eyes." Internment in the dungeon was Lucidor's second round of captivity. The first was on a slave ship. On both occasions he endured nightmarish imprisonment without knowing when or even whether he could leave. When Lucidor entered Bicêtre, it was by lettre de cachet. Because he did not go through the courts, there was (as with the slave ship) no fixed duration to his punishment.[25]

The story about Lucidor in his police file comes from an unnamed informer, who might have spied for the police to avoid being exposed as a sodomite himself; or else he got paid for luring men seeking sex into police traps. The spy relates conversations that seem to be one-sided. It is impossible to know how he lured Lucidor in, what lies he told him, or whether money changed hands. The encounter began at the Porte Saint-Antoine, an archway that divided the Parisian neighborhood of the Marais from the Faubourg Saint-Antoine. The archway stood adjacent to the Bastille prison and near the compound of the musketeers.

> (August 10, 1733) Being at the half-moon at nine in the evening I was accosted by a negro about five feet tall, who began by asking me the time. After a vague conversation, he said there were few women on the walkway. In this conversation he said that he liked men as much as women, that he had consummated the act with men and women, that he got as much pleasure from one as from the other and was

3.1 View of the Bastille, the Porte Saint-Antoine, and part of the Faubourg Saint-Antoine.
Jacques Rigaud (1680–1754), (ca. 1720). Watercolor, pen and India ink on beige paper, 22.3 × 48 cm. Bibliothèque Nationale de France (Paris).

indifferent as to which. He said he was strong and could consummate the act six times in six hours. He said that, were it not so late, he could take me to the Grand Pinte, where they go often, up to thirty of them, and after proposing to go to a timber yard, where he had been several times to consummate the act, and after my refusal, he said he had to go to the Hôtel des Mousquetaires, where he had business, and that he lived in the Rue Saint-Louis with a young bachelor, whom he served, and during all this time he had his hand in his breeches, and after staying with him for about an hour, coming near the Porte Saint-Antoine, I left him and Sieur Simonnet followed him to the Hôtel des Mousquetaires.

(August 15) At eight in the evening I found the said Lucidor, who was looking to hook up, and came up to me smiling, wishing me good evening, struck up a conversation with me, noting that there weren't many people about, because it was still light; he proposed to take a turn and took me near the Pont au Choux to seek a place to satisfy his infamous desires and he was arrested on the way in the name of the king and conducted to the Petit Châtelet prison.[26]

The spy recounted two assignations, neither of which lasted for more than an hour. It is impossible to know whether Lucidor was cruising or selling his services. During the first encounter, Lucidor flaunted his libido and bragged about his stamina. During the second, the police arrested him as he led the spy under a bridge for their sex date. On neither occasion, as recounted here, does Lucidor, age 15, seem like the hapless plaything of other people. He gives the impression of a cheerful hustler with a busy schedule who moves with ease around a secret version of Paris. He was a regular at, a gay hook-up bar called La Grande Pinte in the village of Bercy. He knew a desolate place—a lumberyard—to take men he met there.

Lucidor perfected the art of dueling, which became his life, while working for people who knew about his imprisonment. Getting arrested as a sodomite, in the opinion of Catherine de Salins, was impossible to keep a secret. Salins even claimed that deporting Lucidor would rescue him from a life of squalid destitution, "it being perhaps impossible to find a master after being noted at Châtelet." She either misunderstood the Parisian social world or was pretending.

According to police files from the 1720s through the 1740s, domestics were the leading cruisers and rent boys of the capital.[27] Getting arrested for sodomy did not debar young men from the household staff of top people. For handsome boys, sex was frequently, if not routinely, a condition of employment. The police reported in 1728 that "the Comte de Lisle has long been known as a sodomite to the point that young lackeys who are out of work are advised by acquaintances to go to him."[28] The arrest report (1730) for Desjardins, a tailor's assistant (and ex-servant), notes that his former master, Monsieur Portail (probably Seigneur de Vaudreuil and Léry, chief justice at the Parlement de Paris), "always chose handsome lackeys whom he did not keep for long and always had them educated in trades."[29] While Portail seems to have treated the floating sex personnel with a mixture of benevolence and exploitation, the same cannot be said of Monsieur de Marbeuf (the lieutenant-general of the army, or perhaps his son), who "takes young valets and lackeys, whom he corrupts and fires after a couple of days."[30]

Notwithstanding the class-related exploitation of male servants, the whopping differences in status that otherwise organized Old Regime society did not mean the same thing in this world. Nobles and servants seem, at least from these files, to have attended the same parties. Despite huge inequalities

88   SLAVES IN PARIS

in status and wealth that structured the underground sex scene, there was a leveling effect that came from sharing the same forbidden desires, needing to fulfill those desires in secret, and needing other people, who did not come from the same social class, to make that happen. What was true of class might be said of race. An athletic African teenager was probably as equal in the underground sex scene as anywhere in Paris.

After Lucidor's death, his daughter, Marie-Thérèse, remembered her father as "a native of Africa who being transported to Martinique from there passed to France . . . and always served the king and after obtaining his discharge married and established himself as a master of arms in this capital." When did Lucidor "serve the king" and when did he obtain his discharge?

Army recruiters often enlisted the inmates of Parisian dungeons. Take the 1736–1737 case of a black man known to police as "Baptiste," whose years in Paris overlapped with Lucidor's time there. A slippery Parisian errand boy complained that Baptiste and his wife, together with three other black men, had showered him with insults, threatened his life, and bludgeoned him before witnesses. (He said nothing about what provoked them.) After he was arrested, Baptiste "voluntarily enrolled to serve in the capacity of drummer in the Free Company of Montauban for six years only." The enlistment reads, "knowing how to sign, I have written my name in Portuguese." The illegible signature that follows does not say Baptiste.[31]

There is no mention in Lucidor's file of forced enlistment. At 15, he was below the minimum age for joining the army. He did not need to enlist, moreover, to "always serve the king." At the time of his arrest, he was living among the Black Musketeers (who were white men), cavalry officers headquartered in an immense compound behind the Bastille fortress.

Lucidor's training as a master of arms probably began inside the Hôtel des Mousquetaires. He became an instructor around the time of his marriage. We know that he married at the age of 27 in 1745, although the parish records for that year are unobtainable. In 1871 the army invaded Paris to smash the Commune, a municipal junta led by socialist militants. In the ensuing street battle, a fire consumed the city archive. What survives of Lucidor's marriage certificate is a stub the size of an index card from an attempted reconstruction of parish records after the fire. The stub identifies Lucidor as "negro in origin, domestic of Madame de Blancheton." He married a white woman, Thérèse Richard, the widow of a black Portuguese-speaking army drummer, François Bourval, who died in the Hôtel des

Invalides, a home for injured soldiers.[32] There is no mention of Lucidor's military service here or in any other official document relating to him.

A later document of the same year, 1745, offers a different picture of Lucidor's early married life. It is the death certificate of Louis Lucidor, age one month, who died in November, ten months after Lucidor's marriage, in the care of a wet nurse. The death certificate—from a village located 115 kilometers to the west of Paris—does not mention Lucidor's race or describe him as a servant.[33] It identifies his occupation as dueling instructor (*provôt en salle d'armes*).

Soon afterward he assumed the title "master of arms." He described himself that way in a 1754 affidavit containing sworn testimony on behalf of a friend named Louis Lircot—a black ex-drummer in the cavalry regiment of the Prince of Clermont and a former regimental fencing instructor. Because Lircot wished to marry, but lacked a baptismal certificate, the vicar of Paris allowed him (as other foreigners) to provide sworn statements attesting to his age and religion. Witnesses other than Lucidor who spoke on Lircot's behalf included Jean-Louis Pharaon, an enslaved cook, and Louis-Joseph, no surname, who shared an apartment with Pharaon in Paris. According to French military records, a man called Louis-Joseph, "native of Rata [*sic*], Coast of Guinea, age 32, 5 foot 3," joined the all-black light cavalry regiment of the Maréchal de Saxe on August 1, 1750.[34] In their joint statement, Lucidor, Pharaon, and Louis-Joseph all claimed to know Lircot, "having all lived together as negroes in Cap Français of Saint-Domingue." They vowed he was "30 years of age, free in his person, of the Catholic Apostolic Roman faith." Pharaon is known to have lived in Saint-Domingue. By contrast, there is no evidence that Lucidor set foot there. All three men had other reasons to know each other. Lircot was an ex-army fencing instructor who lived in the same parish as Lucidor and the two men may have worked together. Lucidor, age 36, "master of arms," then resided at a curious location: the courtyard of the Abbey Saint-Martin-des-Champs.[35]

According to the work laws of eighteenth-century Paris, everything from making hats to performing tragedy was a monopolistic privilege, which the king bestowed on groups—guilds—not individuals. People outside the guilds faced arrest and the confiscation of their property for performing illegal work. What was true for hosiers and hairstylists was also true of swordsmen. Both Lircot and Lucidor worked in a highly

90   SLAVES IN PARIS

regulated occupation. Lucidor, though not Lircot, defied Parisian law by usurping the title "master of arms," an honorific reserved for members of the swordman's guild.

Lucidor's name would never appear on a single official list of Parisian fencing masters. Nor would such lists include the name of Guillaume Quenaut, a former slave from Saint-Domingue who registered with the Admiralty in 1762 just after Lucidor. As illegal masters of arms, both men belonged to the criminal class of workers that policemen called *ferrailleurs*. The French word *fer*, from the Latin *ferrum*, means iron. According to the seventeenth-century lexicographer La Curne de Sainte-Palaye, the word *ferraille* denoted both worthless metal detritus and despicable people; the ferrailleur was, according to La Curne, a stealthy weapon-maker. By contrast, Furetière's 1690 dictionary defined the ferrailleur as someone "who constantly fenced with swords" or a quarrelsome person. Similarly, eighteenth-century editions of the French Academy's dictionary defined the ferrailleur as someone "who makes a profession of fighting." The *Encyclopédie* stands alone in viewing the ferrailleur as a form of artisan, and groups this term under the subject heading, "chaudronnerie," a broad category of metalwork, which typically involved making vessels and industrial parts from sheets of tin, steel, copper, or iron. Diderot's volume (but no other book) defined the ferrailleur as a crude tinkerer who made little things like grills, stakes, and tongs. Let us assume that the word ferrailleur in mid-eighteenth-century Paris contained a variety of entangled meanings. Formally, in police correspondence, a ferrailleur was an illegal fencing instructor. In a broader sense, the word ferrailleur called to mind a sleazy hoarder of metal garbage with a violent temper who forged weapons in secret and used them constantly.[36]

Raids by the police on ferrailleurs date back to at least the seventeenth century. As the dueling fad caught on, the police busts grew more numerous. In 1722, one such roundup included ten police commissioners and seventeen illegal dueling instructors.[37] The illegal gyms continued to multiply, as one-handed fencing with slender swords became a popular sport outside the nobility.[38] In 1765, following the arrest of two ferrailleurs, a Parisian court ordered that their school be "sealed and walled up for six months," which hints that illegal gyms resurfaced quickly after each raid.

Unlicensed masters of arms found ways of avoiding arrest. Men who did not belong to the guild could rent the privilege of exercising this trade from an official master.[39] Such contracts were renewable. For two decades the swordsman Hyacinthe Serval, a veteran of the Seven Years War, paid an annual fee—150 livres per year from 1766 to 1787, equivalent to 2,600 modern euros—for the privilege of working as a master of arms. In 1787 a technicality caused a lapse in protection money. The police raided his school and confiscated everything.[40] In Paris, no free exercise of the dueling trade was possible, raising the question of how Lucidor sustained that livelihood.

Some patches of central Paris did not fall under the authority of the guilds. These zones were vestiges of the medieval past, when Paris was a smaller place. French kings had once empowered Church officials to govern ecclesiastical compounds (abbeys, monasteries) in rural areas outside the city's walls and beyond reach of municipal power. When the walls of Paris moved outward, ecclesiastical control over these places endured. Two such

3.2 The Abbey Saint-Martin-des-Champs, as viewed from the bell tower of the Saint-Nicolas Church (1630).

Etienne Martellange (1569–1641). Graphite, light India ink wash, 38.5 × 44.2 cm. Bibliothèque Nationale de France (Paris).

92 SLAVES IN PARIS

zones lay next to one another on the Right Bank, creating a broad swath of earth whose inhabitants claimed exemption from the city's work laws. One was the Temple—a compound owned by the Knights Templar. The other was the Abbey Saint-Martin-des-Champs, a walled monastery. Both enclosures contained private residences and a market.

In the eighteenth century, a visitor to the Temple could spot a sign that read *Marteau, Master of Arms, Student of Monsieur de Liancourt.* At the nearby Abbey Saint-Martin-des-Champs, another dueling master, Gardinier, advertised his gym with the wordless insignia of an arm holding a foil. Gardinier's sign was the official symbol of the fencing guild, to which neither he nor Marteau belonged. They, like Lucidor and Quenaut, were ferrailleurs.[41]

Lucidor lived in the abbey for much of his life. In the eighteenth century, the Martinians, a Benedictine order, converted portions of the abbey into a new neighborhood with modern apartment blocks, a fair, and a market with stalls that looked like garden sheds. Although new housing on the perimeter fell under the power of the police, the courtyard remained under the authority of the abbot, outside the jurisdiction of the king's courts.[42]

The wild and slatternly character of everyday life in the courtyard was an embarrassment to the monks. The court records of the abbey depict a raucous marketplace, where the special character of this jurisdiction, relative to the rest of the city, made life more dangerous. Because of the monks' real estate speculations, more and more people lived there. The abbey was rife with strangers avoiding the police. Jews were legally banned from Paris, but lived in the enclosure and filed suits at the abbey's court.[43] People gambled at the foot of the church, shot into the air, punched barmen and broke into taverns to keep drinking after closing time.[44] Apprentice butchers emptied chamber pots onto the crowd from atop the abbey rampart.[45] The air reeked of homemade alcohol. In 1749, after complaints, the police forbade residents from distilling spirits or making paint varnish in their homes.

One article of the ordinance prohibited, all at once, "the breaking of lanterns, of windows, the singing of dissolute, calumnious or defamatory songs, cursing and blaspheming, gathering in crowds at night to play games of chance."[46] All of the troublemaking in that article boiled down to a single practice, known in France as charivari. This was a folk ritual of humiliation, which the crowd performed by making a horrible din and unleashing its vengeful mockery on members of the community whom they accused of violating their social rules.[47] The *Encyclopédie* mentions "loud sounds of contempt at night made with pots and pans and cauldrons" that (circa 1750) "we have not suffered in Paris for thirty years."[48] At the abbey, in August 1756, residents joined in a charivari that lasted for days.[49]

How did Lucidor come to settle at the abbey? Perhaps on advice from his wife. Her aunt may have sold old hats there in the 1760s. Perhaps through his former owners, since members of the Salins and Prévost families lived on the Rue Saint-Martin, which limned the abbey.[50] But Lucidor had other reasons to know about this place. He knew about hideouts and ill-policed pockets of the city. The abbey was a space for tolerated illegality of every variety. The ubiquity of streetwalkers in the enclosure even found its way onto souvenirs—painted fans—which the abbey's prosecutor decided to confiscate. On one fan, now preserved in the National Archives, the abbot strolls through the market with a harlot.[51]

IT WOULD BE WRONG to picture Lucidor as locked within the abbey enclosure, plying his trade on an island of misrule. His social world extended beyond Saint-Martin-des-Champs. For a few years he and his family may have left the abbey, or at least spent stints of time elsewhere. In 1756 Lucidor bought a house outside city limits in the hamlet of Ménilmontant.[52] It was a hilly village, full of taverns, where workers drank on holidays and master craftsmen kept second homes.[53] Perhaps Lucidor meant the house to become a fencing school. It may have become one, briefly.

The file on Lucidor suggests a man of roguish courage and resourcefulness whose talent, beyond swordsmanship, was getting by. But then we stumble upon the house, which tells a different story. It was a three-story villa with a well, an outdoor furnace, a chicken coop, a woodshed, and a separate walled garden. It cost 8,500 livres—approximately 160,000 modern euros—and suggests a bold new undertaking.

Did the guild laws apply to Ménilmontant? Probably not. Legislation dating back to the seventeenth century applied the authority of the fencing guild to Paris and its suburbs, known as faubourgs (literally, false towns). The formal list of suburbs encompassed by this legislation (Faubourgs Saint-Germain, Saint-Michel, Saint-Denis, Saint-Jacques, Saint-Marceau, Saint-Victor, Saint-Martin, Montmartre, Saint-Honoré, and de la Roule) did

94   SLAVES IN PARIS

not, however, reflect the eighteenth-century expansion of the city into rural areas.[54] The village of Ménilmontant, despite its proximity to Paris, fell under the jurisdiction of lord proprietors until 1789. Lords included the family of Le Peletier de Saint-Fargeau, who became a member of the Committee of Public Safety during the French Revolution. Another lord proprietor was the abbot of Saint-Martin, who owned the courtyard that remained Lucidor's principal residence.

Whether or not the guild laws applied to Ménilmontant, Lucidor's activities there would have been hard to discover. His house stood behind a wall and a *porte cochère* (a large door meant for carriages). You could see and hear little. The neighborhood was noisy, despite the rural scenery. The Chemin de Ménilmontant was a cobblestone thoroughfare clogged with industrial carts hauling plaster to the city from a gypsum quarry that has since become the Buttes-Chaumont Park. Street cleaners used the Chemin de Ménilmontant to haul muck (carelessly) out of the city.[55]

Lucidor did not remain in Ménilmontant for long, if he ever lived there full-time. In 1762 he gave the abbey as his permanent residence. There are quite a few mentions of Lucidor in abbey records from the 1760s. During the final decade of his life, Lucidor appears frequently in court documents as a figure haunted by debt and penury.[56] References to him include eviction notices (1766, 1767, 1768), an unpaid bread bill (1769), and a dispute with a pawnbroker (1770–1771). He was a broken man when he died, at 53.

The genealogist Pierre Bardin has cited documents relating to Lucidor's Ménilmontant house as evidence of Lucidor's social integration and affluence. Bardin's essays in *La généalogie du Caraïbe* and in the *Dictionnaire des gens de couleur* depict Lucidor as a prosperous suburban athlete-businessman. According to Bardin, "the dueling gym of the Rue de Ménilmontant was frequented by many people . . . the inventory made on December 13 by the notary Pierre Rouveau shows that each lesson cost 100 livres." According to Bardin, neither Lucidor's color, nor his foreignness, nor his legal status would hinder his advancement in French society.[57]

Bardin's depiction of Lucidor is based on an incautious reading of the sources. The fee of 100 livres per lesson (the modern equivalent of 1,700 euros) is an impossible hourly rate. A licensed master dueler in Paris charged between 2 and 4 livres per lesson. A day laborer in the building trades earned 250 to 300 livres per year. The annual salary of a Parisian master of arms, on average, was 770 livres.[58] No one paid dueling masters 100 livres per lesson.

The inventory mentioned by Bardin in this rosy depiction of Lucidor's career resulted from the man's severe indebtedness, which required an itemized valuation of his belongings and house prior to sale. We will never be able to see Lucidor, despite the presence of mirrors on the list of furnishings in every room. The inventory does, however, make it possible to sense Lucidor's imprint on the threadbare redingote he left behind. He is there in the piles of old sandals, gloves, and broken sword tips. He died in a bed covered in a worm-eaten quilt embroidered with birds.[59]

The document that inspired Bardin's portrait of Lucidor is a scoreboard of insolvency. The pattern of debts listed in this very source, together with the objects catalogued there, describe a man who had not earned much—perhaps nothing—for a while. He who makes 100 livres per lesson would not pawn his gold watch to cover a debt of 120 livres. A man who charges 100 livres per lesson would not have a wife clad (according to this inventory) in a muff made out of cat fur.

At the end of the household inventory, in the section listing the family's unpaid debts, Thérèse Richard, Lucidor's wife, announced that students owed a total of 100 livres in unpaid fees. Bardin's Lucidor, who has been making his way into tweets and websites, is a fictional being.[60] The inventory is straightforward about the impending seizure of the house for debt. Lucidor's wife even told the notary she had run out of coin. No reader could mistake the subject of this inventory for an affluent tradesman with a flourishing suburban gym except by an act of imaginative projection so forceful as to will the real man out of history.

The most surprising thing about Lucidor's house is that he managed to acquire it in the first place. The house cost a staggering sum—8,500 livres—of which he paid nothing at the time of sale. How could Lucidor buy a house and walled garden, together with everything in the house, on the strength of his word, with no money down? Texts relating to this house, while they record a story of decline, connect him to at least one illustrious member of the Parisian elite—a fact that no one could deduce from his police file, or from the flurry of eviction notices in abbey records. During Lucidor's early career as a dueling master he belonged to a circle of formerly enslaved soldiers and skilled African domestics. The archive of the house shows that his web of acquaintances reached much higher.

Lucidor bought his house with the help of a famed patron and plutocrat, the financier Louis-Claude Dupin de Francueil (1715–1786), a onetime employer of Jean-Jacques Rousseau. Dupin's granddaughter was the writer George Sand. Dupin married Marie-Aurore de Saxe in 1777 when he was 62 and she was 29. They called each other father and daughter in public. After Dupin's death in 1787, his widow survived him by thirty-five years. She recalled her husband to Sand as "beautiful, elegant, soigné, gracious, perfumed, playful, affectionate, and even-tempered until he died."[61]

Slavery was an important ingredient of the Dupin family fortune—a fortune that enabled a life of kingly splendor. The origin of the fortune was Samuel Bernard, a larger-than-life wizard of royal finance whose ancestors plied the ironic vocation of miniaturists, painting very small things. In 1695 Bernard founded the Guinea Company, one of the first French slave-trading firms. Bernard married his beautiful daughter Louise to Claude Dupin père, then a widower, in repayment for Dupin's kindness toward her ailing mother, who was Bernard's mistress. When Parisian financiers resurrected the Guinea Company in 1748, Dupin père, Francueil's father, was one of eight major investors, each of whom contributed between 40,000 and 80,000 livres.[62]

In 1756 Dupin de Francueil sent an emissary to the notary handling the sale of the house to Lucidor, with a letter in which he pledged to act as guarantor. Should Lucidor fail to pay the seller 4,500 livres in the space of a year (more than half the total sale price of 8,500 livres), Francueil would pay the money himself. Given the speed of the payment and the lack of any financial arrangements, like an installment schedule, we must interpret this sum, amounting to about 78,000 modern euros, as a gift. The scale of Dupin's gift to Lucidor exceeded his magnanimity toward Rousseau, although the writer received huge presents from people in Dupin's entourage. In 1756, the year Dupin bought Lucidor half a house, the society hostess Madame d'Épinay, who was Dupin's titular mistress, gave Rousseau a newly renovated cottage, called the Hermitage, on her estate.[63] (According to the letters of Madame d'Épinay, Dupin de Francueil was living apart from her at the time of the Ménilmontant house purchase.)

This gift to Lucidor by Dupin de Francueil makes it necessary to consider how they might have met. There were ties between the Dupin family and Lucidor's original owners. Dupin père, the father of Francueil, and Hugues de Salins, the father of Madame Blancheton, belonged to the same social and professional world. Both were tax farmers, although Salins never

3.3 The Château de Chenonceau (Oct. 1922).
Agence Rol. Photographic glass negative, 13 × 18 cm. Bibliothèque Nationale de France (Paris).

attained to his colleague's stratospheric level of affluence.[64] The tie between the Salins-Blancheton and Dupin families began, but did not end, with how they got their money. The younger generation, who lived on the fortunes of tax farmers—including Francueil as well as Blancheton and his wife—moved in a social world where prestige came not only from lavish expenditure but also from patronage and self-cultivation. They practiced an art of being that could counterbalance, or erase, deficiencies of birth. Blancheton, from a lawyerly family of Burgundian nobles, was a violin player and a collector. The Fonds Blancheton, a collection of musical scores in twenty-seven volumes—301 hand-copied works by 104 composers—is known to scholars throughout the world.[65] As for Dupin de Francueil, the world came to the Palace of Chenonceau, his family's country seat, built by Henri II for Diane of Poitiers. At Chenonceau, Dupin de Francueil maintained "a corps of thirty musicians who executed concerts and operas in a mechanized theater built by his father in a wing of the chateau." His stepmother Louise enjoyed renting out the Paris Opera, which also performed at Chenonceau. According to George Sand, Dupin was an amateur luthier: he made his own

98 SLAVES IN PARIS

violins. He was also a skillful amateur performer. Dupin and Blancheton belonged to overlapping worlds of performance and patronage.[66]

It is worth revisiting Lucidor's teenage arrest file to think through these family connections. I have already mentioned the letter it contains from Catherine de Salins, where she suggested sending Lucidor to some unnamed Caribbean island. The file also contains a note describing a conversation between the police chief and the Marquis de Courcy, the musketeer whom Lucidor served. The missing person in this file is Pierre-Philibert de Blancheton, Salins's husband and the titular owner of Lucidor. Despite Catherine de Salins's observation that Lucidor could not claim anyone, her husband remained in touch with him for several decades after this incident. If authentic, the freedom certificate that Lucidor gave the Admiralty clerk in 1762 bore the signature of Blancheton and dated back to 1750. Blancheton died of sudden illness on his Burgundian estate in 1756, the year Lucidor bought his house. Blancheton did not mention Lucidor in his will, however. If Lucidor's money came from Blancheton, it was not an official part of the succession.

There is no reason to assume that Dupin and Lucidor knew each other well. Nothing except the sale contract for the house suggests a link between them. Yet there is a chance of early and long-lasting acquaintance. According to notes by the police spy, Lucidor worked for a "single young man" in the Rue Saint-Louis who had nothing to do with the musketeers. There were at least two streets in Paris called the Rue Saint-Louis at the time. One was in the Marais near the Place Royal (now the Place des Vosges). The other cut across the Île Saint-Louis, an island in the Seine. In 1726 the Dupin family bought the Hôtel Lambert, on the second of these streets. Dupin de Francueil was 18 years old and a bachelor living in the Hôtel Lambert at the time of Lucidor's arrest.

NEW IDEAS OF RACE became conspicuous in Paris after 1750, and especially toward the end of the Seven Years War (1756–1763). In 1762, all free people of African descent who resided in Paris were obliged to register with the city's Admiralty Court—a requirement that had applied to slaves in the past. According to the prosecutor-general of that court, the point was to monitor people he viewed as racial contaminants as a precursor to

3.4 Entrance to the Hôtel Lambert on the Rue Saint-Louis en l'Île (1900–1901).

Eugene Atget (1857–1927). Photograph on albumen paper from gelatinobromide glass negative, 21.5 × 17 cm. Bibliothèque Nationale de France (Paris).

their removal. "The introduction of too large a quantity of negroes in France whether as slaves or in another capacity has dangerous consequences. We will soon see the French Nation disfigured, if such an abuse is tolerated. Indeed, negroes are generally dangerous men, and there is scarcely one who on receiving freedom has failed to abuse it, and who has not been carried toward dangerous excesses toward society."[67] In 1762, with the expansion of registration to include free people of color, race arrived as an explicit category of Admiralty law and began structuring the activities of its Paris court.

Lucidor watched the emergence of a new racialized policing culture that targeted men like himself. Friends and friends of friends began to disappear. In 1754, as we have seen, Lucidor joined several other men as a witness for

Lircot, a former slave from Saint-Domingue. Another witness was Pharaon, also from Saint-Domingue, who worked for a family of planters in Paris. In 1755 all of the female domestics in his household petitioned for freedom. While their case awaited judgment by the Admiralty, police rounded up the women and dispatched them to a prison in Le Havre pending their removal to the colonies. Pharaon seems to have been arrested in the raid. His later fate is unknown.[68]

Guillaume Quenaut, a master of arms from Saint-Domingue, registered with the Admiralty one day after Lucidor. According to what he told the clerk on May 5, 1762, he was free and a longtime resident of Paris. He came to France in 1718. He did not explain how he exited slavery or mention the person to whom he once belonged. Five months later, the Paris police received an order for the arrest of "Guillaume, negro," whom policemen also called "Guillaume Quenot, known as Guillaume and as Baptiste." After October 13, 1762, the date of his capture, Quenaut disappears from Parisian records.[69]

Anecdotal evidence suggests that intermarriage became harder. In 1765, when François, born in Réunion, sued for his freedom, he did so with the intention of marrying a French girl. His owner, Elizabeth Mitchell Saige, commissioned the Paris police to abduct and deport him. She intended that he be sold. The police only managed to track down François, however, because the family of his fiancée informed the constabulary when he arrived at their home in Alençon.[70] He was embarked as a slave in May 1766 aboard the *Duc de Duras,* bound for Mauritius.

The sequence of events that led to the deportation and eventual resale of François in 1765 would have been unthinkable when Lucidor came to the capital. Lucidor married while still a slave with no objections from the church, his master, the police, or civil authorities. It is striking, in view of later events, that Catherine de Salins, the wife of Blancheton, failed to convince the police to deport "little Lucidor" to the colonies. In the case of François, and of many others, the police were enthusiastic collaborators in slave removal.

The new importance of race in Paris coincided with the flourishing of the French slave trade and French overseas plantations. Yet imperial defeat, and not merely success, played a crucial role in shaping new racial concepts and practices. The rout of French troops during the Seven Years War turned Paris into a gathering place for uprooted colonists, defrocked officials, and soldiers. Many of these refugees from the shrinking French Empire arrived with enslaved domestics. They also carried habits of mind that were common in the imperial places they left behind. Imperial defeat increased the number of people of color in Paris and gave élan to new racial ideas.

Racial hatred would endanger Lucidor's family at the abbey, according to his own testimony. In December 1767 Lucidor recounted a series of assaults and plots by neighbors to the abbey's police.[71] The attacks had been going on for almost a year. The taunts focused on his daughters and, to a lesser extent, his wife. "An assembly of sluts," yelled the women of the enclosure, who mocked the girls as tarts whose parents sold them for money.

> They went to the Saint Claire Fair, they did my dear
> And their mother, to pay for her beer. . . .
> Tomorrow they will have round bonnets and ribbons, my dear
> And there is the father, who grows a horn taking his cows to the bull
> And the mother, too, my dear, and the aunt who hawks the old hats
> You should see them all, my dear.[72]

Amid this taunting, Lucidor's daughter Louise, at age 16, had her first breakdown. She spent one month, from April 12 to May 13, 1767, at the Hôtel Dieu. The attending physician described her condition as "derangement and mental alienation."[73] When Louise returned home, the bullying got much worse. The neighbors joked about her hospital stay, which they depicted as a ruse for concealing a bastard child. They made up songs like this:

> The daughter of Lucidor has quite a strange form of colic,
> Of the two girls, one is sick in a singular way,
> A stomach that aches at ten in the morning.
> Louisonne is having a baby.
> What do you think of that Madame Chemitz?
> Monsieur Bigarre asked Louisonne,
> What is that sickness you have for nine months?
> Lucidor took his daughter to a surgeon, who said it would take
>   nine months.
> The beauty is having a darling little boy
> That is her folly, that is what keeps her from reason
> Louisonne ate peas and she is in for it for nine months.[74]

SLAVES IN PARIS

The imaginary baby became the theme of their taunts. The wife of a cauldron-maker, Madame Chemitz, would scream at the family from beneath their window in a baby voice. "Isn't he charming, the little *morisco*."[75] Children in the enclosure waved a black doll. "Send them a trousseau," yelled someone in the courtyard. The postman delivered an anonymous package in mid-November containing "pieces of paper cut in the shape of shirts, bonnets, and other linen for the use of babies."

Lucidor said nothing when his neighbors plotted to wall up the door to his apartment and immure his family inside (July 1767).[76] Soon, however, prankish bullying changed to violence, and Lucidor began reporting their conduct to the abbey's police. One night in December, Chemitz and his wife screamed at the family while pounding on the door to the Lucidors' apartment. They yelled, "Come out, f—off and scram from your whore-house, I will kill you and your bugger of a wife, who make their daughters screw for money, those whores. Come out, boy. F—off dogs, who do not dare to come out." The Lucidors kept the door closed. The violence resumed the next morning when Louise entered the courtyard to fetch water at the pump. Madame Chemitz followed her, threw stones at her, struck her in different places, and had a group of children follow and insult her. Louise tried to turn back and return to the house. Witnessing the scene, her father tried to help. "Having wished to stop the Chemitz woman from hitting and insulting his daughter, this woman struck him several times on the head and scratched his face and said that the girl would not escape."

The abbey's status as an ill-policed refuge made it a haven for the Lucidor family in the 1740s and 1750s. Inhabitants of the enclosure tended to be strangers who needed to work and live beyond reach of the city's laws. Social dislocation on a world scale, like that wrought by the Seven Years War, probably affected the abbey more than other places in Paris, because it was a magnet for outsiders. As a libertine pocket of the city that beckoned in the world, the abbey offered an ideal ecology for the domestication of ideas and practices that came (like the word *morisco,* in the taunting of Louise) from elsewhere. Racial hatred merged with the culture of carnivalesque violence that had long been a feature of the enclosure. In theory, the abbey was one of the few places where André Lucidor could work. It became a place where he and his family could no longer live in safety.

Chapter 4

JULIEN

IN THE LATE EIGHTEENTH CENTURY, the bridge known as the Pont Neuf was host to a chaotic emporium that drew peddlers, jugglers, street singers, and floggers of bibelots and magic powders. It was a place to sell something, buy a dog, or get a tooth pulled. The bridge was also weedy and waterlogged. Thistles grew around the equestrian statue of Henri IV. Pipes of the famous water pump, the Samaritaine, often clogged, flooding the marketplace.[1]

On March 20, 1787, when Julien stepped onto the bridge, he felt a blow to the head. Two men seized him by the collar and dragged him backward, behind the statue of Henri IV, to a permanent guard post. The soldiers on duty helped to lift him into a carriage. Inspector Poisson, who arranged the kidnapping, drove his charge to the home of Pierre Chenon, an elderly magistrate, to file a report on the arrest. He dropped off Julien at a prison called La Force in time for lunch. Later, around five in the afternoon, Poisson returned for his charge. Bound in irons at the wrists and ankles, the prisoner together with Poisson and a couple of soldiers left in a post chaise for Le Havre.[2]

A French police inspector's baton was a 12-inch polished stump made out of ebony, or something like it, topped by a gold knob and carved with the king's insignia.[3] It resembled an English constable's stick. Both came from rocklike trees that grew in European slave colonies (Brazil, the Antilles, Mauritius) or in places where Europeans purchased captives for plantation work (Madagascar, Gabon). The French inspector's baton differed somewhat

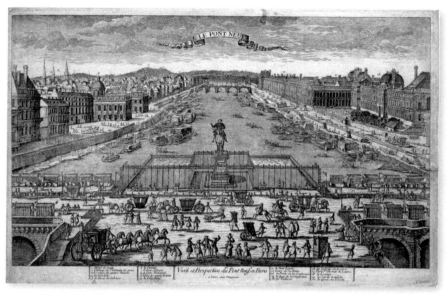

4.1 View of the Pont Neuf (1760).
Anonymous engraving, 35 × 53 cm. Bibliothèque Nationale de France (Paris).

from the English version in being an optional killing stick, topped as it was by a metal ball—gold outside, lead underneath. A version of that baton, in the form of a dangerous cane, was then a popular accessory in Paris.[4] The blow that immobilized Julien or knocked him out must have come from the blunt end of Poisson's truncheon.

Pierre Chenon, who signed off on this arrest, had long accepted the lawfulness of slavery in Paris and defended the interests of slave proprietors. Years earlier, in January 1762, Chenon had questioned Louis-Pierre Hazard, a Martinican slave, in Paris's Grand Châtelet prison. The owner of the slave, Duchesse de Langeac, together with her servants, accused him of stealing pocket-sized treasures. Hazard denied stealing but admitted to selling the buttons and braid of his jacket. Chenon then schooled him about the rights of enslaved domestics. "It was represented to him that, as a negro slave owned by La Comtesse, he could not own anything, much less a suit given him to wear in her service."[5]

People of color in eighteenth-century Paris who vanished by lettre de cachet typically came to the city as slaves and were battling for freedom at the time of their arrests, or thought they had already become free. Born into slavery in Martinique, Julien was just like them. He was seeking freedom through legal channels at the time of his arrest. There was, however, a surface difference between Julien and other slaves who disappeared. Africans, Indians, and Creoles were generally conspicuous in Paris because of their skin color. By contrast, Julien, an apprentice wigmaker (*garçon perruquier*), looked more or less European. He was whitish and blended in.

Under oath, at the home of Commissaire Chenon, "he said he was named Julien Mestif, age 22, native of Saint-Pierre (Martinique)." "Mestif" looks like a proper noun here. But Mestif was not a surname. It was an epithet—as in "Charles the Bald" or "Pepin the Short"—that Julien used to describe himself to officials. In the Martinican racial lexicon, the word *mestif* referred to the child of a white person and a mixed-race person who had one black grandparent. Julien's enemies in Paris claimed he was lying. An unsigned note in navy archives observes that "the mulatto claims to be mestif."[6]

Why should Parisians, a famously uppity people on the cusp of revolution, stand by idly as a youngster was ambushed, clubbed senseless, dragged, and heaved into a carriage? With the acrobats, the balladeers, the dentists, the churning water pump, the clatter of wheels and hoofs, and all the puppies—it was a dog market—this was a loud place. It was also a hub for the demimonde, and brimmed with police spies, called *mouches* or *mouchards*. In exchange for help from informants, police turned a blind eye to illegal conduct. The *mouches* and petty criminals were often the same people. As for non-spies among the bridge bohemians, they could hardly be expected to martyr themselves to the Pont Neuf's permanent military guard.

Julien Rose Baudelle, a white bachelor from a family of planters, was supposed to be Julien's father (2). The bachelor's white sister, Reine Ruste de Rezeville (née Baudelle), was his owner. Reine Baudelle made two trips to France with her enslaved nephew—the first in 1777, when he arrived by way of Marseille, and the second in 1783, through Le Havre. Julien Rose Baudelle joined his sister and son in Paris for the second of these sojourns and lived on the same street, the Rue du Mail, until he died in 1786. The death of Julien père may have brought about a rupture between Reine Baudelle and her nephew, which led Julien to petition the Admiralty for freedom. He was still living in her house on March 5, 1787, when the Paris

106   SLAVES IN PARIS

Admiralty Court declared him free (3). Reine Baudelle and her lover, Pierre Ozenne, a banker and slave trader, immediately began plotting Julien's capture and removal to Martinique. Informed by servants of their intention, he fled the house and took shelter with a formerly enslaved hairstylist who had belonged to Julien's father. On March 17, 1787, at the invitation of Baudelle's lover Ozenne, Julien visited his aunt's residence with his lawyer, Jean-Pierre-Louis Delaval, expecting to settle the dispute out of court. During the visit, Delaval learned that police henchmen were "waiting to seize Julien the moment he went outside." The lawyer protected his client by "sending someone to fetch a cab and taking Julien inside the cab with him" (8). In view of how much there was to lose, it is striking that Julien should venture three days later onto the Pont Neuf—a famous nest of spies with its own police station and nowhere to hide. It was the only bridge in the city without houses, where no one lived, from which you could actually see the water.

At the time of his arrest, Julien and Delaval believed him to be safe. The previous day, March 19, Delaval had obtained a writ from the Paris Parlement that provisionally recognized Julien's free status pending a hearing on Friday of that week (8). After this temporary judicial triumph, Delaval believed Julien's capture to be impossible—at least until the hearing. The next day, Julien ventured onto the Pont Neuf with a pocket full of freedom papers and disappeared. He was probably returning from a visit to Delaval. The Pont Neuf connects the island called Île de la Cité to both banks of the Seine. Many lawyers lived on the Île de la Cité, which was home to the bustling and labyrinthine Palace of Justice that contained most of the city's courts.

Notwithstanding the seeming indifference of the bridge crowd to Julien's fate, his losing struggle for liberty became a cause célèbre in Paris. *Les Mémoires secrets,* a highbrow tabloid, published blurbs about the case as it moved through Parlement during the spring and summer of 1787 and into the royal council for a last, futile appeal in September 1787. Read in sequence, these snippets about Julien's case reveal striking changes in public opinion. In April 1787, under the heading "There are no slaves in France," the paper noted "a pending matter before the Great Chamber [of Parlement] that supposes this maxim to be false." One month later, Julien's exit from slavery lost all connection to the freedom maxim. To the newspaper and its readership, the Julien affair began as a story about free soil; it became a story about skin. Julien's future now seemed to hinge on the secret of his racial identity. "The affair of Julien, pursued as a negro and a slave, though he be white and free, was pleaded on Saturday, May 19, by Advocate-General Hérault, with a great crowd of spectators and universal applause." Until the end of the summer, albeit with diminished conviction, Julien figured in the press as a wrongfully enslaved white man. Reine Baudelle was "the mistress of this so-called negro." And then whiteness dropped out of the story. In the entry for September 10, 1787, we read of "unhappy Julien, the negro who has struggled for so long to become free."[7]

As accounts of Julien's complexion changed from month to month, so did the identity of his persecutors. Reine Baudelle began as the villain of the piece and Parlement was, originally, his protector. Soon, however, the Julien trial became a rallying point for planters and slave traders. As colonists arrayed themselves against him, the gossip-mongering *Mémoires secrets* ceased to portray magistrates in Parlement as impartial embodiments of legal rectitude; magistrates instead became toadies of the colonial lobby. The presiding judge in the May trial, Président de Gourges, from a family of magistrates in the slave port of Bordeaux, was *gagné par les adversaires*—won over, or bought by, Julien's opponents. The press soon exposed the Maréchal de Castries, minister of the navy, as another staunch ally of slave owners. While awaiting the ruling of Parlement in Julien's case, Hérault conferred with Castries and then leaked their interview. He exposed the minister's intention to subvert Parisian justice in defense of colonial interests. Castries had warned Hérault, "The Parlement will do what it wants. But if the court finds Julien free, I will still send him back to the colonies."[8]

A letter to Castries by Reine Baudelle's lover, Pierre Ozenne, lends credence to allegations in the press about backdoor maneuvering on the part of the city's (albeit informal) pro-slavery lobby. "This affair has become so public that all the planters here foresee horrific consequences in case of a judgment in Julien's favor; and will join together to present a petition to [you]."[9] Ozenne's faction wielded power over Crown officials due to France's ever-increasing dependency on colonial slave labor. The English traveler Arthur Young observed of France in 1790, "The only branch of industry in the kingdom that remains flourishing is the trade to the sugar-colonies."[10]

The Julien affair rattles commonplaces about France's rights culture on the eve of the French Revolution. Defenders of Julien inveighed against despotism and decried influence peddling by slave holders in the capital. And

108   SLAVES IN PARIS

yet racial categories played an uncomfortably central role in this story. The universalism that became so striking a feature of revolutionary culture just two years after this legal battle was strangely absent here. Read against the 1790s, the Julien affair underscores the transformative role of the Declaration of the Rights of Man and Citizen, which permanently changed how people talked about rights and freedom. Yet it would be a mistake to picture 1789 as an absolute break with the past. Central figures in Julien's struggle for freedom later assumed prominent roles in the French Revolution. Their careers during the 1790s draw attention to the limits of the revolutionary project, geographical and moral, when it came to slaves in the empire.

WHEN JULIEN SOUGHT freedom before the Paris Court of Admiralty, he did so on the grounds that "there are no slaves in France." Skin only became pertinent to this case when Reine Baudelle and her lover Ozenne sought to retain Julien in bondage. They attempted this by two methods. The first was judicial, by appealing the decision to Parlement. The second was extrajudicial, by appealing to the minister of the navy for a lettre de cachet, as many a slave owner in the capital had done before them.

On March 12, 1787, Baudelle and Ozenne obtained an unprecedented court order from Parlement that duplicated the effects of a lettre de cachet. This writ blocked Julien's freedom sentence while ordering his removal to Martinique as a slave and remittance to Ruste de Rezeville, Reine Baudelle's husband. According to Delaval's memoir about this affair, "This decree even authorized Dame Ruste to have Julien arrested and kept in La Force prison until his departure." (4).

Judges at Parlement proved willing to authorize Julien's arrest and deportation on racial grounds, because (according to Delaval) Baudelle and Ozenne "described Julien as a negro in the request that resulted in the judicial decree of March 12" (30). Delaval reacted by producing facts to contest the court's racial assumptions. Passenger manifests for both ships that conveyed Julien to France—first in 1777 and again in 1783—identified him under false names as white. Reine Baudelle's lover Ozenne was duly summoned by Parlement to account for Julien's abduction on the grounds that "it was a white and not a mulatto."[11]

What should we take from this? Parlement evidently deemed the subversion of legal rulings by assault and kidnapping to be violations of essential rights when it came to white Frenchmen circa 1787. Those rights did not apply to black or brown colonials, however. In the Julien affair, the magistrates of Parlement treated whiteness as a necessary condition for acceding to basic legal protections in France. When Parlement made race into a point of law, every particularity of Julien's body acquired judicial significance. In Delaval's unsigned memoir about the case, Julien became a man whose skin tone, hair texture, and facial morphology met the standard required for citizenship.

> It suffices to know that he is born of a Frenchmen to know that he could only be a mulatto. But in seeing him, one would even doubt that he is one—a very light nuance of brown covering his skin, hair that is not frizzy wool, but instead long and supple. It is clear that his origins are black, but at the same time one is convinced that the generation that will issue from him, if he marries a white woman, will also be white, and the slight brown tint that covers his visage will disappear entirely in his children. We need not fear that the mixture of races will alter *la couleur nationale* [the national color] (26).

This was not the first time that racial categories figured in a freedom suit. Years earlier, in 1758, a youngster named Francisque, from India, had been freed from slavery on the grounds that his European-like features and place of birth proved he was "not a negro," despite the color of his skin. The Julien case was, by contrast, all about skin. There were several quirks to Delaval's portrait of Julien; not least was the phrase *la couleur nationale*, which he employed as a metaphor for white skin. Normally this was something one said (and could still say) about flags, uniforms, and regimental hats, but not about bodies. Noteworthy exceptions to this general rule would include *La Traité de la couleur de la peau humaine* (Treatise on the color of human skin; 1765), by Claude-Nicolas Le Cat, professor of surgery and anatomy at Rouen. Le Cat's book refuted the idea, widespread among naturalists in his day, that nonwhite skin was a degenerate condition caused by climate, with whiteness being the original, ideal state of man. Africans in Europe, noted Le Cat, did not change color after moving there. Likewise, Portuguese, Spanish, French, English, and Dutch travelers who lived close to the equator retained what he called their "national color."[12] In Delaval's brief for Julien, "national color" was a term in which different strands of meaning converged. First, this term owed something to the burgeoning world of anatomical and racial science. Second, it gestured to the newfangled, quasi-sacred collective body that became the foundation of politics in 1789 (e.g., "the nation is the origin of everything . . . it is the law itself").[13] Third, "national color" denoted the hue of national military regalia. An essay about army textiles (with great tips for stain removal) from the *Encyclopédie méthodique* (1787) made the case for keeping French troops in white uniforms: "To the concrete reasons we have advanced in favor of white, we add a moral reason. The French have long regarded the color white as la couleur nationale."[14] In eighteenth-century France, "national color" meant white. This began as a way of describing cloth. It became a way of describing skin.

And yet this text is not a court transcription. The sole comment in *Les Mémoires secrets* about Delaval's unsigned judicial chronicle was that "it was not bad, as a legal brief; it summarizes the case, though flatly; it is little suited to making a sensation in public; it is hoped that a more eloquent pen will take up this cause and give it the merit it deserves." No published text ever rose to the newspaper's standard of eloquence. A later attempt, by the barrister Godard, was "neither more eloquent, nor clearer, nor more methodical, nor more dialectic; we learn nothing new."[15] Godard recycled Delaval's earlier physiognomic portrait of Julien as a man on the brink of whiteness, changing nothing. It was the oratory of Hérault de Séchelles, advocate-general at Parlement and future co-author of the 1793 constitution, that drew applause from the newspaper. It was his speech, of which no copy seems to survive, that led the journal to describe this case as "the affair of Julien, pursued as a negro and slave, despite being white and free." Julien's whiteness entered the public narrative of this affair through Hérault's performance. The lawyer Delaval had not described Julien as white, but as someone whose lineage would be white, whose almost-whiteness should allow him access to the rights of white people.

Both Delaval's published description of Julien and Hérault's speech were part of a broader transoceanic conversation about the threshold that defined whiteness as a legal category. Until the Julien affair, however, the question of who was and was not eligible for whiteness remained a colonial debate, not a matter for domestic French courts. The whiteness question overseas arose in response to the hardening of France's colonial race regime for free people of color. Reform-minded administrators sought a way of accommodating wealthy light-skinned people without changing a single race law. The answer? People who looked white should count as white. One year after the Julien trial, the Marquis de la Luzerne, the new minister of the navy, informed Governor du Chileau in Saint-Domingue that legal handicaps for free colored people should cease "at the moment that signs attesting to colored origin disappear."[16] For most whites in the colonies, however, those signs never vanished. To Moreau de Saint-Méry, it was not the actual hue of skin but undertones and glisten that distinguished true whites from people he called *sangs mêlés* (mixed bloods), whom he calculated to be 1 part black to 8,191 parts white.[17]

Colonial reformers were not the only people who embraced the whitening program. In the 1780s, wealthy light-skinned men in Saint-Domingue sought to acquire the status of whites to escape the colonial race regime and obtain civil equality. As Dominique Rogers observes, men of color in Haiti "did not ask to be integrated [into French society] in the capacity of men of color; they wanted instead to be whitened, recognized officially as white." The mouthpiece for men of color in that campaign was Julien Raimond, a wealthy indigo and cotton planter who owned slaves. With encouragement from the governor of Saint-Domingue, he wrote four reports for the ministry of the navy about the emancipation of light-skinned men through their reclassification as "new whites."[18]

The Crown's management of a defamation case in Saint Lucia, which overlapped with the Julien affair, suggests that royal counselors at Versailles defined whiteness more loosely than planters did. In 1787, a resident of Saint Lucia, Antoine Delpech, sued a local black woman after she accused him of passing. The Superior Council of Martinique ruled against him by privileging "testimonial proof" (local knowledge) over "the extract from the baptismal certificate and other titles attesting to his whiteness." The Crown moved the matter from the Martinican judicial system to the Privy Council, because colonial courts "lacked the perspective required to pronounce justly on an affair of this sort."[19]

To return to the Julien affair: Hérault pushed race to the center of the case and managed, through his courtroom performance, to remove all trace of African origin from Julien's countenance. Hérault descended on his mother's side from the Magons, a well-known family of Breton slave traders and financiers.[20] His grandfather, Magon de la Lande, owned at least seven slave ships; twenty-three recorded voyages by the Magon fleet delivered nearly 10,000 slaves to Cap Français, now Cap Haitien, in the eighteenth century. Hérault was also an acolyte of Johan-Casper Lavater, a celebrity physiognomist and mystic. The young lawyer made a pilgrimage to Lavater's Zurich home in 1783, and the two corresponded afterward. In a 1784 letter to Hérault, Lavater promised, "I will soon take the liberty of addressing to you a plan for a secret personal physiognomic correspondence, which we can never make public."[21] Whatever Hérault said in court, his ability to portray Julien as "white and free" mimicked a liberal-seeming strain of opinion among pro-slavery courtiers who were willing to define whiteness by looks, not blood. That suited Hérault, the physiognomist, since he judged everything by looks (and thought that was science). On the day of his speech, Hérault told the court that he "had nothing ready" and then delivered a stirring ex tempore address to rapturous applause. Hérault (age 27) had a cult following, helped by his shocking handsomeness. He approached courtroom oratory as theater. Tutored by the actress Mlle Clairon, he memorized everything—including his gestures (always the arm, not the hand). The spontaneity was staged, but the speech was his.[22]

In discussions around the Julien affair, racial categories and proto-revolutionary politics converged. The case brought together elements of late eighteenth-century French life that scholars usually keep apart but that belonged to the same experiential world. In Paris of the 1780s, radical politics constantly mingled with the prurient scrutiny of racialized bodies. Consider the experience of book buyers or window shoppers at the famous Palais Royal, the ducal residence qua shopping center that its proprietor, Louis-Philippe-Joseph d'Orléans, refurbished to create even more storefronts in the 1780s. The Palais Royal brought together bordellos, gambling saloons, luxury boutiques, gimmicky cafés, bookshops, and live entertainment. It was where one went to gamble and fornicate, pick out a dangerous cane, see a freak show, and buy the latest pamphlet by the Comte de Mirabeau. In the spring and summer of 1787, during Julien's failed bid for freedom, the French police made frequent book busts at the Palais Royal in an effort to stem the flow of seditious political tracts. Among the dangerous books that circulated that summer, at least three were attacks on the use of lettres de cachet to subvert the legal system—the mechanism by which Julien disappeared.

These included *Une lettre de Monsieur le marquis de Beaupoil à M. de Bergasse sur l'histoire de Latude, & sur les ordres arbitraires* (A letter by Monsieur the Marquis de Beaupoil to Bergasse about the history of Latude and about arbitrary writs) and a satirical pamphlet about the police entitled *Confession général d'un homme exécuté au caveau du Palais Royal* (General confession of a man executed in the vault of the Palais Royal).[23] But the same customers who frequented the stalls of booksellers, including the widows Dubois and Vanfleury (both the target of police raids), might also stop at "arcades #7 and #8, at the sign of the Fat Man," to see Sieur Curtius's exhibit of waxworks and wonders of nature. Here are excerpts from a handbill posted by Curtius in January 1787:

> EXTRAORDINARY LIVING PHENOMENON. Penetrated by the liveliest gratitude toward the public, Sir Curtius hastens to please them, having had the honor of presenting the pied children (half black, half white), he now wishes to make them available to a larger public, by diminishing the price of seats. . . . They can be seen from 10 A.M. until 2 P.M. and from 4 to 10 P.M. People who wish to see the pied children in their homes can arrange to do so one day in advance, so long as this does not conflict with the hours they are on display to the public. Women can see them without fear.[24]

The Julien affair coincided with a transatlantic explosion of interest in monstrous whiteness on the part of slave-owning societies. In Europe and the Americas, wondrous human specimens of this sort included people of African descent with piebaldism or vitiligo, like the children whom Curtius owned or rented for his parlor show; a second, linked embodiment of white monstrosity in these years was the so-called *nègre blanc* (white negro).[25] Scientific interest in the "white negro" began in the 1740s and flowered at the end of the Old Regime, to inspire a one-act comedy, performed at Versailles in 1780, in which a social-climbing collector of natural history specimens is duped into acquiring her own daughter's lover, a Frenchman, for her home museum ("This will draw all of Paris to my door!").[26] The historian Andrew Curran notes the influence of the Comte de Buffon's *Histoire naturelle* (1749) on racial thought in France during the second half of the eighteenth century. Buffon and his followers attributed black skin and African traits to species degeneration under the influence of climate. Neither the phenomenon of the

4.2 Publicity for the 1787 Palais Royal exhibit of two 6-year-old children by Curtius, billed as *Phénomènes extraordinaires de la Nature: Enfans vivans*.
C. Coulubrier. Wax engraving, 35.6 × 24.5 cm. Musée Carnavalet (Paris).

white negro nor the piebald children in Curtius's boutique required anyone to abandon belief in common descent from Adam. Another pioneer of degeneration theory, the naturalist Pierre-Louis Maupertuis, described atypical whiteness among people of African descent as a marvelous atavism—a resurgent fragment of mankind's lost bodily perfection. "The primitive color [white] is not so completely effaced as it might seem," he wrote in *Vénus physique* (1745). But there was no going back. According to this theory, albinism and vitiligo were signs of irreversible decline. Whiteness could never be recovered by degenerate branches of the human family; it could only resurface in odd and monstrous forms. During the 1770s and early 1780s, as Curran observes, French thinkers continued to subscribe to Buffon's degeneration theory while placing new emphasis on "the discernible and measurable anatomical differences separating blacks from whites."[27] This new fixation on the minutiae of physical dissimilarity made albinism all the more sensational—especially to slave-owning naturalists like Thomas Jefferson, who canvased his friends about their albino slaves. Henry Skipworth, who owned three albino sisters, described the girls to Jefferson as "disagreeable chalky white, their hair perfectly similar to short sheep's wool" and their bodies free of "color seams, or spots."[28] The contemporary poet Natasha Tretheway writes of the impetus behind slave owners' anatomical obsession with albinos: "We still know white from not."[29]

THE JULIEN AFFAIR was not merely the product of France's race culture at the end of the Old Regime. Julien's struggle began as a family problem. For several years before this legal suit, Julien had lived on Paris's Rue du Mail as the nameless domestic slave of his own aunt and as a neighbor of his father, who neither acknowledged nor freed him. Julien's disavowal by his father was the root cause of his subsequent legal battle.

The repudiation of mixed-race children and the erasure of family links across the color line coincided with a general decline in the status of free people of color in France's overseas empire. In the course of the eighteenth century, free people of African descent were banned from guilds, forbidden to receive property from whites by will or gift, and excluded from all dignities of state, including nobility. In 1724, Martinique followed Louisiana in illegalizing interracial marriage.[30] The 1685 Code Noir promised freed slaves

SLAVES IN PARIS

and their descendants the same rights as other naturalized French subjects. Planters responded by attacking the rights of emancipated slaves in decrees that differed from one island to the next; the navy, for its part, devised statutes aimed at preventing masters from freeing slaves in the first place.[31]

Within Martinican society, there was nothing secret about the lineage of mixed-race people. Their disavowal by white fathers needs to be considered in light of how much everyone knew about everyone else in these small plantation societies. Planters were under continuous surveillance by their slaves. Local curates, for their part, were notorious for publicizing the sexual exploits of white masters.[32] In 1752 Charles-Marin Hurson (1712–1783), intendant of Martinique, denounced the clergy's repeated exposure of interracial family ties. "In almost all the parishes, in the baptismal certificates of mulattoes, mothers are obliged to declare the father of the child and his name is written into the baptismal register, on the strength of the declaration by a negress or mulatress." Curates justified their recordkeeping practice by noting the obligation of unwed mothers "to declare themselves . . . and identify the father" to both the prosecutor and the curate. They further insisted on the need to "humiliate those who abandon themselves to such shameful congress." To Hurson's further dismay, parish priests were known to broadcast the names of these men during the reading of the bans for affianced couples.

> It has even happened that on the strength of declarations in the registers, when mulattoes and mulatresses are of age to marry, and the bans are published, the name of the father is also published, though there is no other proof than the declaration of the mother. This happened to Monsieur de Poincy when he was governor of Marie-Galande, who was very surprised to hear himself named during mass as the father of a mulatress he did not know. This happened at the beginning of this year in Fort Royal, where the curate published the bans of a mulatto, natural child of the deceased Monsieur Le Merle, former royal prosecutor to the Royal Council of Martinique, in the presence of his children and nephews who later complained to Messieurs Bonpar and Hurson.[33]

Hurson expressed indignation that declarations by female slaves and freed women contained the names of the men who impregnated them. Hurson's own solution was simple; no longer would unwed expectant mothers be permitted to name the white fathers of their children. No longer would curates write those names into parish records. When a white man failed to attend his mixed-race child's baptism, the resulting certificate would list the child's father as unknown.

In domestic France, declarations of pregnancy often included the names of fathers together with lurid details about seduction and false promises. Yet the original 1556 decree by Henri II that made hiding pregnancy a crime did not require a declaration. As Julie Hardwick has shown for France, the initiative for declarations of pregnancy did not come from the state. It came from people who had a personal stake in making those stories known. In principle the colonial clergy had everything to gain from these revelations. According to the Code Noir, enslaved illegitimate children and their enslaved mothers were supposed to be confiscated by the Crown and "donated to the nearest hospital without the capacity ever to be freed." All colonial hospitals were under the control of the clergy.[34]

Suppressing the names of fathers in baptismal records did not resolve the problem of public notoriety. Mixed-race people continued to identify their white lineages in everyday life, despite the disappearance of white fathers from birth certificates. They did so by using their white fathers' surnames. A 1773 ordinance, issued by the king, explained "that a great number of people of color, of one and another sex, impudently usurp the names of whites, even of the most notable people established in these islands, that not only do they call themselves by these names, but they also have the audacity to assume them in public and juridical acts; as this abuse spreads confusion in the families of whites, It seemed important to us to remedy this circumstance promptly."[35] A law of the next year prescribed the creation of new registers that would record the retraction of old white names and their replacement by invented substitutes.[36]

How did Julien feel about the Baudelle family? The recollections of another man of color, who also lived in Paris during these years, convey what it felt like for a small child to be disavowed by his rich white family and then forced to live among them. "At the peace in 1763, I was sent to France and given the name of Anson."[37] Born in Port-au-Prince, Louis-Joseph Anson arrived in Paris at the end of the Seven Years War. For Louis-Joseph Anson, it was never a question of taking the name of his father, who was the judge Charles-François-Antoine Saillenfest de Fontenelle. According to Fontenelle's personnel file, "During the twenty-seven years of his professional service, this judge has spent ten in France, and we were obliged in 1768 to order him back to resume his functions."[38] Notorious for enjoying long stretches of restorative leave in Paris, Fontenelle was there when Joseph, "father unknown," arrived in the capital at the age of 8.

Writing during the Revolution, Anson recommended that the legislature undo the stigma attached to men of color by issuing them new birth certificates on which the words "bastard" and "father unknown" were removed. To make this possible, Anson proposed an expedient fiction: all men of color should be given new birth certificates with the names of invented fathers. "We should in all justice be allowed to repudiate our natural fathers, since they repudiated us, by taking the name of a truly unknown and imaginary father who will be supposed to have borne the name we have chosen." The point of this proposal was to give official status to the surnames that illegitimate people of color invented for themselves. His naming proposal was a perfect reversal of colonial race law as it applied to family lineages during the Old Regime.

People who took the name of their white families did not picture this as tribute. It was a way of demanding recognition and combating erasure. White families, in their turn, viewed the unauthorized use of their names as a crime. On July 13, 1792, the former soldier Pierre-Philippe de Grouchet complained to a Parisian policeman about Claire dit Calalou, age 16, whom he called his slave. Claire lived in Paris with Grouchet from the age of 6. In May 1792 she moved in with a neighbor, a local engraver, who became her tutor and legal advisor. Under the alias Marie-Elisabeth Bonne, she petitioned the court of the second arrondissement in Paris to claim Grouchet's family as her own and to choose a trustee from the family. She identified herself as "the minor natural child of Sir Pierre-Philippe de Grouchet, former officer, and of Marie-Claire, free negress."[39]

A SLAVE HUNT in the aftermath of the Seven Years War, coinciding with Pauline's struggle, anticipated the Julien affair by two decades in depicting whiteness and slavery as incompatible. Hélène, age 16, disembarked at Bordeaux in 1765 with her owners, who falsely identified her to port authorities as their impoverished ward. They did so to avoid the hefty fee required of masters who brought slaves into the country. When the girl fled and sued for freedom in Paris, her master, a colonial judge, demanded and received a lettre de cachet. The prosecutor-general of the Admiralty Court, Poncet de la Grave, became incensed by the police hunt for Hélène. His efforts to save her, which failed, were all the more striking because of his enthusiastic collusion in the removal of dark-skinned people who sued for freedom before his court.[40] Writing to Antoine de Sartine, lieutenant-general of police, Poncet described Hélène as "white not negro, and her whiteness is even superior to that of many women in Paris and the countryside."[41] In his futile, desperate campaign to shelter Hélène, Poncet hid her in his mother's apartment at the Château de Vincennes. He warned Sartine that, because of her whiteness, arresting Hélène would incite a popular revolt.[42] The racial language used to describe Hélène varied considerably between officials. For Poncet she was "the very white Creole." For the Duc de Choiseul, minister of the navy, who conducted a relentless campaign for her capture, she was "the negress of Mister de Ronceray" (August 13, 1765) and finally "their enslaved negress" (November 2, 1765).[43]

The Julien affair differed from the earlier Hélène scandal because of the particularity of the late 1780s. The new dynamism of public life at the end of the Old Regime turned Julien's struggle for liberty into a public event, whereas the circle of interested parties in the Hélène case did not reach beyond a few benevolent grandees and clerks. More important still was the new, openly racist legislation that applied to people of color and slaves in France. In 1765 the notion that white and nonwhite people enjoyed fundamentally different rights on domestic French soil was an expression of Poncet's white supremacism, not a fact of law. That changed with the race laws of the late 1770s, which took effect under the leadership of Sartine, formerly lieutenant-general of police, who became minister of the navy in 1774.

The first of these new decrees, the Royal Declaration for the Policing of Blacks (August 9, 1777), banned "blacks, mulattoes, and other people of color," whether enslaved or free, from domestic France.[44] Next was the Decree of the Council of State for the Policing of Blacks, Mulattoes, and Other People of Color in the town of Paris (January 11, 1778), which applied to people who happened to be in the capital at the promulgation of the new travel ban, or who received special exemptions from the new law.[45] Finally, the Decree of the Council of State concerning Marriages of Blacks, Mulattoes, and Other People of Color (April 5, 1778) banned mixed marriages.[46]

"Other people of color" needs to be read in light of the famous Francisque trial of 1758, which freed a teenager from Pondicherry largely on the grounds that he lacked an African nose and came from a civilization with "long and beautiful hair, similar to that which decorates the head of Europeans." In view of that trial, it seems reasonable to read "other people of color" to encompass—without being limited to—Indians from the subcontinent.[47]

The mere existence of these laws is not proof of their enforcement. Colonists who wished to bring enslaved retainers into France did their best to evade the travel ban just as they had sought to avoid earlier impediments to slave movement. Well before the 1777 decree banning "blacks, mulattoes, and other people of color" from the kingdom, the navy obliged masters to supply huge cash guarantees (3,000 livres, or about 31,000 modern euros) for every nonwhite servant, free or enslaved, they brought into the country. Some masters avoided the fee by passing light-skinned slaves off as whites with the likely complicity of port officials. Such was the case of the slave Hélène, in 1763, when she came to France with the Ronseray family. Such was also the case of a woman called Olive, who told her story to police officials on Paris's Left Bank in 1791. She claimed to have entered France just after the Seven Years War (like Hélène) with her owner, Madame Aubry, and "another mulatto, whom Madame Aubry hid under her bed." After entering the port of Rochefort, Olive and the other slave remained concealed for eight days. Aubry then traveled with her two slaves to Versailles, where Olive was "coiffed in the European style, as a white woman" and "called by the name of Mogens, her father."[48] France at the end of the Old Regime was the rare country where racial passing was encouraged by slave proprietors.

The ruse that allowed the owners of Hélène and Olive to dodge hefty fees when taking their slaves to France would later enable Reine Baudelle to smuggle Julien into the kingdom despite the territorial exclusion of "blacks, mulattoes, and other people of color." In 1777, the year the travel ban took effect, Julien sailed to France with his aunt, arriving through the port of Marseille, where she passed him off to Admiralty officials as her orphaned ward. In 1783, Julien returned to France and disembarked at Le Havre, where the Admiralty recorded his identity as "Pierre Julien, native of Martinique, age 17, son of Pierre and Dame Rose Gauthier." Of the seventeen passengers who sailed to France aboard that ship, five were sailors from Le Havre; nine of the remaining twelve were the minor children of elite Martinicans traveling without their parents. The ship's young travelers included Paul-Augustine Elie de Luynes (age 14) and his sister, Marie-Thérèse (age 10); Christophe-Thomas Legendre (age 10); Caroline Ruste de Rezeville (age 9), who was Reine Baudelle's niece; Michel-Louis Brière de Bretteville (age 8); Pierre-Antoine Durand de la Villesegue (age 8), traveling with Bibianne, a free black woman; Dominique-George-Marguerite Durand Hautbourgneuf (age 7); Reine Gautier (age 18); and Julien himself (age 17). When Julien's aunt identified him to the Admiralty as a member of the Gautier family, she gave him the same surname as another passenger and probably hoped to pass him off as the girl's cousin—another youngster traveling alone from the same family.[49]

In 1778 the French Council of State imposed a ban on interracial unions. That decree, like the travel ban, faced both resistance and avoidance. For the lawyer Joly de Fleury, who preceded Hérault de Séchelles as advocate-general at Châtelet, the 1778 decree concerning mixed marriages did not outlaw those unions but instead left the matter to the discretion of bishops. For Joly de Fleury, lay authorities could not impose their law on the clergy when it came to the sacraments.[50] The scant evidence for Paris from this period indicates that mixed unions continued to take place despite the decree. In 1780 and 1785, the Parisian notary Lhomme drafted two marriage contracts for daughters of André Lucidor.[51] Neither of these contracts described the girls as "mulatresses," whereas similar documents drafted in Paris from the same period included racial epithets. The marriage contract between the naturalist Fusée-Aublet and Armille Conan in 1775, which predated the interracial ban, described the bride as "a negress of age."[52] Perhaps the absence of racial epithets after 1778 in legal documents relating to mixed people bespoke a discretionary willingness on the part of officials to overlook the ban when it came to light-skinned people.

In 1778 two of the most powerful men in France quarreled about the legality of mixed-race marriage, prompted by a small village dispute. The quarrel arose when an elderly former slave of the Marquis de Rumont who had inherited property at his master's death sought to marry a young local woman. The Rumont heir knew Sartine. He instructed the curate of his fief to consult the minister about the legality of the union. Rumont lay near the country seat of Guillaume-Chrétien de Lamoignon de Malesherbes, newly retired from his post as minister of the royal household. Malesherbes, who hoped the marriage would go forward, instructed his own curate to marry

122   SLAVES IN PARIS

the couple. He did not believe the 1778 act to be a compulsory or inflexible law. "This prohibition is imposed by a decree of the Council of State; and if the king meant to prohibit curates from marrying [mixed couples] this would have required a royal edict or declaration." Only an unmediated speech act, directly from the king, not through the mouthpiece of his council, could prohibit clergymen in France from administering the sacraments. Malesherbes argued that the 1778 decree left room for curates to exercise their own practical and spiritual judgment. He could not believe that the curate of Rumont "understood the letter of Monsieur de Sartine as an absolute prohibition against marrying this unhappy man and firmly believes that if he does otherwise, he will be put in the Bastille, or at least exiled."[53]

Black men needed help from powerful courtiers when they sought to marry in spite of the ban. In 1785 Charles-Louis Almanzor, who came from Coromandel in India, married a French laundress in Versailles through the intercession of Madame (Adélaïde de France, the king's aunt) and of her valet. Baptized in Paris, Almanzor had once served in the famous black and brown-skinned regiment created by Maurice de Saxe.[54] Permission for the couple to wed came straight from the king, as a favor to Madame; but the union needed to take place in secret. The public should not know of the ceremony, lest they "seek exemption from his majesty to obtain the same favor."[55] The couple married on May 9, 1785, in Versailles's Saint-Louis church, with witnesses including the bride's brother, the security guard of the church, and Jean Aubert, Madame's valet. By contrast, the very next year Antoine Tassime failed to obtain permission to marry the mother of his two daughters, who was pregnant with another child. His lifelong partner petitioned the minister of the navy, observing that "Tassime is black, but free and virtuous," and could claim "no other homeland than France." The Vice-Admiral Count d'Aché, his former master, had bought him in India as a boy of 5; he became a slave in France immediately thereafter. The Countess d'Aché sought assistance from the Princesse de Lamballe, a favorite of the queen, to no effect. As the widow of a disgraced admiral, she lacked the stature at court to be worth bending rules for.[56]

Julien's struggle for freedom makes it plain that these laws did not need to be enforced rigorously to matter. Judges at the Parlement together with Julien's own supporters understood whiteness to confer a right to protection from police violence. No one, including his staunchest allies, condemned the extrajudicial removal of "blacks, mulattoes, and other people of color."

After the Admiralty declared Julien to be free, Reine Baudelle sought orders for his arrest both from the Paris Parlement and from the minister of the navy at Versailles. Addressing the court, she quoted the 1777 Royal Declaration wherein "blacks or mulattoes who were taken to France or who came on their own accord after this publication will be arrested and conducted to the nearest port to be embarked for our colonies."[57] In Julien's case, Parlement acted more hastily than Versailles in supplying Baudelle with an order for his capture. It did so for the nominal purpose of enforcing the country's new law banning nonwhite people from the kingdom. That law set the scene for the Julien affair by racializing the whole system of justice in domestic France. With the exclusion of "blacks, mulattoes, and other people of color" from the country, the mere fact of living under French law and enjoying its protection became the exclusive privilege of white people. Ultimately, in March 1787, Julien's lawyer Delaval managed to stay the warrant issued by Parlement for Julien's arrest; but no lawyer could deactivate a lettre de cachet that came from Versailles. Ultimately it was a royal writ that enabled Julien's capture on the Pont Neuf. Parlement's order for Julien's arrest on racial grounds proved central to this affair, nonetheless, because it provoked a courtroom debate over Julien's racial identity.

AFTER 1789, men involved in the Julien affair, including the slave trader Ozenne and the lawyer Hérault de Séchelles, assumed prominent roles in the French Revolution. Both were powerful men before 1789, and they were bitter opponents during Julien's trial. They later became allies. Each had ties to France's dictatorial leadership council, the Committee of Public Safety. Hérault de Séchelles joined the committee in May 1793. Less than a year later he was guillotined in a purge of prominent legislators that inaugurated the bloodiest phase of the Revolution, known to historians as the Great Terror. Pierre Ozenne, by contrast, proved immune to danger. He spent the Great Terror working as an arms consultant to the Committee of Public Safety and kept the same job after the fall of Robespierre.

Julien, too, made a mark on the Revolution at its bloodiest hour. As the guillotine churned, the National Convention, diminished by purges, chose to annul the 1787 ruling by the Parlement of Paris in his freedom case. Three months after the beheading of Hérault de Séchelles, the French legislature vindicated Hérault's case for Julien by repudiating the verdict, "which condemns him to serve Citizen Ruste, creole, wife of the ex-deputy of Martinique, as a slave." The world described by this decree had long ceased to exist, however. Revolutionaries suppressed the Parlement of Paris in September 1790. Julien had been free for years.

The overlapping stories of Hérault, Ozenne, and Julien after 1789 invite questions about the relationship between the monarchy and the New Regime. The careers of Hérault and Ozenne both underscore the limits of the revolutionary project with respect to slavery; that of Ozenne further reveals the importance of slavery and the slave trade to one man's revolutionary success story. The revival of the Julien affair in the spring of 1794 carried the slave past into the revolutionary present for the purpose of annulling it. That decree, as we shall see, draws attention to the uncanniness of life in the 1790s for people of color in the French Atlantic world, for whom remaining free was an art that required deft maneuvering through space and time.

Hérault de Séchelles was not an opponent of transatlantic slavery before the Revolution and never became one. In 1788 he declined an invitation to join France's new Society of the Friends of the Blacks, modeled on the British Antislavery Society (and created with British encouragement). He congratulated the society's founder, Jacques-Pierre Brissot (1754–1793), for advocating on behalf of "the eternal rights of humanity," while declining membership on professional grounds. He argued that membership would force him to recuse himself from "causes of this sort" and "deny him the ability to defend that same liberty." Hérault was thinking of freedom trials before Parlement, like the Julien affair. Brissot walked away in disbelief. He intended the club to combat a global evil that enjoyed the sanction of national law and flourished outside metropolitan France. He did not understand how Hérault could picture slavery as "the sort of cause to defend before a tribunal."[58] Hérault was an opponent of slavery insofar as this meant championing the cause of slaves nearby. This pre-Revolutionary exchange between Brissot and Hérault revealed stark differences in the geography of their respective forms of idealism.

A few years later Hérault made quite a spectacle of his ardor for liberty during the festival honoring the Constitution of year II, which he wrote. (Year I began with the arrest of the king.) At the Place de la Bastille on August 10, 1793, he addressed the crowd while standing near a fountain shaped like a naked goddess of Nature. During the ceremony, her breasts spurted (apparently potable) water, which Hérault collected in a chalice and sipped after declaiming at her feet. "Sovereign of savage and enlightened nations! . . . It is in your breast, it is from your sacred source, that they recover their rights and are regenerated."[59]

Despite the apparently universal character of the goddess, Hérault did not embrace a global form of revolution. His views shared something with those of his political comrade Robespierre, who denounced Brissot for attempting to "break the chains of the universe" without achieving liberty on domestic soil. (Robespierre's faction also arranged to have Brissot executed.) The 1793 constitution, written by Hérault, abolished slavery, but the document only applied to domestic France. "All men can engage their time and their services; but they cannot sell themselves, nor be sold. Their person is not alienable property." The limited reach of Hérault's constitution and its irrelevance to the colonies became central to political debate in February 1794, when deputies in the Convention, confronted by circumstances in Saint-Domingue, abolished slavery. On that occasion an unidentified deputy tried to obstruct the emancipation decree by yelling "It is decreed!" to which another retorted "Not for the colonies!" Reflecting on Hérault's constitution, the deputy Lacroix remarked: "We were selfish in the constitution and forgot about men of color. Let us remedy our oversight in the name of posterity by declaring slavery abolished in all the colonies."[60]

Ozenne's bond to the republic had none of Hérault's fervor. He later became a Bonapartist and ended as a nobleman during the Bourbon Restoration under the title Ozenne de Boismorel. As an accidental revolutionary, Ozenne had expertise that made him indispensable to the state; he cared little about what regime he served. Reading his earlier and later careers through the prism of the Julien affair underscores the connection between his involvement in transatlantic commerce and his professional life after 1789. Slavery helped to anoint him as a steel specialist who stood above politics. It was the making of a technocrat.

Ozenne and his partner Charette acted as correspondents for *La Négresse,* an especially murderous slave ship that ended its three-year, misbegotten journey at Nantes in 1780. The memoir of its captain, Jean-François Landolphe, in which Ozenne plays a supporting role, helps to situate Ozenne's professional activities before 1789 in relation to his later career.

A sailor with a background in slaving and smuggling, Captain Landolphe, in his prime, was the kind of man who dressed his dogs in nail spikes and

126 SLAVES IN PARIS

named them after famous gangsters.[61] During the Revolution he became a notorious privateer, who preyed on British slave ships and took the slaves he pillaged to Guadeloupe. When he died at home in 1825, on Paris's Rue des Fossées Saint-Jacques, what remained of that world came down to a spyglass, the *Dictionnaire de la Marine,* and a swept-hilt silver saber engraved with the phrase, "Given by the merchants of Pointe-à-Pitre to Captain Landolphe in recognition of his service in year II of the Republic."[62]

Landolphe's account of the ship *La Négresse,* on its maiden voyage, presented the slave trade as a romance about consumer goods. The text passed in silence over the fate of captives aboard that ship, a remarkable omission in view of their fate under Landolphe's command. Nearly half (47 percent) of the 396 people imprisoned in this ship, who came from Benin, died during the Middle Passage—shocking, unexplained, and anomalous for the period. His approach to the slave trade, as an adventure story about commodities, makes this text a particularly useful introduction to Ozenne. Landolphe's observations about Africa do not resemble a travelogue so much as a stockroom inventory. Among the Warri (Itsekiri), the king was "enveloped in rich white Indian muslin," whereas in Senegal and Whydah "one uses blue."[63] Alongside textiles and Brazilian tobacco, *La Négresse* carried huge iron bars, pistols, rifles, sabers, and even delicate items for the male toilette—scissors and razors—that were an English specialty.[64] In exchange, Landolphe acquired slaves and an immense quantity of ivory. At Nantes, Ozenne's firm oversaw the removal and sale of 60,000 pounds of elephant tusks, from hundreds of slaughtered animals—to become things like crucifixes, snuffboxes, and pianofortes.[65]

The commodities that defined Ozenne's later career, steel and smelted iron, were just as connected as ivory to the transatlantic slave trade. At the height of the sugar boom in Saint-Domingue, Ozenne invested in the Royal Steel Manufacture at Amboise, a joint public and private venture. A 1786 advertisement for the new business in the *Gazette de France* promoted its utility for commerce with the West Indies. The factory's location on the Loire would simplify the production and shipment of "agricultural instruments for the colonies." Like the royal manufacture at Essonne, the Amboise factory produced machine components in both iron and steel.[66] The new steam-powered sugar mills, pioneered in the 1780s, required pieces in both metals. A short notice about the Amboise venture in *La Feuille du*

Cap Français, published in Saint-Domingue, also mentioned the manufacture of slave irons for the colonies, together with cauldrons, axles, and cylinders.[67]

Ozenne's involvement in the manufacture at Amboise made him an expert in metallurgy at the outbreak of war between France and Austria (1792). His former employer, the Duc d'Orléans, was killed at the guillotine in 1793. Ozenne became ever more unassailable as the war dragged on.[68] In the autumn of 1794 he became the envoy of the Committee of Public Safety to a new school of military engineering; the École de Mars.[69] He later briefly served as the assistant director of a new engineering school: the École Polytechnique.

What of Julien's experiences after 1789? On 23 messidor year II (July 11, 1794) the National Convention revoked the 1787 decision by the Parlement of Paris that had declared him the slave of "the Citizeness Ruste, wife of the ex-deputy of Martinique." At the time of this decree, Julien had been free for at least three years, although the status of enslaved domestics in Paris remained murky at the outbreak of the Revolution. In February 1790 the slave trader Jean-Baptiste Nairac reported, "People are posted along the streets to stop negroes and men of color, conduct them to notaries, make them protest against their servitude, and reclaim the rights of man."[70] Notwithstanding this burst of solidarity with slaves in the city, domestics still had reason to fear for their safety. In August 1791, in response to a complaint by the planter Boullonier de Saint-Simon about his fugitive housekeeper, the new chief of police ordered "that the said Françoise negress be arrested by the commissioner of police from the section of the Louvre, assisted by the National Guard." The newly elected commissioner Nicolas Chépy, a distinguished lawyer, refused to enforce the order.[71] On September 28, 1791, the National Assembly decreed, "Every individual is free the moment he enters France."[72] Just over a month later, in November 1791, a newly arrived fugitive in the city named Jacques Pascal worried (reasonably) that his masters, who had fled the capital for Brussels, would arrange for his capture.[73]

Six months after proclaiming the emancipation of slaves throughout the French Empire, on 23 messidor year II (July 11, 1794), the National Convention revoked the pre-Revolutionary verdict by the Paris Parlement in Julien's freedom trial. Why did deputies of the legislature bother correcting a miscarriage of justice that dated back seven years when all

128 SLAVES IN PARIS

courts mentioned in the original act, together with slavery, the monarch, the Gregorian calendar, the seven-day week, and even the twenty-four-hour day, had disappeared? The most obvious purpose of this decree was financial. This decision by the legislature empowered Julien "to seek an indemnity before the courts for the oppression he experienced."[74] He signed away that right in December 1795, perhaps after receiving a cash settlement. He was then living with Ruste, Reine Baudelle's ex-husband.

A second explanation for this decree opens from the perils of sea travel in the Age of Revolution for freed slaves and especially for people who owed their freedom to the French Revolutionary government. At the time of the Convention's decree, Julien was preparing to leave for Martinique. At the time of his departure he might not have known about the conquest of the island by British troops (March 20, 1794). He did know, however, that sailing directly to Martinique was impossible. He needed to travel by way of the United States.

The French decree abolishing slavery of 16 pluviose year II (February 4, 1794) was not recognized by Great Britain, Spain, Holland, Portugal, the United States, or planters in Martinique, then under British occupation, where the 1794 abolition decree never went into effect. For Julien to board a ship during the war with Great Britain would expose him to attack and interception at sea by enemy ships. People of color who sailed around the Atlantic without freedom papers risked falling into the hands of privateers. With capture came the risk of being enslaved and sold at auction. At the time of Julien's departure, the freedom he enjoyed from the fact of living in France circa 1794 was not enough. He needed to obtain documents attesting to a liberty that did not originate in Revolutionary law. He certainly needed a letter of manumission that came from his original owners. Julien could not board a ship for the Americas without a kit of legal documents that accorded him freedom in a form that the world would recognize. The decree by the Convention annulling his freedom trial gave him a right to sue his family. By sanctioning future legal proceedings for financial damages, the 1794 decree gave Julien the leverage to extract whatever document he wished from his aunt. It gave him access to the equivalent of a passport.

At which point Julien disappears from view in French archives. In 1815, under the name Julien Baudelle, he married a Haitian woman in Paris.[75] He gave the name Baudelle to his own son, Henri. In 1833 he died near his brother, also named Baudelle, in Port-au-Prince, the capital of newly independent Haiti. During the 1820s, Baudelle prospered in the Haitian capital at the ironic vocation of town auctioneer from a large building opposite the Vallière market in the city center, where he sold the property of the dead, naval salvage, and newly arrived merchandise.[76] He became an importer of luxury consumer goods from France. In 1837, four years after his actual death, Julien reappeared in the city archives for a final act when notaries conducted an inventory of his estate. As they walked from room to room, there was not a single book. Nor a testament: his wife had burned it. What remained of Julien were pocket squares, 37 white cravats, closets full of summer suits, and chairs made of Haitian mahogany.[77]

Chapter 5

OURIKA

THE CHILD WHO BECAME known as Ourika left Senegal for Paris in 1786 and died during the Revolution at the age of 16. Kidnapped or orphaned by a slave raid, she became the property of Stanislas de Boufflers, the governor of the colony, who bought her at the age of 2 or 3. In Paris, Boufflers bestowed her as a gift on his uncle, the Maréchal Prince Charles-Juste de Beauvau. Ourika was not her birth name.[1] Boufflers, an admirer and occasional house guest of Voltaire, is best known as an epigrammatic noble with liberal views. In 1789 he sat as a deputy in the National Assembly. He attended one meeting of the Society of the Friends of the Blacks, an abolitionist group, founded by the journalist and politician Jacques-Pierre Brissot.[2]

In documents relating to Parisian slave hunts, the reader feels a sudden blast of thereness as otherwise silent people break through the surface of those texts while being tracked by the police. Ourika is different. She became an embodied presence in state archives through her own death. She died in the evening of 8 pluviose year VIII (January 27, 1799) in western Paris, amid citywide celebration of the death of Louis XVI. Witnesses to the death of Ourika included a self-described money manager who was really an old valet of the prince and Ourika's legal guardian.[3] At the time of her death, Ourika lived in a palatial townhouse belonging to the prince's widow, Marie-Charlotte de Rohan-Chabot. The princess had not lived in the house for years. The building where Ourika died is now the seat of the French Ministry of the Interior.

130

Two days after Ourika died, someone carted her corpse to Saint-Germain-en-Laye, a village to the west of Paris. The The Princesse de Beauvau had a chateau there, which revolutionaries seized, but she remained in the suburb nonetheless. Ourika's body was inhumed in the village graveyard. The only person mentioned in the burial record is the village clerk.[4]

Ourika's story is that of a child who never reached adulthood. Police records are of no direct use in researching her life. She was too young to make official complaints and never was at risk of being captured in Paris. Nonetheless, her experiences echo those of other people in this book. Bodysnatching and orphanhood were the primal scene of the slave trade. Random and sudden abduction, the experience of falling outside everything in an instant, was central to black experience in the eighteenth-century Atlantic world. Ourika is far from being the only African person in this book. Lucidor and Jean both survived the Middle Passage at young ages. Nonetheless, surviving documents provide few clues about their lives before they set foot in Paris. The fragmentary record of Ourika's brief life at least makes it possible to see the workings of the slave trade at close range, and to glimpse something of the world she came from.

A generation after her death, the salon hostess Claire de Duras published *Ourika* (1823), a short historical novel that incorporated elements of the real girl's biography. The tale by Duras was briefly a bestseller. During the fleeting *Ourika* craze, the book inspired stage plays and fashion accessories—such as novelty canes and hats with black flowers.[5] The first sections of this chapter focus on Ourika, the historical person. Then I grapple with the rebirth of Ourika in story. My approach to the novella by Duras is that of an historian. I begin by separating the historical Ourika from her literary avatar. Next, I consider the novel and its protagonist as social artifacts. I argue that Duras's story was birthed by a particular milieu. The slave-owning elite that converged on Paris in the eighteenth century, which I have followed throughout this book, incubated this novel. That group was a hodgepodge; it included minor and high nobles, naval officers, planters, salon hostesses, bankers, and slave traders. In a genealogical and social sense, the author of *Ourika* grouped all of those people in and around her person.

Problems that wind through earlier chapters of this book recur with particular starkness in Ourika's brief life and in her posthumous resurrection as a literary protagonist. Slaves are always dismayingly silent and disfigured by the written record. With respect to Paris, the very sources that reveal their presence typically counterfeit their desires and general character. Actual speechlessness may have been Ourika's original condition when she reached Paris. Boufflers claimed she could not talk.

An inclination toward ventriloquism—speaking, becoming, feeling, and otherwise ventilating through Ourika—defined Boufflers's conduct toward her from the very beginning. Ventriloquism would also define the relationship between author and protagonist in the novel *Ourika,* which Duras wrote mostly in the first person and read to her social set before publication. Boufflers and Duras laid claim to Ourika to accomplish similar ends. They pictured her as an instrument for the attainment of virtue and used her as a vehicle for enacting benevolence. In Ourika's life and in her rebirth through story, violence was always the sustaining force behind compassion.

THE GIFTING OF SLAVES is an ancient practice, common to all slave societies. Nonetheless, Ourika directs attention to a variant culture of slave gifting, involving extremely young children, which seems to have been on the rise at the end of the Old Regime. In 1777 Louis XVI issued a declaration banning "negroes, mulattoes, and other people of color" from entering the realm. The new law did nothing to halt the influx of children. In 1783 the Maréchal de Castries, minister of the navy, complained that officials routinely flouted the travel ban, arriving with four or five slaves at a time, consisting of "negro children aged 4, 5, or 6 years old, even younger."[6] It is difficult to substantiate this claim by Castries; officials had no problem keeping their own names and hence the names of people in their entourage out of ship passenger lists and port archives.

In France's Atlantic and Indian Ocean colonies, the gifting of children of tender age arose from conditions on the ground that put colonial officials into contact with a surfeit of orphans. Conditions favorable to this gifting practice included war, famine, and the destruction of villages by slave raiders. The very young children who became the property of Stanislas de Boufflers came from a region of Africa where all three of these conditions came together. The slave trade threw Senegambia into famine and tumult. The supply needs of slave ships drained the country of millet. The slave trade armed warlords and triggered jihads.[7] To the north, on the edge of the Sahara, lived the Arab-Berber tribes, known as Moors (*Maures*—hence

Mauritania), who expanded their political and military authority over the Senegalese River region in the eighteenth century.[8] They enslaved local peoples. They also controlled the harvest and export of sap from acacia trees, known as gum arabic. The gum was an essential adhesive in paints and textile manufacture. It fastened colors to paper and cloth. It was almost as vital to European economies as the trade in humans.[9]

The gifting of very young children in the eighteenth century further resulted from new patterns of human mobility. New roads and the mushrooming of the merchant marine quickened the pace of travel while enabling a huge increase in the number of people moving around. The frequency of imperial war with Britain, from the 1740s to the Revolution, increased soldiers' and administrators' to-and-fro between France and the colonies. Perhaps most importantly, the rise of child gifting coincided with a spike in the volume of the French slave trade during the final years of the Old Regime.

During Boufflers's time in Senegal, France outpaced Britain and Portugal as the world's top slave-trading power. The available numbers for the French trade for the years 1781–1790 are limited to the Atlantic region, and do not

Table 5.1

Transatlantic Slave Trade—Number of Slaves Transported by Ships under the Flag of France, Great Britain, and Portugal-Brazil, 1671–1790, by Decade

DECADE	FRANCE	GREAT BRITAIN	PORTUGAL-BRAZIL	TOTALS
1671–1680	6,407	48,384	2,909	57,700
1681–1690	10,595	102,209	7,767	120,571
1691–1700	4,539	79,808	31,033	115,380
1701–1710	14,047	132,209	29,395	175,651
1711–1720	54,220	149,280	32,555	236,055
1721–1730	70,422	193,214	73,641	337,736
1731–1740	95,431	226,266	73,039	394,736
1741–1750	111,682	164,485	129,258	405,425
1751–1760	93,754	233,527	64,831	392,112
1761–1770	129,531	336,990	126,938	593,459
1771–1780	154,962	279,876	66,132	500,970
1781–1790	266,398	278,640	107,739	652,777
TOTALS	1,011,988	2,224,888	745,237	3,982,113

Source: Trans-Atlantic Slave Trade Database.

134 SLAVES IN PARIS

Table 5.2

Transatlantic Slave Trade—Number of Slaves Transported by France, Great Britain, and Portugal-Brazil, 1781–1790

YEAR RANGE	FRANCE	GREAT BRITAIN	PORTUGAL-BRAZIL	TOTALS
1781	686	12,503	13,514	26,703
1782	2,856	17,853	19,069	39,778
1783	9,471	22,782	12,030	44,283
1784	29,612	40,775	11,287	81,674
1785	29,314	32,403	9,089	70,806
1786	33,073	30,153	14,152	77,378
1787	39,637	28,995	6,723	75,355
1788	36,280	35,864	5,868	78,012
1789	34,189	30,162	10,613	74,964
1790	51,280	27,150	5,394	83,824
	266,398	278,640	107,739	652,777

Source: Trans-Atlantic Slave Trade Database.

include statistics from the Indian Ocean trade. During the final decade of the Old Regime, at least ninety French ships—chiefly from Bordeaux—delivered slaves from Mozambique, India, and Madagascar to the Mascarene Islands.[10]

To understand the gifting of young children, we must examine the eighteenth-century slave marketplace. Enslaved children were considered highly perishable commodities. In Africa or the colonies, small children could be obtained for little or nothing—as naval prize or as a gratuity to officials from sea captains. The numerical abundance of young captives together with their inutility as laborers and tendency to die made it easy and inexpensive for colonial administrators to buy them up as gifts.

The use of children as gifts also gained ground through officials' efforts to curry favor with their patrons. A fracas from the 1760s involving Étienne-François Turgot, brother of the famous statesman, reveals the ordinariness of this practice in the eyes of officialdom. Turgot wrote to defend himself against the following complaint: "Why did he take away a negro boy belonging to the king from his parents to make a present of him in Paris?" He was indignant: "Believe me, if I wanted to make the gift of a negro boy, I would be able to pay for him myself." As for the origin of the rumor, "I chanced upon Monsieur Morisse, who informed me that he had asked Monsieur de Behague (NB: former governor), at the time of his passage to France, to take a negro boy back with him and give him to the Comte d'Hérouville, for whom [Morisse] paid 150 livres with a view to this present." For Turgot, this smear on his character had nothing to do with the use of children as gifts and everything to do with his alleged pilfering of state resources (slaves of the king).[11]

Children of color who became enslaved domestics in Paris typically ranged in age from 8 to 12. They were invariably boys, to whom French people referred by the derogatory epithets *petit nègre* and *négrillon*. Boys needed to be old enough to follow orders and young enough not to mind. On August 9, 1786, within days of Boufflers's arrival in France, a slave-owning American wrote to Thomas Jefferson for advice about a "boy, 8 or 9 years old" who was "very useful to his wife." He wanted to know whether to comply with French law, which required that incoming slaves be declared to the Admiralty. Jefferson, who was then living with two slaves in Paris, thought it best to say "nothing about it," adding, "the boy is so young that it is not probable he will think of claiming freedom."[12]

While child gifting was a fad of the later eighteenth century among Parisian nobles, the trend did not typically include newly weaned females. The three boys Boufflers sent to France were also younger than other child slaves in Paris—too young to follow instructions or train for work. Zimeo, whom Boufflers gave to Madame de Blot, sister of the former governor of Martinique, fulfilled the household function of "caressing everybody" (though he shrieked at the sight of Madame de Blot).[13] Vendredi, whom Boufflers gave to Eléonore de Sabran, was "like a cat with sequins on its tail" and provided "comedy all day long."[14]

Boufflers took inspiration in his gifting practice from the household of the Duc d'Orléans, the head of his social set (apart from his uncle). In the words of Madame de Genlis, who educated the Orléans children, "Scipion is seven and he is the *petit nègre* who is the most caressed and the most spoiled from the four parts of the world. He has been reigning for four years in the salon of the Palais Royal in the midst of the most refined circle. He walks on all fours, he does somersaults on the carpet, he slides under the chairs of women to remove their shoes."[15] An apprentice knave since the age of 3, Scipion understood his job, eventually. Madame de Genlis later noted his social acuteness. He was there to flaunt the status of the Orléans family by pranks and buffoonery. As the clownish proxy of his masters, he paraded his (and their) indifference to social constraints and forms of propriety that applied to everyone else. As the gifts of Boufflers, Zimeo and Vendredi landed among people who emphasized their detachment from the vulgar cares of life by seeking to outdo one another in displays of ludic excess. In this group, the functionless superfluity of baby jesters was a status marker.

What about the status of these children? Did they count as slaves in France? In contrast to the people who wound up in police archives, there was no moment of reckoning. Because of their youth, their status did not need to be clarified. Boufflers, for his part, described Ourika as a thing. He made this explicit in a letter to his lover, Eléonore de Sabran, about the usual discomforts of sea travel—vile food, bleeding gums, and contrary winds. While he complained about the food, African animals cooked alive in the hold. By the time they reached the Azores, the monkeys, a green parakeet, the white spoonbill African spatula, and at least five parrots had died. What remained alive on the ship? "A parrot for the queen, a horse for the Maréchal de Castries, a small captive for Monsieur de Beauvau, a sultan chicken for the Duc de Laon, an ostrich for Monsieur de Nivernais." Since Boufflers referred to this child by the generic term *une jeune captive* (a young captive) and signaled her presence in an inventory of surviving animals, we can dismiss the possibility that he pictured her as his ward, or adoptive daughter, or even as a particularized individual.[16]

Ourika was one of two, perhaps three girls of tender age that Boufflers acquired in Africa.[17] Like the boys, they were much younger than black children who served as domestics in Paris. Moreover, noble houses did not include girls in their front-of-house retinue, even as pets. There is a further oddity to the Ourika story. Boufflers bestowed her on his uncle, the Maréchal de Beauvau, a man of high character and a founding member of the Society of the Friends of the Blacks (1788), to which Boufflers briefly belonged. Beauvau's best friend and his permanent house guest, the writer Jean-François Saint-Lambert, was also an opponent of slavery. Beauvau gave Ourika the invented surname Benezet. In the context of late eighteenth-century abolitionism, this name commanded instant recognition. It was the name of the Frenchman who founded the Pennsylvania Abolition Society, the world's first antislavery group.

The prince opposed slavery before the founding of Brissot's society. Yet the convictions of the prince do not make Boufflers's original purchase of

Ourika, or her transfer to France, into an abolitionist story. Boufflers's letters and journals, together with ministerial correspondence from Senegal, make it impossible to view his acquisition of Ourika as a rescue effort. Boufflers's serial purchase of small girls and boys needs to be understood as a fetish practice. These special things (who were people) gave him access to feelings of spiritual elevation. Boufflers's child fetish developed when the guiding purpose of France's colonial presence in Africa, which was the slave trade, collided with the moral code he followed as a nobleman and aesthete.

TO SITUATE BOUFFLERS in relation to the slave trade in Senegal, and to the people he purchased, requires that we take measure of the man before he arrived in that colony. In Africa he hoped to attain to manly distinction after a career that had hitherto focused on sketching, gambling, and the writing of poems and fables. While a young seminarian, he published *Aline: The Queen of Golconde* (1761), a bawdy tale (which opens with a rape scene) that became a bestseller.[18] Obliged to forsake the priesthood, he joined the order of Malta. In exchange for a vow of celibacy, Maltese knighthood allowed Boufflers to take a cut of the rent that peasants paid to abbeys throughout the kingdom. He staked the rent on card games. Membership in the order of Malta fed his gambling habit.[19] He then fell back on the only career that was left to him: the sword. In 1765, at the age of 27, he became a captain in the personal guard of the king of Poland, who was his godfather. One year later he rose to the rank of *mestre de camp* (similar to colonel) in the Esterhazy Hussars, a French cavalry unit.[20] In Paris he outfitted Theleman, his black domestic, in a "short scarlet jacket with silver epaulettes and uniform buttons of the said regiment of Hussars."[21]

During his stint in Senegal, Boufflers bantered about military gear in a letter to his sister, Marie-Catherine de Boisgelin, when asking that she commission a sword befitting his estate. He wanted something "known commonly as a battle sword, in silver: for this you must consult a man of the sword [e.g., full-blooded nobleman] and not of the robe [such as a judge or an ennobled officeholder], because the blade of the law and our blade do not resemble one another." Real people do not fight with silver sabers. This object, no less than the sword worn by a courtier, was an ornament. Boufflers evidently wanted his sister to believe that this sword would be destined for his use as a mark of his noble lineage. It is extremely unlikely that he intended to keep it, however. In the 1780s, silver swords were frequent gifts from European slave traders to African kings.[22]

Boufflers's desire to abandon his past as an amiable parasite and make a mark on the world, which led him to Africa, had earlier propelled him to the marches of Poland. He had ties to the Polish court. He grew up in Lorraine at the palace of Stanislas I, the exiled Polish king.[23] In 1769, when Polish and Lithuanian noblemen began rattling real swords at Russia, Boufflers traveled eastward. In Poland he saw a stage for heroism or, at least, somewhere less embarrassing to learn the soldier's craft.[24] After the disgrace of his friend, the Duc de Choiseul, Boufflers sought help from his uncle, the Prince de Beauvau, in obtaining the king's approval of his service in a foreign army. "It is a unique opportunity for me to develop my talents; if I am successful, I will become useful to France without costing her anything; if I am beaten, all the misfortune will fall on Poland."[25] Court intrigue delayed the letter of the king's consent. Boufflers lost interest. The Poles did not take him seriously. "The Polish marshals laugh at the confederation, take the money of everybody, and orders from no one."[26] Deflated in his prospects, Boufflers hastened to the nearest version of his natural habitat: the salons of Vienna. In May 1771, a mere two months after receiving authorization to fight for Poland, he sulked to Beauvau. "I tumble back into the obscurity that I had hoped to leave."[27]

Historians who write of French elites have discovered a lively debate in the eighteenth century over the proper role of the nobility. At stake was whether nobles could abandon their original function as a warrior class to engage in useful tasks, especially commerce. Where did Boufflers fall in this debate? It is plain from his writings before and during his stint in Senegal that it was *éclat*, personal attainment, and not helpful service to his (or any) country that mattered to him. On the topic of commerce, his conduct did not match his doctrine. He ruled over slave-trading posts in Africa but viewed commerce as debasing.[28]

When Boufflers reached Senegal, every man in uniform, down to the lowliest official, participated in the slave trade. They plundered the government stores of rifles and gunpowder. They trafficked medical supplies. Three top officials, including Cornet, captain of the battalion, co-owned a boat for collecting gum arabic and slaves as well as water and wood.[29] Cornet later explained that he had no choice. In Senegal "we receive our salaries in raw materials and merchandise from the royal storehouse. This method of payment, fixed in the governor's instructions and approved by the sovereign, makes it necessary to convert into cash whatever merchandise one does not consume."[30] The trade in slaves and gum arabic by officials, he claimed, took place with the knowledge of the home government, because the navy paid its staff in things, not money. Perhaps the surgeon who admitted to "going dutch with Mister Dubois, resident of Senegal in the trade," really did barter for slaves with hospital blankets.[31] A clamor arose among French merchants in 1783 over the monopoly exercised by the governor, Dumontet, as the agent of Le Normand de Flaghac, a Parisian banker and personal friend. (Le Normand's son was the governor's aide-de-camp.)[32] A replacement governor, Repentigny, sent to root out corruption, soon began trading himself.[33] At the time of Boufflers's arrival, Repentigny was preparing to leave the colony with one hundred captives, whom he purchased with a plantation-owning sea captain. They would "not leave Saint-Domingue until they were sold, down to the last."[34]

In Senegal, the navy protected Boufflers—son of a field marshal, grandson of a duke—from the need, felt by all other officials, to hawk government wares to realize his salary. The navy gave him "an extraordinary bonus of 12,000 livres to cover the cost of his establishment."[35] The problem for Boufflers, on arriving there, was how to reconcile the refinement he vaunted in letters to Eléonore de Sabran with the work of ruling a slaving entrepôt, for which he had, after all, volunteered.

At no point in his correspondence with his lover and future wife, Eléonore de Sabran, or in his private journals, did Boufflers denounce the slave trade. Boufflers did not attack local officials because of the vileness of buying and selling people. Instead his disgust arose from the betrayal of caste by officials, including nobles, who wore the costume of honorable men while disporting themselves with the baseness of salesmen. "They all have the heart of a merchant while wearing an officer's uniform."[36] The slave trade, rather than being singularly vile, epitomized the vileness of commerce in general.

Although Boufflers adhered to the nobleman's code of unprofitable indolence, it was retail sale that counted as dishonorable, not shopping. The moral license he enjoyed to purchase anything helps to explain his role in a slave transaction on behalf of Louis-Philippe, Comte de Ségur (1753–1830), during his first weeks in the colony. This transaction is essential to

140   SLAVES IN PARIS

understanding the context for Boufflers's original encounter with, and purchase of, the child whom I believe to be Ourika.

The father of the Comte de Ségur was Philippe-Henri, Marquis de Ségur, minister of war (1780–1787).[37] His mother was a plantation heiress from Saint-Domingue. The count himself was the French ambassador to Russia. During the 1780s he lobbied the navy for help in obtaining slaves on the cheap to replenish the family sugar estate. In 1783 Ségur asked for permission to use royal cargo vessels to transport "169 negroes from Cayenne that are being offered at an advantageous price" against a promise to pay for the slaves' food during the voyage. That arrangement, which the minister of the navy refused to countenance, would further have required a grant of legal impunity, because "it is forbidden to transport slaves from one colony to another."[38]

Boufflers helped the count to secure slaves from Senegal. On February 4, 1786, he wrote to Eléonore de Sabran about the imminent arrival of a special slave convoy. "Tell *la petite Ségur* [NB: the countess] that I am waiting for the ship Monsieur Beudet is supposed to send from Bordeaux on her behalf, and, if it arrives, I could, despite the current high prices, give her about fifty strapping negroes for half the going rate, so that in Saint-Domingue they will end up costing [individually] only 100 pistoles." One pistole was probably equal to 10 livres tournois or 12.8 modern euros. The countess acted for her husband, who could not make these arrangements from his ambassadorial residence in St. Petersburg.[39]

Ségur's ship, *La Pourvoyeuse,* left Bordeaux on January 10, 1786, began trading in April, and left Africa with ninety captives. The captain, Jacques Bedout (not Beudet, as Boufflers wrote), was a Canadian-born sailor of distinction, who became vice admiral during the Revolution. His brother, Michel-Antoine, was a planter in Saint-Domingue. After Napoleon's ascension to power, gout-stricken Bedout conveyed 5,000 Polish soldiers to Saint-Domingue for the Leclerc mission (1801–1802) aimed at restoring slavery. On return, he was appointed to the Legion of Honor.[40]

La Pourvoyeuse was not a slave ship. It was a small warship that the navy struck from its rolls the year of Bedout's mission to Africa.[41] The ship stopped at Saint-Louis, the headquarters of the colonial government, before continuing to Albreda on the Gambia River. Ten captives died before the ship reached the port of Saint-Marc in Saint-Domingue that October. Until 1786 the talented Bedout, a commoner, could not enter the naval officer corps because of his low birth. After the Africa trip, he was raised to the rank of second lieutenant (the lowest commissioned rank).[42]

Boufflers agreed to help the Ségurs with their purchase scheme before he left Paris. He believed their ship would arrive close on his heels, just after he assumed his duties in the colony. (One cannot help wondering whether he got the post of governor in exchange for a promise to make this happen.) He told Sabran that his friends should expect "about fifty strapping negroes," cheaply priced, which means that he played some role in examining and haggling for them. Four days later, Boufflers told Eléonore about his purchase of a beautiful child, whom he supposed to be incapable of speech.

> Feb. 8, 1786. I am buying a little negress of 2 or 3 years of age to send to Madame the Duchesse d'Orléans. If the merchant ship that must carry her is delayed in leaving, I do not know how I will part with her. She is pretty, not as the day, but as the night. Her eyes are like little stars and her manner is so gentle that I am moved to tears thinking that this little child was sold to me as a little lamb. She does not yet speak, but she understands what one says in Wolof: kay filé, come here; toura man, kiss me. If you see her at the Palais Royal, do not fail to speak her language to her and to kiss her, knowing that I have also kissed her, and that her face is the meeting place of our lips.[43]

Boufflers had just been looking at slaves to buy for the Ségurs. There were no new captives coming to the island. In December, when the dry season began, it became impossible to travel between Saint-Louis and the continent. The notorious barre of the Senegal River prevented ships from approaching the shore. Ocean currents made northward trips to Saint-Louis from the Gambia, or even from the island of Gorée, dangerous and slow. Boufflers must have purchased this young girl on the island of Saint-Louis, the seat of the colonial government. She might have come from a family of household slaves on the island; she might have been conveyed to a slave pen before the dry season. We cannot know if Wolof was her mother tongue; Africans sold to Europeans on the Senegal River were not necessarily local to that region. Captives in Galam, the most remote location frequented by Europeans on this river, were often made to travel great distances, reaching the trading post after "sixty, seventy, and eighty days of walking."[44]

142   **SLAVES IN PARIS**

In February 1786, Boufflers spoke of his intention to bestow this small girl on the Duchesse d'Orléans. That gift never happened. He had immediate second thoughts about sending her away and resolved to keep her should "the merchant ship that must carry her" (presumably a slave ship) delay its departure. Given the abandonment of Boufflers's planned gift to the duchess, and his need to bestow a particularly wonderful token of esteem on his uncle, it seems likely that Boufflers kept her and took her to France for the prince.

Boufflers did not bother to mention the name of this child when writing about her. Instead, he used the generic phrase *une petite négresse.* He depicted her as physically distinctive in her beauty but morally indistinguishable from other beings in her racial category. Ourika could not talk—he said; yet she understood several words in Wolof. Boufflers gave two sample phrases that he wanted Sabran to address to her. He correctly translated the first phrase, *kay filé,* as "come here." He translated a second phrase, *toura man,* as "kiss me"—which is not merely incorrect, but also a strange invention. In Wolof, *toura man* means "tell me your name / what is your name / do you want to know my name."[45]

Boufflers urged that Sabran "kiss her, knowing that I have also kissed her, and that her face is the meeting place of our lips." To make sense of this recommendation, and unlock the puzzle of his moral compass, requires that we parse the language of love in other letters by Boufflers, with special attention to fetish-like objects. Boufflers envisaged his amorous communion with Sabran as unfolding in an insular country of the mind, where there was neither trade nor any form of work. "Our life may appear empty to others, but it is full to us. What others call business, employment, occupation, is nothing to us. Leisure, love, and intimate complicity, detachment from everything, is what fills our heart."[46] While incompatible with worldly life, such countries are everywhere in art and literature—the land of Cockaigne of medieval myth, the enchanted islands in Ariosto's *Orlando Furioso* (1516), Shakespeare's Forest of Arden. This sphere of unhurried thought and pleasure to which Boufflers and Sabran belonged was a literary utopia, sealed from every feature of life in a slave-trading post. Their insular paradise was the opposite of Saint-Louis of Senegal, the island he governed.

How might Boufflers attain to this detached land of pure feeling while Sabran remained in Paris? He could get there, or near there, through the mediation of special objects. They were special because they were distinct from saleable goods. They had a *je ne sais quoi* of uniqueness and were completely un-useful, making it impossible to estimate their value in exchange. In a sort of echo of the slave trade, Boufflers describes these objects as carrying people inside them. "Your charming portrait has arrived . . . It says everything I know that you think. I believe I hear you, and your voice penetrates to the bottom of my heart."[47] Special objects contained the essence of loved ones (and of himself). Their allurement further hinged on their apparent valuelessness. "I am sending . . . these strands of hair that you requested as a gauge and symbol of the sweetest and most enduring bond. If there remains some vestige of sensation in what is separated from us, if what was part of me still participates in my nature, they will fly to you like iron to a magnet and straw to amber."[48] Boufflers's particular theory of the love fetish conformed to that of other high-ranking Parisian noblemen. Because of, and not in spite of, this caste's consumerist excesses and buying power, the most precious tokens were valueless things worn about one's person or otherwise connected to one's body. Letters, as much as hair strands or pictures, were objects of this special type. Like the talking portrait of Sabran, they revealed inner secrets. They also made it possible in a tactile way to feel the imprint of another person's body. While letters are distinct from renewable ex-body parts, such as hair strands, they bore the scratches and smudges of fingers and retained vibrations of touch.

Boufflers's ability to commune with Sabran required the mediation of love tokens, which he needed to keep coming as a sign that love endured. In practice, this meant that his special country of "love, leisure, intimate complicity" was parasitic on the triangular traffic of commercial ships during the 1780s, at the trade's historic acme. In relying on the slave trade to supply him with love tokens, Boufflers depicted the to-and-fro of ships as a normal postal system and awaited new ships with nervous expectancy. Of the *Gustave Adolphe,* a ship aboard which half of the captives would die, he wrote, "I begin to despair at this accursed Gustave . . . the weather was appalling and it might have suffered at sea and been thrown far from my imperceptible colony."[49] The despair was not for the people in the ship, but for the mail bags. On October 1, 1786, he wrote of expecting "one or two ships from Bordeaux" armed for Senegal and begged that she learn the date of their departure as proof of her love.[50]

In his letter of February 8, 1786, Boufflers described Ourika in the same terms as other love fetishes. She met all the criteria. Through his kiss, she

144 SLAVES IN PARIS

became imbued with his person; in the commodified world of Saint-Louis, she was worth nothing. For opponents of slavery, including Boufflers's uncle, the Prince de Beauvau, humans were not commodities. People did not have prices. For Boufflers, however, as a noble aesthete who reviled trade, a selection of captive children, exuding a *je ne sais quoi* of uniqueness, became poignantly desirable. Boufflers never varied in describing these children as things rather than people. Their pathos was that of beautiful objects that the world deemed worthless. Their cheapness made that pathos collectible. We are now able to decode what Boufflers thought he was doing when he gave Ourika to the Prince de Beauvau. She was his love letter to an abolitionist.

THE FIRST PUBLISHER of Claire de Duras's *Ourika* (1823) was the Imprimerie Royale, which otherwise produced edicts, national statistics, rulings of the Court of Cassation, and the occasional museum catalogue. *Ourika* first made history as the only novel ever published by a French king. The first reviews of the book—by salon insiders, sycophants, or venal critics—did not describe it as fiction. When presenting the story to her own set, Duras did not describe it that way, either. An early review in the *Mercure* (1823) by the poet Pierre-François Tissot described *Ourika* as "based in fact, or at least so it would seem from the truthful depiction of movements of the heart in this victim of ill chance and misplaced generosity."[51] The next year, when the book came out commercially, the reviewer for *Le Constitutionnel* wondered "why we give to this pretty little book that Ladvocat put up for sale yesterday the qualification of novel." The tale was "authentic," and its author simply related the story "with the charm and talent that are particular to a woman who unites amiability with wit."[52]

Later in the nineteenth century, literary biographers of Claire de Duras ceased to view the story as a factual recounting of Ourika's life and presented the tale instead as a stealth version of autobiography. In an 1834 essay, written seven years after the death of Claire de Duras, the critic Saint-Beuve speculated that the novelist had channeled her inferiority complex and sense of taint, as a parvenue duchess, into the character of Ourika. He wrote that Duras was chronically afflicted by a "sense of inequality, either in nature or in social position."[53]

At the turn of the twenty-first century, *Ourika* became "a canonical anticolonial text" in France and the Anglophone world.[54] Carol Sherman has praised Duras's "imaginative sympathy by showing suffering felt by a person generally seen . . . to be radically other."[55] Critics have vaunted the text's political message, declaring *Ourika* to be "a progressive work with respect to slavery" that "speaks vehemently against racial prejudice."[56] A 2007 Gallimard teaching guide to the novel *Ourika* for French students lists four topics of classroom emphasis, including "the rebirth of abolitionism in nineteenth-century France," "the reappraisal of African culture," "the movement for racial equality," and "the Revolution in Saint-Domingue."[57] A 2022 edition of *Ourika* for French high school students lists themes of the book, which include "demonstrating the absurdity of racial prejudice" and "a meditation on alterity."[58]

My own reading of this novel opens from a comparison between the real Ourika's past and the fictionalized version of her life in Duras's book. The two Ourikas belong to distinct temporal worlds. In the novel, Ourika is a teenager in 1789. It is crucial to Duras's story that she reach adolescence under the tutelage of Madame de B (or Beauvau), a haughty salon hostess at the pinnacle of aristocratic society. At the age of 16, fictional Ourika is the product of a Pygmalion-like noble world to which she can never belong. In the words of Madame de . . . , Beauvau's confidante, "who would ever want to marry a negress?"[59] The plot of the story centers on Ourika's inability to marry the white man she adores, and her epiphany of horror when she sees herself as others do. This plot device is possible, however, only because Duras has aged Ourika by ten years in order to educate her as a gentlewoman, sexualize her body, and insinuate nubile desire into her person.

None of this speaks to the experience of the real girl, who came to Paris in 1786 at the age of 3. Ourika lived in the Beauvau residence in a western neighborhood of the city, on the Rue du Faubourg Saint-Honoré, where new aristocratic townhouses of shocking splendor dotted a landscape of medieval ruins, garden plots, barns, and orchards. The destruction of the nobility during the 1790s emptied this semi-urban precinct of its top-tier inhabitants. In the 1790s, people in the social orbit of the Beauvau family were dead, eking by in obscurity, abroad, or on the lam. Anne-Louise, the daughter of the Prince de Beauvau, was an exception. She remained with Ourika in her father's house. Her husband, Philippe-Louis de Noailles, Prince de Poix, fled the country. Born with a weak leg and lamed by illness, Beauvau's

146 **SLAVES IN PARIS**

daughter needed to remain for both physical and financial reasons. During the Revolution, she struggled to save what she could of their estate.[60]

The Paris of the real Ourika was a city in upheaval. It is no wonder that Marie-Charlotte de Rohan-Chabot, Beauvau's widow, chose to live in the countryside. Historians remember the patriot society near her Parisian townhouse—the section de la République—for its unsurpassed zealotry in the adulation of Revolutionary saints. After being murdered in the bathtub by Charlotte Corday, the journalist Jean-Paul Marat became the center of a religious cult devoted to the martyrs of liberty. In July 1793, after a delegation of local women sprinkled petals on Marat's decomposing corpse, an orator from this section rallied mourners in the voice of the martyred man: "I seem to hear him tell you in his energetic language . . . Avenge the republic and disappoint their ferocious hopes by strengthening the indissoluble knots of civic brotherhood." The section's splendiferous party for Marat, in December 1793, took place inside and at the foot of the Beauvau townhouse, where Ourika and Beauvau's daughter lived. Receipts from the festival include an invoice for windowpanes shattered by the vibration of cannon salvos. Ourika (age 11) could not have failed to notice explosions, broken glass, outdoor festoonery, and hundreds of revelers in and around the house. Planners of the festival commissioned a "Monument to the Glory of Marat." The ceremony featured a sarcophagus, 385 feet of flower garlands, 120 wreaths, liberty trees, an arc of the covenant, and an allegorical figure of the Law. The section paid tribute to Marat with musical entertainment from a band with twelve drums, fourteen violins, bassoons, trumpets, and four French horns. Inside the Beauvau residence, people feasted. The grocery list included forty-five pounds of ham. The soldiers alone drank 200 bottles of wine and broke a lot of rented crockery.[61]

The real Ourika died just over five years later, in January 1799, the same year that Bonaparte overthrew the Republic. According to the Princesse de Beauvau, she was then 16.[62] The demise of her literary avatar happens later, in 1802, after the false Ourika takes holy orders. Postponing Ourika's death made it possible for Duras to stage her character's final days in a setting that would have been impossible during the real girl's lifetime: the Revolution had abolished religious orders. It was not until March 1802 that nuns began returning to convents in Paris. By cloistering herself in a picturesque ruin on the Rue du Faubourg Saint-Jacques, the false Ourika volunteers to renounce the body that is the cause of her wretchedness from which, in October, she disburdens herself through death.

If we turn from the pages of this historical novel to the archives of the police from the period the novel describes (the spring of 1802), we discover an unsettling concatenation of events at the instant the fictional Ourika takes the veil. On March 13, 1802, the police transmitted news that the Carmelites were returning to their old convent on the Rue du Faubourg Saint-Jacques. Six days later, on March 19, 1802, police spies in Paris reported a rumor (which was not just a rumor) "that the government was going to expel all the negroes and mulattoes in France. Several of them, it is said, have gone into hiding."[63] As this police document suggests, the disappearance of Duras's Ourika into the cloister and tomb coincided with a period of disturbing change for people of African descent in Paris and on French soil more generally. Those changes were of inestimable significance to the author of this novel. Duras reaped huge pecuniary benefits from Napoleon's pro-slavery policy, which held the key to her status in French society.

After eight years of British rule, Martinique returned to France under the Treaty of Amiens (April 1802), which established peace, however briefly, between the two belligerents. Bonaparte responded by issuing a decree that preserved slavery where it had never been abolished (Martinique) and reviving the slave trade. He had already dispatched administrators to Guadeloupe and French Guiana with instructions to re-enslave the inhabitants. In the spring of 1802, more than 30,000 soldiers converged on Saint-Domingue under the command of Charles Victor Emmanuel Leclerc for the purpose of restoring slavery there (resulting in the independent state of Haiti). In 1802 and 1803, Bonaparte enacted a modern version of the 1777 edict banning "black, mulattoes and other people of color" from the kingdom. He also revived the 1778 ban on interracial unions.[64]

Duras's Ourika locks herself up and wastes to death just as people of color were being hunted, stripped of citizenship, and reduced in law to the equivalent of saleable objects. The British conquest of Martinique in 1794, which prevented revolutionaries from abolishing slavery, saved the slave fortune of Claire de Kersaint and enabled her marriage to the Duc de Duras. According to the Princesse de Boigne, "The fortune of Mademoiselle de Kersaint, without being very considerable, was very much to the liking of Monsieur de Duras. Hardly has she disembarked that they wed."[65] Her fortune then included more than 100,000 livres (the equivalent of about two

148   SLAVES IN PARIS

million euros) in the Bank of England, plus the profits from two and a half slave plantations. In principle, Martinican proprietors had everything to lose in 1802. It would have been reasonable to suppose that the return of Martinique to France by the Treaty of Amiens would result in the emancipation of slaves on that island. Napoleon's colonial policy, which preserved slavery in Martinique, allowed the author of Ourika to retain her slave wealth.

Texts that offer an illuminating counterpoint to this novel include not only police reports and laws of the period but also the marriage contract of the Duchesse de Duras. Her actual marriage to the Duc de Duras took place in 1797, during their exile years in London.[66] Newly returned to France, they visited a Parisian notary in April 1802 to regularize their earlier agreement. The resulting contract empowered Claire de Duras to testify, make contracts, initiate legal suits, buy and sell movable property (slaves), and perform all manner of transactions except for alienating land without the duke's consent.

The French marriage contract typically requires a list of assets to be held in common or kept separately by each party. This 1802 document did not mention a single asset of the duke.[67] It did, however, list the property of Claire de Duras. Her assets included "half of the plantation des Anglais in the Saint Anne quarter of Martinique, held indivisibly with her mother as a legacy from the deceased Jean-Louis Monnel, her great uncle by marriage; she also stated her "rights to the succession of the defunct Comte de Kersaint, her father, for whom she is the sole and unique heir." We know from her father's seized papers that he served as custodian of two plantations in Saint Lucia on her behalf during the 1770s and 1780s.[68] Those estates had since been sold.[69]

In Duras's story, Ourika withdraws into a nunnery and shrivels up from unrequited love for a white man. The period of Ourika's cloistering and physical demise—the spring of 1802—matches the period, outside the novel, when the French government repudiated revolutionary emancipation. That occurrence harmonized with the interests of Duras and everyone she knew.

The fictional Ourika's suffering was the downbeat of Duras's actual life. The author became newly visible and prominent in Parisian society as her character, inside the novel, disintegrates in tormented solitude. Duras returned from exile, thereby becoming newly visible in France, as her character vanishes into the cloister. Duras's legal empowerment during the spring of 1802 coincided with her character's physical wastage in a monastic cell. What do we learn from reading Duras's novel against her life? The death of Ourika was a submerged form of the author's story of becoming.

FOR REASONS she could not control, slavery created the physical being and social self of Claire de Duras. Slavery also shaped her literary voice, which developed out of her career as a salon hostess. Without plantation wealth, she could not have written *Ourika*. To understand the importance of slavery in constituting her world and art, we can begin by examining her family history. As it happens, the lineage of the Duchesse de Duras links her, directly or indirectly, to every theme and nearly every episode in this book. Hers is a story that includes child gifting, slave trading, and the wartime seizure of ships laden with slaves. Both her father and her grandfather were naval officers. During the War of the Austrian Succession, the elder Kersaint served in the East Indian theater alongside Bouvet de Lozier, the owner of Pauline (Chapter 2). While in Mauritius, the novelist's grandfather staved off an English attack through his clever placement of ships so as to give the illusion of a heavily defended colony. In 1748, Governor David conveyed his gratitude to the elder Kersaint with gifts including coffee beans and a naked boy.

> Sir I know that you desired to have *un petit négrillon* and as I just came across one with a rather handsome face, I am hastening to satisfy the first desire of yours that became known to me. I send him just as he was when he arrived. I hope he pleases you because it is my inclination to wish happiness to everyone. A councilor from the island of Bourbon sent me coffee that is said to be excellent. As I hope to enhance the reputation of these islands, I am sending my present to you and bid that you savor it and spread the word among the people to whom you have it served.[70]

In this letter bestowing two local commodities—boy and coffee—we are left to wonder whether the governor pictured the naked child as a brand emissary for the French Indies Company or whether the boy was meant to be savored, with the coffee, as a complementary exotic stimulant. The elder Kersaint spent the remainder of his career fighting England in defense of French slave colonies, which chimed with family interests. On his mother's side, he descended from the powerful Eustache family in Le Havre. During the period 1728–1741, the Eustache family was owner or part owner of at least five slave ships that transported more than 1,300 slaves to Martinique and Saint-Domingue.[71]

In 1756 Duras's grandfather left Brest for Africa on a secret mission: to prey on British slave ships, sink as many as possible, seize their cargoes, and "sell these slaves for the benefit of the king at the most advantageous price" in Martinique and Saint-Domingue.[72] One-third of the profits went to the crew. At the age of 15, Armand-Guy, Comte de Kersaint, the father of Claire de Duras, joined his father on that mission at the rank of officer in training (*garde de la Marine*). His first act of valor in the navy was an assault by canoe on an English slaving vessel at Cape Mount in modern Liberia.[73] Years later, while stationed in Martinique, he married Claire d'Eragny d'Alesso, from a Creole family of planters.[74] Through that marriage, with help from his affectionate uncles in the Eustache-Lecouteulx family—bankers and slave traders—Kersaint became the owner of plantations.[75] A few of the slaves he purchased came from the merchant Ruste de Rezeville, master of Julien Baudelle (Chapter 4).[76]

In 1784 Kersaint père moved into an opulent apartment in Paris with his enslaved attendant, Crispin Loff. The boy soon disappeared. We know of Loff from three documents. The first is an unpaid haberdashery bill from 1787 going back three years. Merchandise on the bill includes "a hat for his negro" (12 livres) from November 29, 1784. The second is a 1785 receipt for the boy's roundup by a police inspector. The third is a letter from Kersaint's plantation manager about Loff's misdeeds on the ship back home. "Loff the negro of whom you rid yourself in my favor is the greatest scoundrel and I would hang him if my humanity did not spurn the idea."[77] Loff may be an abbreviation of Wolof, an ethnicity in Senegal—probably that of Ourika. Loff and Kersaint lived on the Rue Saint-Honoré, a prolongation of the street where Ourika lived, beginning in 1786.

How should Claire de Duras's family history shape our reading of *Ourika?* The author herself came into being through a violent transoceanic imperial story that appears shapeless at first, involving uncoordinated action among people diverse in station and livelihood, strewn through provincial France and the two hemispheres, who eventually fused in the person of a new-fangled duchess on Paris's Rue de Varennes. What gave momentum to that family story, enabling far-flung disparate elements to

5.1 Northeastern view of the Château d'Ussé at Rigny-Ussé (1934). View from the northeast.
Marcel Maillard (1899–1977). Photographic negative on film, 9 × 6.5 cm. La Médiathèque de la Communauté Urbaine d'Alençon.

converge in Claire de Duras, was the activity of buying, moving, selling, and intercepting African captives, defending colonies, and extracting labor from slaves.

Transatlantic slavery created this family lineage and would also embed Claire de Kersaint in a new lineage, assign her a higher social rank, and accord her a better name. Viewed this way, all of the things that slavery removed from African people, it gave to her.[78] The status that Claire de Kersaint attained through her marriage to Duras, a peer close to the king, meant that her subsequent overlapping roles, as an elite hostess and a writer of tales about elite society, stemmed from her Martinican slave fortune. In 1807 Claire de Duras and her mother sold their plantation to buy the Château d'Ussé, a storybook palace in the Loire Valley—purchased jointly with the Duc de Duras's mother. The plantation buyer paid in installments and still owed money when Claire de Duras died in 1827.[79] The lapse in years between the chateau purchase and the writing of *Ourika* does not diminish the importance of slavery in furnishing the physical setting and material surroundings of Duras's social self.

The lineage of the Duc de Duras was no less crucial to the making of *Ourika*. His mother was Charlotte-Louise de Noailles. His uncle, Philippe de Noailles, Prince de Poix, was married to the only child of the Prince de Beauvau. Marie-Charlotte de Rohan-Chabot, Beauvau's widow, was the duke's great aunt. Through her marriage, Claire de Duras came into direct contact with people, including her own husband, who had spent long periods with Ourika in the late 1780s and early 1790s. The Princesse de Beauvau (1729–1807) was alive at the time when Claire de Duras returned to France under Napoleon. They socialized at the Château du Val, Beauvau's estate in Saint-Germain-en-Laye—the town where Ourika was buried.

The Marquise Henriette-Lucie Gouvernet de la Tour du Pin, née Dillon, became a close friend of Claire de Duras in London during the late 1790s. In her memoirs, La Tour du Pin recalled her evenings at the Château du Val at the beginning of the French Revolution. "We made music, accompanied by Madame de Poix, who was an excellent musician. Madame the Maréchale [de Beauvau] amused herself by arranging me in a tableau vivant with her little negress Ourika. I took her on my knees, she put her arms around my neck, and she pushed her little face, black as ebony, against my white cheek. Madame de Beauvau never tired of this performance, which annoyed me in the extreme, because I detest factitious sentiment."[80] The participants in this scene, with the exception of Ourika, later became the Duchesse de Duras's inner circle. It is consistent with the liberal spirit of the Beauvau household that the Princesse de Beauvau, as hostess, should enlist La Tour du Pin, a sleek blond countess, to snuggle an African orphan in a tableau connoting high moral principle—or as a nod to the Revolution, since the year is 1790. The scene here pays homage to the antislavery movement while denaturing it. Through this tableau, abolitionism ceases to be a campaign against a murderous global profit scheme involving millions of people; it becomes a philanthropic allegory embodied by two adoring females who stand for Africa and France. In recounting this incident, La Tour du Pin seems so out of sympathy with the girl on her lap (who was probably 6) as to hint at Ourika's guile in pressing "against my white cheek" to make the visual contrast more striking in their mutually unfelt staging of moral sentiment.

At several points in this chapter I have insisted on the need to distinguish the historical Ourika from Duras's fictional character. The same kind of distinction needs to be made with respect to Duras herself. Claire de Kersaint's first literary masterpiece was the person she became in Restoration society. On marrying the duke, she adopted a style of talk and bearing that looked back to a time she had not experienced, and marked a social category to which she had not belonged. She spent her early married life "studying high society" in order to replicate "the conversation of the Old Regime, a time of graciousness and beautiful words."[81] Her niece, Léontine de Noailles, would recall "her old courtly ways." The society that Duras described in *Ourika* was one she taught herself to inhabit.[82]

Saint-Beuve's essay about the Duchesse de Duras draws frequent comparisons between the salon of the Princesse de Beauvau and that of Duras. Claire de Duras spent years cultivating that resemblance. She spent the decade after her marriage studying the aphoristic language and manners of courtiers and famous hostesses. The books she mentioned in letters to friends included the correspondence of eighteenth-century salon hostesses—Julie de Lespinasse, Madame du Deffand—and the journals of Philippe de Courcillon, Marquis de Dangeau, in twenty volumes, about the reign of Louis XIV.[83] The metamorphosis of Duras into a grande dame of the Old Regime was soon so complete that the narrator of *The Memoirs of Sophie,* her novelized autobiography, identifies herself in the book's fourth paragraph as the lineal descendant of Germanic princes, exactly like the Beauvau family.[84] Claire de Duras's family ties to Ourika provide an essential context for interpreting curious lines in a notebook (newly discovered) that she kept in the 1820s. She wrote, on November 20, 1821: "I would like someone with talent to treat another subject, an event that happened in our own time to which I was witness. The chevalier de Boufflers brought back from Senegal . . . a little negress hardly 2 years old . . . She died before she was 20 and was glad to die."[85] What to make of this claim, which she ventured nowhere else, to have seen Ourika? Duras was born in 1777. She was 9 years old when Ourika reached Paris, 12 at the start of the Revolution—too young to be out in society, making her an improbable guest at the Beauvau salon. Neither the Duc de Duras nor his cousin, Henriette-Lucie de la Tour du Pin, who both frequented the Beauvau house, knew Kersaint before 1797, when they met her in London. In a wry letter to Duras from 1824, the Duc de Lévis praised the novel for its skillful mimicry of an alien social milieu unknown to its author. "I lived in that world, which you only know by stories, and I admire your sagacity in guessing its true character based on hearsay."[86] The Duc de Lévis was thirteen years her senior and married to her first cousin.[87]

Duras may have met Ourika at the house of Madame Blot (sister to Duras's uncle by marriage), on whom Boufflers bestowed another child,

154 **SLAVES IN PARIS**

named Zimeo. Perhaps she encountered Zimeo in her girlhood. Her line about witnessing Ourika remains an imposture, however, which projected her into the past of a family she had recently joined.

Why confabulate in a private journal? Assuming this notebook is both authentic and correctly dated, there are three possible answers to this question: the notebook had another function than a diary, Duras could no longer tell when she was making things up, or she had an elastic notion of witnessing, which included what people close to her saw. Marie-Bénédicte Diethelm, who has published many learned editions of Duras's work and who found the notebook, dates the writing of *Ourika* to December 1821. By contrast, the nineteenth-century editor of Duras's correspondence gives an earlier date—between winter and spring of 1821.[88] The published correspondence of Countess Swetchine, a friend of Duras, refers admiringly to *Ourika* in April 1821.[89] These nineteenth-century volumes add further complexity to the newly discovered notebook. If Claire de Duras wrote *Ourika* in early 1821, this phrase from November 1821 exhorting "someone with talent to treat an event . . . to which I was witness" was written months after Duras wrote the story.

In his 1834 essay "La Duchesse de Duras," Saint-Beuve describes the genesis of *Ourika* as recollected by Claire de Duras's daughter: "Having one evening recounted the real anecdote in detail of a young negress brought up by the Maréchale de Beauvau, her friends, charmed by this story, told her—but why don't you write that tale?"[90] Propped against Saint-Beuve's essay, Duras's notebook reads like a preparatory script: "I would like someone with talent to treat another subject, an event that happened in our own time to which I was witness" is the kind of thing you say to house guests that hints at lifelong companionship with Old Regime princes. Guests would probably urge that you write the story yourself. Maybe you had. These texts draw attention to the blend of fact and fiction that distinguished Duras's conversation. More importantly, the notebook together with Sainte-Beuve's essay hint at the back-and-forth between writing and talking that structured Duras's life in language as a salon hostess.

Duras read versions of *Ourika* aloud in her salon for several years before publishing it. The novel needs to be read as something more than an individual work of imagination. People who listened to this story played a role akin to that of editors in shaping what the book became. Duras's desire to oblige, to impress, and above all not to enrage her public would shape the book's content. Written to delight a specific group, *Ourika* was a social product. While it is impossible to recover the precise social interactions that shaped the story, it is comparatively easy to know who gathered at Duras's house. We cannot know what they said; but we can surmise what they did not want to talk about.

Duras wrote *Ourika* in 1821, a watershed year in the history of French abolitionism. In that year, English antislavery activists, joined by a handful of French statesmen, denounced the French government for complicity in the flourishing of the illegal slave trade and recounted scenes of mass murder at sea. Duras was one of the first people to learn of these horrors. On January 13, 1821, the naturalist Alexander Humboldt sent Duras a pamphlet written by William Wilberforce about atrocities aboard the French slave ship *Le Rodeur* (1819).[91]

Duras's salon was a gathering place for cabinet ministers, not for antislavery liberals. The marquee figure at those parties was the writer and statesman François-René de Chateaubriand. The funds of the Chateaubriand family came entirely from the slave trade. His father, René-Auguste, captained two slave voyages early in his career. Later he controlled the family business out of Saint-Malo. Chateaubriand's uncle, Pierre-Anne, sailed the family slave ships, including the *Saint-René,* the ill-fated *Amaranthe,* and the *Roi de Juda.*[92] Chateaubriand's diplomatic career, promoted indefatigably by Duras, often kept him from Paris. He probably encountered *Ourika* first in written form, not in Duras's salon. Chateaubriand, whom Duras esteemed to the point of idolatry, was, nonetheless, her most important interlocutor and ideal reader.

Many cabinet ministers of Louis XVIII had ties to slavery. The Baron Portal, who became director of colonies in 1815 and minister of the navy three years later, descended from a family of slave traders in Bordeaux. Under his protection, merchants in French ports openly prepared ships for Africa despite French assent to abolition at the Congress of Vienna, confirmed by royal edict in 1817.[93] Officials and legislators in France, including Chateaubriand, denounced British abolitionism as a cynical plan to subvert French sovereignty and destroy the French Empire. While Chateaubriand served as ambassador to London, he promised to "stay on my guard and not be the dupe of British philanthropy."[94] In 1821 the naturalist Alexander Humboldt warned William Wilberforce, the English abolitionist, that "no bookstore in Paris would pay to print your pamphlet."[95]

156 SLAVES IN PARIS

Frequent visitors to the Duras salon included Joseph de Villèle, president of the council of ministers. Villèle and his brother emigrated to the Mascarenes during the French Revolution and married plantation-owning sisters on the Isle of Bourbon (now Réunion). During the Restoration, the Villèle family plantations depended on the illegal trade.[96] Amable-Guillaume-Prosper Brugière de Barante—liberal peer, bureaucrat, historian—was married to the heiress Césarine-Marie-Josephine de Houdetot, from another family that emigrated to Mauritius during the 1790s. Barante was a member of the Christian Moral Society (Société de Morale Chretienne), which opposed slavery, and a friend of Benjamin Constant, a leading abolitionist of the day. Barante did not, however, sit on the society's abolition committee or address the topic in the Chamber of Peers during the 1820s.[97] Mathieu de Molé, an occasional visitor to Duras's salon, served as minister of the navy from 1817 to 1818; he presided over the reoccupation of Senegal and a singularly lackluster campaign against the slave trade. Molé later claimed, plausibly, to have been sabotaged in his efforts to suppress the trade by every minister but one (Richelieu).[98]

Claire de Duras was a genealogical product of sugar and slavery, which she could not cleave from her identity without destroying herself. Yet she wrote *Ourika* in the voice of a dying African woman after Humboldt informed her of slave ship atrocities. Ourika's monologue in the story begins, "I was taken from Senegal at the age of 2 . . . my mother was dead, I was being taken onto the ship despite my screams."[99] How should we understand the relationship between author and character in this utterance? To answer this question, we must picture these lines in their original form—as part of a spoken-word performance to a crowd of cousins, friends, and ministers, many of whom had ties to slavery, with a sprinkling of liberals who kept their cards close.

From a technical point of view, Duras did not express compassion for the character Ourika in her story. The concise reflections of William Hazlitt on human character make it easy to spot the problem. In self-love, he writes, "it is I who feel (sympathy), and who am the object of it. In benevolence or compassion, it is I who still feel the sympathy, but another (not myself) is the object of it."[100] In public readings of *Ourika*, Madame de Duras spoke in the voice of her protagonist and embodied the intended object of sympathy. As an author, she bestowed sympathy on a figure whom she enjoyed channeling before house guests. The diagram of affect here is that of self-love.

What of the audience for this minstrelsy? Chateaubriand wept—but for whom, or what? The ingeniously apolitical character of *Ourika* began with Duras's choice of subject. The story's protagonist was the rare African infant saved from a slave ship by the French monarchy. For Stephanie Félicité du Crest, Comtesse de Genlis, the work was admirable precisely because of its refusal to embrace radical politics. "A vulgar author seeking to conform to the fashion (much too enduring, since it started more than thirty years ago) would not have failed to make Ourika into a passionate lover and to declaim with vehemence against slavery, servitude, distinctions of birth and rank; finally, this author, in place of imagination, would have lifted incidents and phrases from other works and inserted them in his own, to create a novel full of plagiarism, exaggerated sentiment, dangerous and false ideas." For Genlis, the perfection of Duras's novel stemmed from its exclusive focus on the "development of thoughts and sentiments of Ourika." She praised the book for being uncontaminated by radical proselytizing. The concepts she derided as "dangerous and false ideas" were those of the Declaration of the Rights of Man and Citizen. The source of the overused fashion that "started more than thirty years ago" was the French Revolution. For Genlis, a "vulgar author" (the opposite of Duras) was someone who declaimed against slavery and trumpeted human equality. The book's lack of a political message was the source of its literary merit.

For Duras's story to be political, there would need to be injustice. And yet the cause of Ourika's distress is irremediable. In Duras's novel, slavery and the slave trade are out of the picture and racism is beyond redress. According to the elusive Madame de . . . , a confidante of Ourika's guardian, the African girl's entry into the Beauvau household shattered the order of nature. Madame de . . . continues: "She was placed in society without its permission and society has avenged itself." Duras's protagonist espouses the same doctrine. After the Terror, "the more society returned to the order of nature, the more I felt like an outsider."

In Duras's story, nature and society are one. Notwithstanding this text's superficial borrowings from the Old Regime, the phrase *l'ordre de la nature* (order of nature) expresses a nineteenth-century worldview. Duras's book denies a central claim of Enlightenment philosophy, in which nature and

158   **SLAVES IN PARIS**

society were distinct categories and typically opposed to one another. In *Ourika*, the racialized hierarchy of elite Paris is nature. Inequality is the foundation of this inalterable, plantlike order of things. The quality that makes Ourika unmarriageable and untouchable is not a product of human artifice according to the doctrine that stands as truth in this story, and cannot be undone by man.

The cultural historian Robin Mitchell characterizes Duras's protagonist Ourika as "an actual black body."[101] Contemporaries of Duras did not agree. The novel's popularity with French readers hinged on the whitening of its central character. According to the critic Eusèbe Girault de Saint-Fargeau, in his survey of major French literary works (1839), the reader "cannot refuse a tear to this young girl—good, loving, sensitive, whom the imagination strips so easily of her color, of her native country, to dress her in the seductive forms of our lovely French women. As we read, Ourika ceases to be black, and that is why we care so much about her fate."[102]

Ourika "ceases to be black" because Duras employs literary devices of transfiguration. Most obviously, she hides Ourika from our gaze. Because the text is mostly a monologue by Ourika, we scarcely see her. A total of four sentences in the book explicitly refer to her blackness.

At rare and crucial instances when race comes to the fore, it does so as a prelude to the character's metamorphosis. After zapping Ourika with physical uncanniness, the text disintegrates and de-races her. This happens first at the top of the story in the short first-person narrative of a doctor attending Ourika, then a dying nun, in the garden of her cloister. Unsettled by the gothic ruins, he gasps when the nun, draped "in an enormous black veil that covers her almost completely," turns around to reveal her face. "I was strangely surprised to perceive a negress!" His surprise at the nun's black face increases when he hears her and discovers a voice redolent of the old nobility. Her speech belongs to the pre-Revolutionary past and hence to the dead.

At which point Ourika disappears. "Her thinness was excessive, her brilliant big eyes, her gleaming white teeth, were the only things that lit her physiognomy; the soul was alive but the body was destroyed." The surface of her face—flesh in general—goes missing. Instead of skin, we see eyes, bones, and teeth. As the story continues, once Ourika takes over as the narrator, the reader learns nothing of her appearance except this: "I was often noted for the elegance and beauty of my figure." What of her face? While performing the comba, a Latin American dance that Duras mistakes for African, Ourika's partner "wears black crêpe on his face: alas! I did not need to, but I did not yet have this thought." To imagine your own skin as black fabric, you would need to see it as a removable film of concealment—a black pall over your body. The person underneath could not be black.[103]

Race enters the consciousness of Duras's character during her accidental invisibility while seated in a parlor behind a decorative screen. Unaware of her presence, Madame de B and her companion, the story's brutal truth teller, discuss the girl's doomed fate to remain unmarried and alone. "As fast as lightning, I see all, I see myself as a negress." Although Ourika voices revulsion at her appearance in this episode, the reader sees nothing but her hands, which Duras depicts as monstrous alien appendages. "My face horrified me, I no longer dared look at myself in a mirror; when my eyes glimpsed my black hands, I thought to see the hands of a monkey." Through the enactment of horror-stricken disbelief at her own deformity, Ourika exits her body. She withdraws outside blackness by heaping rebuke upon herself ("I exaggerated my ugliness"). By her exhaustive ventilation of self-disgust, Ourika steals the script of the racist reader by thinking his thoughts. She disburdens herself in loathing from her anatomical body to become pure voice, which functions in the novel as a new body. Sound (if read aloud), or the materiality of the printed word, give a sense of dimension to her de-raced soul.

In 1824 Duras commissioned the artist François Gérard to paint a scene from the book.[104] The printmaker Henri-Alfred Johannot, who illustrated the works of Chateaubriand and Walter Scott, created the print in aquaforte, a traditional technique with acid that creates images with remarkable depth and texture.[105] A color reproduction of Gérard's lost work, by the porcelain artist Marie-Adélaïde Ducluzeau, survives on a large Sèvres vase at the Château d'Ussé.[106] Gérard's lost painting, the vase, and Johannot's print all depict the opening scene, where the doctor encounters Ourika in a huge black veil, discovers her black face, and watches her skin and flesh disintegrate. The translation of Duras's text into visual media required artists to invent a body and a countenance for the novel's largely concealed heroine. In a faithful rendering of the opening scene, Ourika would be almost invisible.[107] A bungled version of Johannot's aquatint in the collection of the Musée d'Aquitaine in Bordeaux—abandoned in mid-process—represents Ourika with white hands and a white face.[108] Yet even unflawed renderings of

5.2 Ourika during the doctor's visit to her convent.
Alfred Johannot (1800–1835). Etching, 43 × 29 cm. Musée d'Aquitaine (Bordeaux).

this scene looked wrong. An otherwise admiring reviewer of Ducluzeau's work complained, "Since it is a question of painting a black woman, could one not have chosen a religious habit in a different color than her face?"[109]

The popularity of Duras's novel depended on the title character's unseen-ness, and on the whitening effect of self-flagellating racial insult. Moving Ourika out of the text and onto the stage turned her body and face into a problem. "The color black does not please in the theater, it does not interest one; it often disgusts," pronounced a critic of one such performance, at Paris's Gymnase Theater.[110] The fame of the Duchesse de Duras as a salon hostess, the duke's preposterous sinecure as the head of the Comédie Française, and the marketing genius of her publisher, meant there were a few weeks in 1824 when at least four theaters staged one-act Ourika plays in Paris.[111] More Ourikas were composed than staged.[112] Actresses in the title role performed in blackface. Unintentionally, melodrama became low comedy. The plays flopped. A performance by the Comédie Française, much awaited, never happened. The leading starlet of her day, Mademoiselle Mars, pulled out of the role. "We hope that Mlle Mars will conquer her repugnance to assume the hue of a negress," remarked the *Journal des débats*.[113] Meanwhile, carved female African heads became a novelty decoration on canes.[114] To the outrage of the playwright Duval, who frequented the salon of the Duchesse de Duras, the Comédie Française retained its privilege to his Ourika play but never staged the work. Nor could anyone else. The troupe asserted its proprietary right by entombing it.[115]

In 1847 an unsigned theater column in the *Feuilleton du Journal des débats* recalled the story of Mlle Mars. "She was horrible: picture the clamor, the maledictions, the laughter." This author used the anecdote to launch a screed against black actors on the Parisian stage. The debut of three actors of African descent at the Théâtre des Variétés led the author to observe, "By what unnatural fantasy does a theater of pleasure permit itself to afflict our eyes with these deformed beings . . . these three black things, blackish, yellowish . . . have produced an experience of disgust so vivid that it would be impossible to give you an idea. Yes, woolly hair! Yes, enormous swollen lips!"[116] One might be tempted to dismiss this article as the ravings of a fringe maniac, had it not appeared on the first and second pages of a leading daily—the second most popular newspaper in France. *Ourika* went unperformed at the Comédie Française because black women could not appear on the French stage except as figures of vulgar buffoonery.[117] In 1837 the inventive Monsieur Lherie performed four roles in a comic one-man show, including the Actor, the Roué, Jacquot the Oarsman, and "Ourika, young Negress."[118] To the degree that Duras's book had an afterlife in French popular culture, it provided a name for black horses, black dogs, newly arrived African slaves, and fictional slaves, including one with a tail, from the "tribe of the *niams niams*," who eats her master's dog in an 1854 story.[119]

5.3 Oval medallion designed by William Hackwood and manufactured by Josiah Wedgwood for the Society for the Abolition of Slavery (ca. 1787).
White jasper with black relief set in gilt metal, 3 × 2.7 cm. © Victoria and Albert Museum (London).

The bestialization of black people in French high and low culture shaped Duras's novel. In her outpourings of self-disgust, Ourika channeled the attitudes of her day. Nineteenth-century racism provided a context for Duras's concealment of Ourika's body and for her character's ineluctable, anorexic shrinkage.[120] The annihilation of Ourika's physical self does not belong to the past, however. It is part of any reader's experience of this book.

According to a recent critic, *Ourika* teaches us that "black women feel like white women."[121] Identification with Ourika by modern readers does not result from the novel's anti-racist universalism, however. It is a product of the book's remorseless violence—a violence that becomes evident by setting Duras's depiction of Ourika beside the most famous antislavery image in the Western hemisphere. In 1787, to promote the abolitionist cause, the commercial potter Josiah Wedgwood produced jasperware cameos emblazoned with the figure of a kneeling, mostly naked black man in chains and the legend "Am I not a man and a brother?"[122] Thousands of these medallions circulated in England as buttons, hairpins, brooches. In Revolutionary France, the short-lived Society of the Friends of the Blacks adopted the Wedgwood image as its insignia. Notwithstanding French uses of this symbol in the era of the Rights of Man, it seems plain from the slave's supplicating posture that abolitionism was not a struggle for equality. The Wedgwood cameo made a different point. It exhorted the spectator (or wearer) to recognize himself, and mankind, in the flesh of the kneeling figure.

Duras's book repudiates the most basic claim of the Wedgwood image. Her novel does not suggest that a black person's body could ever stand for humanity. It does not enjoin readers to recognize themselves in the physicality of the book's protagonist. It is through Ourika's unseenness, through her disavowal of the black body wherever its fragments appear, and through her resurrection as pure voice, that she becomes mankind. At the time of the novel's publication, moreover, the fact that Ourika in her agony made no complaint or claim against the world made it easy to weep. De-raced, asking nothing, she is universal humanity, whom we gratify with compassion without consequence.

CONCLUSION

IN THIS BOOK I have drawn a picture of five people who came to eighteenth-century Paris as slaves. Two of those people were free when they left the capital. Two were free when they died there. Jean, alone among the protagonists, left as a slave. The freedom that Pauline, Lucidor, Julien, and Ourika wrested from the city did not result from abolitionist sentiment. Lucidor enjoyed de facto freedom from a young age, yet spent his life dodging the police for other reasons. While harbored by slave-owning peers, Pauline became free by a concealed form of self-purchase. Julien lost his trial in 1787 and became free during the Revolution. Ourika was gifted to a quietly abolitionist grandee. The fate of these people raises the question of what importance, if any, we should assign to the legal maxim *There are no slaves in France.*

During the years covered by this book, slaves sued for freedom before the Paris Admiralty Court. They always won. Beginning in the 1760s, decisions of that court routinely mentioned that *all who set foot in France are free.*[1] As we have seen, attempts by slaves to become free through Parisian courts provoked a violent reaction from masters and the Crown. Legal maneuvering by slaves and their lawyers called forth a need for extrajudicial weapons—orders of the king—that came from the police or Versailles. The result was spying, trickery, stakeouts, and (often) capture.

Freedom suits did not help the people who most needed rescuing. Masters easily arranged for their domestics to disappear. Nonetheless, legal battles between slaves and masters held a significance unrelated to their efficacy. When Governor Bouvet de Lozier first complained about Pauline's misconduct, he warned the police that she frequented "those of her sort most likely to suggest a spirit of independence."[2] Freedom petitions, though formulaic, required people to relate their stories to a lawyer, knowing that

164

versions of those tales would become part of the public record. The strength of bonds between people in Paris and the overseas empire meant that the struggles of slaves in the city escaped the limits of the master's household. The lieutenant-general of police at the time of Pauline's trial, Antoine de Sartine, complained about the noise around freedom trials after he became minister of the navy. "Printed memoirs full of declamations against slavery and the tyranny of their masters are spread profusely throughout Paris." Publicity around the trials spilled into the streets. "Judgments become public by posters alerting negroes that they are free, independent, and equal to those they once regarded as superior beings whom they were fated to serve."[3] Sartine believed the posters and printed trial accounts to be more toxic than the courtroom events behind them. He worried about how events in Paris would reverberate in the colonies, because he lived in a time of heightened imperial mobility. As minister of the navy, it was his job to intensify links between metropolitan France and the wider world while policing those connections. He thought publicity about freedom cases would undermine the moral foundations of colonial society by carrying "a spirit of liberty, independence, and equality" across the ocean and preparing "a revolution for which neighboring colonies have already provided examples."[4] (In 1777, Sartine was thinking of slave rebellions in Surinam and Jamaica.)[5]

Freedom trials in Paris, and the noise they made, should not be mistaken for evidence of an antislavery consensus in the capital. Notwithstanding the righteous clamor that worried Sartine, the city's elites were more connected to sugar and the slave trade at the outbreak of the French Revolution than at any time in the capital's history. In 1790 the lawyer Louis-Lézin de Milly, a planter from Martinique, informed Parisians that, while "there was nowhere in the kingdom that could be indifferent to the abolition of slavery and the slave trade, Paris was one of the places that would suffer most."[6] He lived in the District of the Filles de Saint-Thomas, centered on the Rue de Richelieu, dominated by finance.[7] As we have seen throughout this book, this neighborhood was thick with bankers, planters, and investors in the slave trade. At the time of Milly's speech, the nearby Place des Victoires— Pauline's hiding place—served as headquarters for the Club Massiac—the country's most influential pro-slavery lobby.[8] Milly was not the only mouthpiece for colonial interests to note the dependency of Paris on the colonial world. An anonymous pamphlet warned, in 1789 or 1790, that Paris would be ruined by abolition. The capital flourished as a hub of consumerism, focused on luxury trades, which planters used as a stage for opulent self-display. They came there to "dispense most of their wealth, like an ever-renewed spring of water" on "fashion, jewels, tailoring, carriages, books, and tools of all sorts."[9]

Parisian nobles have figured in this book as slave owners and helpers of slaves. Each chapter recounts acts of benevolence by people of rank from the mid-eighteenth century to the Revolution.[10] Those acts conformed to a recognizable pattern. Excluding Beauvau—whose opposition to slavery was a matter of conviction—helping slaves did not arise from, or stimulate, opposition to slavery as an institution; nor did helping slaves entail a repudiation of racial concepts in a categorical way. Elite encounters with enslaved people—even when marked by friendship, tenderness, and physical intimacy—were not political in nature or effect.[11]

The ease of researching the people who helped slaves, like the Duc de Noailles or the Castellane family, underscores the incompleteness of every biographical sketch of a slave in this book. The writers of traditional biographies use sources like letters and memoirs that scholars now call ego documents. Nothing written by slaves survives in the French language. It is also important to recognize that the materiality of ink and paper, and the act of inscription, meant something else to enslaved and freed people. They experienced the link between writing and identity in a way that no European diarist could fathom. For someone exiting slavery, the self became immanent on paper, for the first time, in the form of a freedom certificate. This was a text written by someone else that typically bore the signature of a slave master; it was paper one carried close to the skin, especially when traveling, like a talisman; and it was something that, with a bit of luck, might allow one to be recognized as an ego.

Conventional ego documents do not appear in this book until Chapter 5, about Ourika. I have shown that Boufflers acceded to feelings of lightness, purity, and inner authenticity through the vehicle of commercially value-less objects, including letters. He pictured the letters and trinkets he sent to Eleanor as living matter, the stuff of his higher being. He viewed the letters she sent (via slave ship) in precisely the same way, as bits of her. Ourika and the other children were letter-like. He bought them and turned them into ego documents. I do not mean that the children lacked selves—an absurdity. But Boufflers did not think they did. He pictured them as material emanations of his unsullied conscience. As for Duras, the transformation of Ourika into a kind of ego document—a fictional text in the first-person voice of *I*—accompanied the girl's agonizing death at the hand of an author who did not know what she was doing.

For the French writer Alain Robbe-Grillet, who wrote in the 1950s, the erasure of inwardness and personal distinctiveness was the crux of literary modernity. In manifesto-like essays about the *nouveau roman* (new novel), Robbe-Grillet championed writing in which people lacked "surname and first name," a "hidden soul," "parentage," and "a face that reflects his character." In his own writing, Robbe-Grillet placed particular emphasis on surroundings and inanimate things, to which his depthless figures, who represent humanity, seem curiously attentive; and from which they are always estranged. "He sees them, but he refuses to appropriate them, he refuses to have any connivance with them; he asks nothing of them."[12]

What the new novel stripped from narrative is everything that I could not include in this book's portraits of enslaved and freed people. Rudimentary details about their lives, like parentage, remain unknowable. What I did learn about my subjects came from examining their encircling stuff of life. The late Richard Cobb wrote about the need for historians of ordinary people (*petits gens*) to develop a granular knowledge of the past, involving things like "the contents of pockets," "the softness of corduroy," "the texture of stone," and "how many people sleep to a room."[13] He advised this because people's outer worlds cannot be meaningfully separated from what they do and think. Locks, pocket change, trousers, beds, types of stone are not decorative schema on a strikable set—as Robbe-Grillet seemed to picture them. They are not really surroundings. They are integral to identity. They are composite elements of the human subject.[14]

To adopt a composite approach to subjectivity requires that we recognize the embodied nature of oppression as the exterior world remakes the flesh. Jean, in Chapter 1, fled determinedly. It is no less important, however, that people who saw him found his woundedness to be shocking; that he slept on the floor without bed linens, mattress, or blanket; and that he survived on kitchen scraps. We do not know much about Jean and will never manage to. We can, however, be certain that, already, at the age of 22, he was watching his body become a body made by slavery.

No one, regardless of their status and personal myth, is a truly autonomous agent whose days unfold as thrusts of an unfettered will. No one is purely acted upon. The scholarly project of recovering the agency of oppressed peoples—whether slave, worker, peasant, or prisoner—is a worthy one. In practice, however, this historical endeavor is beset by problems. As Walter Johnson observes, "giving people back their agency" or "humanity" suffers from the redundancy of proving that people are people.[15] There are other defects. An agency-centered approach to history rests on a model of the human subject that screens out the compositeness of being and omits the disquieting complexity of life.

The broken bits of steel in Lucidor's house at the time of his death, and the forge in his Ménilmontant courtyard, are not important as instantiations of the man's agency. The bins of sword tips matter because they are the man. We surmise that he was the kind of swordsman who also fixed and forged metal. We see the breaking and making of things. We sense that he has not been doing any of this work for a while. These bits of metal also make it possible to mourn the man differently. We recognize in this debris the devastating expressiveness of little things that lie around the house at the end of a life.

Because of the composite nature of the subject, people are not just agents or units of will. They merge with their outer worlds. They undergo involuntary change in new spaces of life. They adjust their gait in different shoes. Their bodies mutate by friction, burn, rot, or puncture, depending on what they lay or do not lay on their skin. People are consubstantial with their surroundings. They are inseparable from what they wear, eat, and own. One has only to skim the archives of the poor, and see the lists of threadbare clothes, unwearable shoes, and unpaid houses to see that people inhabit their belongings and can be destroyed by them.

Notes

Acknowledgments

Index

NOTES

ABBREVIATIONS

AB	Archives de la Bastille
ADCO	Archives départementales de la Côte d'Or
ADR	Archives départementales de la Réunion
ADY	Archives départementales des Yvelines
AN	Archives nationales (all are Paris, unless marked Pierrefitte)
ANOM	Archives nationales d'Outre-Mer
AP	Archives privées
digi	digitized records
LGP	lieutenant-général de police
NAM	National Archives of Mauritius
SHD	Services historiques de la Défense, Vincennes
SHDL	Services historiques de la Défense, Lorient

INTRODUCTION

1 The name, For l'Évêque, refers to the building's medieval function. "For" (like "forum") meant "public place for the exercise of a jurisdiction." The building once functioned as the court and prison for the bishopric of Paris. See Claude Irson, *Nouvelle méthode pour apprendre facilement les principes et la pureté de la langue françoise contenant plusieurs traitez* (Paris, 1662), 245; Frantz Funck-Brentano, *Bastille des comédiens: Le For l'Évêque* (Paris: A. Fontemoing, 1903), 17–18.

2 Archives de la Bastille (hereafter AB) ms. 11,830, fol. 281 (description); fol. 283 (capture, 16 May 1753); Archer and Linsens to lieutenant-général de police (hereafter LGP), 21 May 1753, fol. 289; and Desbrières et fils to LGP, 4 June 1753, fol. 291. A decade earlier, on 24 May 1743, Charles Desbrières, banker, declared the arrival in Paris of Elisabeth, *une jeune mulâtresse,* age 8 or 9, on behalf of a Martinican planter. See Z^{1D} 139, Archives nationales (hereafter AN; all AN cites are for Paris unless marked Pierrefitte).

172 **Notes to Pages 1–4**

3 The full maxim was "Toutes personnes sont franches en ce royaume, & si tost qu'un esclave a atteint les marches d'iceluy, se faisant baptiser, il est affranchy" (All people are free in this kingdom, and as soon as a slave crosses its borders, and is baptized, he is freed . . .). See book I (*Des personnes*), title I, art. 6, in Antoine Loisel, *Institutes coutumières, ou Manuel de plusieurs et diverses règles, sentences & proverbes tant anciens que modernes, du droit coutumier et plus ordinaire de la France* (1608; Paris: H. Le Gras, 1637), 2. On this maxim and its rephrasing in the eighteenth century, see Sue Peabody, *"There Are No Slaves in France": The Political Culture of Race and Slavery in the Ancien Régime* (New York: Oxford University Press, 2002), 30–31.

4 Dudresnay-Desroches to LGP, 11 April 1753, AB ms. 11,814, fol. 61–62.

5 Dian Wolfhal, *Household Servants and Slaves: A Visual History, 1300–1700* (New Haven, CT: Yale University Press, 2022); on attendants, see Anne Lafont, *L'art et la race: L'Africain (tout) contre l'œil des lumières* (Dijon: Les presses du réel, 2019); David Bindman, Henry Louis Gates, and Karen C. C. Dalton, *The Image of the Black in Western Art: From the Age of Discovery to the Age of Abolition,* vol. 3 (Cambridge, MA: Belknap Press of Harvard University Press, 2010–2011), pts. I and II.

6 On the translation quandary relating to French racial epithets, see Gregory Pierrot, "Nègre (Noir, Black, Renoi, Négro)," *Small Axe: A Caribbean Journal of Criticism* 26, no. 2 (68) (July 1, 2022): 100–107. This phrase comes from royal legislation (1777–1778) banning people of African and South Asian descent from entering France, subjecting nonwhites in Paris to special policing measures, and forbidding people of African or South Asian descent to marry white people. These laws are discussed briefly in this Introduction and receive more detailed examination later in the book, especially in Chapter 4. See Déclaration du roy pour la police des noirs, 9 August 1777, in *Le Code noir ou Recueil des règlements rendus jusqu'à présent concernant le gouvernement, l'administraiton de la justice, la police, la discipline, et le commerce des nègres dans les colonies françaises, et les conseils et compagnies établis à ce sujet* (Paris, L. F. Prault, Imprimerie du roi, 1788), 489–500 (digi); Arrêt du Conseil d'état pour la police des noirs mulâtres ou autres gens de couleur, qui sont dans la ville de Paris (11 January 1778), in *Le Code noir,* 510–513 (digi); Arrêt du Conseil d'état du roi concernant les mariages des noirs mulâtres et autres gens de couleur (5 April 1778), in *Le Code noir,* 518–520 (digi).

7 Frantz Funck-Brentano, *Légendes et archives de la Bastille,* 2nd ed. (Paris: Hachette, 1898), 1–12. See also Marie-Élisabeth Jacquet, "Vie et mort d'un dépôt d'archive: Les archives 'de la Bastille' dans les années 1780," *Circé: Histoires, savoirs, sociétés* 16, no. 1 (2022).

8 For general works, see Paul Fabre, *Les lettres de cachet* (Béziers: J.-B. Perdraut, 1878); Claude Quétel, *Les lettres de cachet: Une légende noire* (Paris: Perrin, 2011); Frantz Funck-Brentano, "Les lettres de cachet," *Revue des deux mondes* (1829–1971) 113, no. 4 (1892): 821–853.

9 On uses of lettres de cachet in eighteenth-century Paris, see Arlette Farge and Michel Foucault, *Le désordre des familles: Lettres de cachet des Archives de la*

Notes to Pages 4–5   173

Bastille au XVIIIᵉ siècle (Paris: Gallimard, 1982); published in English as *Disorderly Families: Infamous Letters from the Bastille Archives,* trans. Thomas Scott-Ralton (Minneapolis: University of Minnesota Press, 2016). On eighteenth-century denunciations of this practice, see Hans-Jürgen Lusebrink and Rolf Reichardt, *The Bastille: A History of a Symbol of Despotism and Freedom,* trans. Norbert Schürer (Durham, NC: Duke University Press, 1997).

10   For the story of free soil in the eighteenth century, see Peabody, *"There Are No Slaves in France."* On people of color in eighteenth-century France, see Erick Noël, *Être noir en France au XVIIIᵉ siècle* (Paris: Tallandier, 2006); Pierre Boulle, *Race et esclavage dans la France de l'Ancien régime* (Paris: Perrin, 2007); Dwain C. Pruitt, "The Opposition of the Law to the Law: Race, Slavery, and the Law in Nantes 1715–1778," *French Historical Studies* 30, no. 2 (2007): 147–174; Marcel Koufinkana, *Les esclaves noirs en France sous l'ancien régime, XVI–XVIIIᵉ siècles* (Paris: L'Harmattan, 2008); Julie Duprat, *Bordeaux métisse: Esclaves et affranchis de couleur du XVIIIe à l'empire* (Abbeville: Mollat, 2021). For the nineteenth-century history of free soil, see Sue Peabody, *Madeleine's Children: Family, Freedom, Secrets, and Lies in France's Indian Ocean Colonies* (New York: Oxford University Press, 2017). Martha Jones has turned up a case of arrest and detention—consistent with the pattern I describe—in the person of Abigail, enslaved to John Jay. Martha Jones, "Time, Space, and Jurisdiction in Atlantic World Slavery: The Volunbrun Household in Gradual Emancipation New York," *Law and History Review* 29, no. 4 (2011): 1040–1042; see also Jones, "Enslaved to a Founding Father, She Sought Freedom in France," *New York Times,* 23 November 2021.

11   Peabody, *"There Are No Slaves in France,"* 41.

12   On Corinne, Marie-Jeanne, Fanchon, and Louison, see AB ms. 11,941 and Colonies B 104, fols. 10, 11, 110, 152, ANOM. Compare with Peabody, *"There Are No Slaves in France,"* 55. See also Léo Elisabeth, *La société martiniquaise au XVIᵉ et XVIIIᵉ siècles, 1664–1789* (Paris: Karthala, 2003), 344. Elisabeth is one of the few scholars to mention slave arrests by order of the king, which he researched using navy archives.

13   Médor petitioned the Admiralty in January 1763 and was granted freedom on 28 March; navy documents reveal, however, that Médor was imprisoned soon thereafter in Chalons (in eastern France). In April, a lettre de cachet ordered his transfer to a French port pending deportation to Gorée. See De Par le Roy, 12 April 1763, Colonies B 117, fol. 126, ANOM. Compare with Peabody, *"There Are No Slaves in France,"* 91.

14   On his expulsion from Paris, and exclusion from Saint-Domingue, see Peabody, *"There Are No Slaves in France,"* 40. For non-Admiralty sources on Boucaux, see AB mss. 11,380, 11,407; see also the lettre de cachet that enabled his exit from Grand Châtelet, Colonies B 69, ANOM. On the annulment of the freedom judgment, and the convocation of the case to the Conseil du Roi, see "Arrêt qui évoque au Conseil du roi l'appel interjeté par Bernard de Verdelin, maréchal général des logis, des camps, et armées du roi, d'une sentence de la Table de Marbre de Paris,

174   **Notes to Pages 6–7**

déclarant libre Jean Boucaux, nègre esclave, que Bernard de Verdelin a emmené de Saint-Domingue en France, et qui en interdit l'exécution" (no. 10), 12 September 1738, Colonies A3, fol. 71, Archives nationales d'Outre-Mer (hereafter ANOM); and Colonies E 384bis, ANOM (digi).

15 For a chronology of Francisque's case, including his extrajudicial detention, see Joly de Fleury, ms. 1833, fol. 258–259. On the racial theme in the case, see *Mémoire signifié pour le nommé Francisque, indien de nation, néophyte de l'Église Romaine, intimé, contre le sieur Allain-François-Ignace Brignon, se disant écuyer, appellant,* ms. 1833, fol. 282. Ethnicity, not skin color, would determine the status of *une jeune arabe enlevée de sa patrie* in Saint-Domingue. See *Gazette des Tribunaux,* 1 January 1784, 71–76.

16 On Jean-Baptiste, see petition of 27 July 1763, in Z^{1D} 132, AN; for details of his roundup, see Colonies C^{8B} 12, no. 103, ANOM; Colonies B 124–125, fols. 354, 407, 439, 449, 533, ANOM.

17 On Ambroise Lucas, see AB ms. 12,228, and preliminary sentence of 27 January 1766, Z^{1D} 133, AN. Lucas is identified as a doorman in livery by his employer, Pierre-Augustin de Beaumarchais, in his supplicating letters to the lieutenant-general of police, Antoine Sartine, after he struck the agents who arrested Lucas. See fols. 75–76, AB ms. 12,228. Additional materials concerning Beaumarchais's involvement in this affair are in Fonds Beaumarchais, carton 8, dossier 9, NAF 29073, Bibliothèque Nationale de France. Lucas's next master, Louis-Auguste Félicie de Castillon, Baron de Saint-Victor, freed him on return from Saint-Domingue in 1770 before the Parisian notary Ledoux on 21 April 1770 under the name "Ambroise Lucas dit Deschamps." See petition of 25 April in Z^{1D} 134, AN.

18 On Luce, see interrogation of Marie-Françoise Laperle, 12 December 1777, Police des Noirs, Colonies F^{1B} 4, fols. 190–192, ANOM; on 10 April 1760 she obtained a declaration of nonregistration from the Admiralty (Z^{1D} 139, AN); see also interrogation of Luce Diancra, who gives her age as 57 and mentions *qu'elle avait cinq cents livres de rentes qu'elle tenait de Madame de Castellane, mère de Madame Berger.* See perquisition chez la femme Corbin, 8 November 1792, W 246, AN (Pierrefitte). She obtained a *certificat de non-déclaration à l'amirauté,* on 4 October 1760. See Erick Noël, ed., *Dictionnaire des gens de couleur dans la France moderne,* vol. 1 (Geneva: Droz, 2011), no. 116, p. 30.

19 Rapport au conseil des dépêches par Monsieur de Sartine du projet de déclaration sur la police des noirs, 9 August 1777, Recueil des pièces relatives à la législation sur la police des noirs, Paris 1778, ms. Fr. 13,357, Bibliothèque nationale de France.

20 Farge and Foucault, *Disorderly Families,* 26–27.

21 I include Boucaux, Francisque, Médor, Ambroise Lucas, and the four women, including Corinne, in this list. See also Louis, AB ms. 12,160 and Colonies B 115 (1762), ANOM; Petitjean AB ms. 12,193 and Colonies B 117 (1), fol. 113 (1763); Pierre Scipion, AB ms. 12,196 (1763); Pauline, AB ms. 12,252 (1765); Narcisse, AB ms. 12,252 and Colonies B 122, fol. 130 (1765); Aza, AB ms. 12,230 and Colonies

B 122, fol. 146 (1765); Pedre Alengin, AB ms. 12,230 and Colonies B 122, fol. 147 (1765); Charles-Dominique Lazy, AB ms. 12,247 and Colonies B 122, fols. 161, 314 (1765); Anne-Philippe Hector, AB ms. 12,245 and Colonies B 122, fol. 216; Hélène, AB ms. 12,245 and Colonies B 122, fols. 232, 263, 316, 350, 401, 403 (1765); François, AB ms. 10,748 and Colonies B 122, fol. 315 (1765); Valentin, Colonies B 124–125, fols. 140, 207 (1766); Barnabé dit Raymond, Colonies B 124–125, fol. 205; Cupidon, Colonies B 124–125, fols. 501–502 (1766); Acajou, Colonies B 131, fol. 315 (1768); Pierre Avril, Colonies B 134, fols. 106, 114; Sertorius dit Auguste, Colonies B 134, fol. 209 (1769); Ali, Birame, and Boucary, Colonies B 137, fol. 77 (1770). I include Ali because he was enslaved to the same master, Ménager / Esmenager, as two domestics— Birame / Birance and Boucary—who filed freedom suits that overlapped with his own flight; Jupiter, Colonies B 137, fol. 77 (1770); Williams / Ramsay, Colonies B 137, fols. 168, 186; Julien Baudelle (1786), whom I discuss in Chapter 4.

22 Peabody, *"There Are No Slaves in France,"* 49; Boulle, *Race et esclavage,* 76.

23 Gratia is listed as two different people in Noël, *Dictionnaire des gens de couleur.* For his registration as a free man, see 1 August 1777 and 31 January 1778 in Z^{1D} 139, AN. See Courcelles to Poncet de la Grave, 1 November (1777), in Régistre des déclarations des nègres et mulâtres commencé le 3 mai 1777, Z^{1D} 139, AN; letter from Dom Grassiat to Bottée, Paris Court of Admiralty, 8 July 1778, Havre de Grace, Z^{1D} 138, AN.

24 Quite reasonably, in the absence of anything else to count, both Peabody and Pierre Boulle based calculations for the Paris black community on Admiralty records. See Peabody, *"There Are No Slaves in France,"* 83; Boulle, *Race et esclavage,* 126. My purpose here is simply to point out the inaccuracy of that resource and to signal equal problems with Erick Noël's nonetheless invaluable and broadranging *Dictionnaire des gens de couleur.* My own chance discoveries suggest there were more nonwhite people in Paris than historians have previously recognized.

25 "Vol d'une veste de drap écarlate (galonné)," 1 January 1774, Y 9813A–B, AN. Theleman may have remained in Boufflers's service until the latter's death in 1815. There is an allusion to racial prejudice in Boufflers's testament. Addressing his stepson, Louis-Marie-Elzéar, Comte de Sabran, Boufflers notes his concern for "my oldest servant whom I do not wish to leave without bread after I die; in the meantime, I leave in my son's hands the fate of this man who has always been very attached to me. Of course my son will overcome *his repugnance if he has any, out of friendship for me, and his feelings will overcome his prejudices*" (my italics). Testament de Monsieur le Marquis de Boufflers, 20 January 1815, MC / ET / XLIII / 681, AN.

26 Kersaint papers, E-1428, Archives départementales des Yvelines (hereafter ADY). For the letter about Loff, see Carrère to Kersaint, Saint-Pierre de la Martinique, 30 May 1785, Kersaint Papers, E-1430, ADY.

27 See documents dated 9 January and 18 March 1765, Z^{1D} 132, AN.

28 This approach to space is informed by Akhil Gupta and James Ferguson, "Beyond 'Culture': Space, Identity, and the Politics of Difference," *Cultural Anthropology* 7, no. 1 (1992): 6–23.

176   **Notes to Pages 10–12**

29   For a global approach to Africans in the Francophone world, see Lorelle Semley, *To Be Free and French: Citizenship in France's Atlantic Empire* (Cambridge: Cambridge University Press, 2017).

30   Saidiya Hartman, "Venus in Two Acts," *Small Axe* no. 26, vol. 12, no. 2 (June 2008): 3–4. On the relationship between historians of slavery and the archive, see also Brian Connolly and Marisa Fuentes, "Introduction: From Archives of Slavery to Liberated Futures?," *History of the Present* 6, no. 2 (2016): 105–116; on the bookkeeping archive in the era of the slave trade and its echoes in modern quantitative history, see Jennifer Morgan, "Accounting for 'The Most Excruciating Torment': Gender, Slavery, and Trans-Atlantic Passages," *History of the Present* 6, no. 2 (2016): 184–207.

31   On the lack of slave narratives, and uses of alternative sources, see *Hearing Enslaved Voices: African and Indian Slave Testimony in British and French America, 1700–1848,* ed. Sophie White and Trevor Burnard (New York: Routledge, 2020); see also Sophie White, *Voices of the Enslaved: Love, Labor, and Longing in French Louisiana* (Chapel Hill: Omohundro Institute and University of North Carolina Press, 2019).

32   The remarkable Atlantic story of Rosalie and Elisabeth, as reconstructed by Jean Hebrard and Rebecca Scott, bears witness to the scarcity of institutions in Saint-Domingue relative to Cuba and nineteenth-century Louisiana. See Jean M. Hebrard and Rebecca J. Scott, *Freedom Papers: An Atlantic Odyssey in the Age of Emancipation* (Cambridge, MA: Harvard University Press, 2012). The richness of Iberian municipal institutions is manifest in Alejandro de la Fuente, "Slaves and the Creation of Legal Rights in Cuba: Coaracion and Papel," in *Slavery and Antislavery in Spain's Atlantic Empire,* ed. Josep Fradera and Christopher Schmidt-Nowara (New York: Berghahn, 2013), 101–133; on Spanish ecclesiastical courts as a forum for slaves, see Michelle McKinley, *Fractional Freedoms: Slavery, Intimacy, and Legal Mobilization in Colonial Lima, 1600–1700* (New York: Cambridge University Press, 2016). On the structure of the French Empire and the making of its archive, see François-Joseph Ruggiu, "Colonies, Monarchy, Empire, and the French Ancien Régime," in *Crowns and Colonies,* ed. Robert Aldrich and Cindy McCreery (Manchester: Manchester University Press, 2016), 194–210; and Marie Houllemare, "La fabrique des archives coloniales et la naissance d'une conscience impériale (France, XVIIIᵉ siècle)," *Revue d'histoire moderne et contemporaine* (1954–) 61, no. 2 (2014): 7–31.

33   Lynn Hunt, "The Self and Its History," *American Historical Review* 119, no. 5 (2014): 1576–1586; S. G. Magnússon, "Views into the Fragments: An Approach from a Microhistorical Perspective," *International Journal of Historical Archaeology* 20, no. 1 (2016): 182–206; Mary Fulbrook, "Life Writing and Writing Lives: Ego Documents in Historical Perspective," in *German Life Writing in the Twentieth Century,* ed. Birgit Dahlke, Dennis Tate, and Roger Woods (Woodbridge, UK: Boydell and Brewer, 2010), 25–38.

34   Denis Diderot, *Rameau's Nephew and D'Alembert's Dream,* trans. Leonard Tancock (London: Penguin Books, 1966), 172, 181.

35 Roman Jakobson, "Two Aspects of Language and Two Types of Aphasic Disturbances," in *Studies on Child Language and Aphasia* (Boston: De Gruyter Mouton, 1971), 49–74.

36 Marisa Fuentes likewise reconstructs the lives of fugitives in Barbados with particular attention to architecture, maps, movement, and bodily experience. See Marisa J. Fuentes, *Dispossessed Lives: Women, Violence, and the Archive* (Philadelphia: University of Pennsylvania Press, 2016).

37 On the intersection of family history and imperial history, see Emma Rothschild, *An Infinite History: The Story of a Family in France over Three Centuries* (Princeton, NJ: Princeton University Press, 2022); Rothschild, *The Inner Life of Empires: An Eighteenth-Century History* (Princeton, NJ: Princeton University Press, 2013); Jennifer L. Palmer, *Intimate Bonds: Family and Slavery in the French Atlantic* (Philadelphia: University of Pennsylvania Press, 2016). On Parisian high society and sugar plantations, see Paul Burton Cheney, *Cul de Sac: Patrimony, Capitalism, and Slavery in French Saint-Domingue* (Chicago: University of Chicago Press, 2019). On lawyers, the imperial bureaucracy, and the imperial character of Paris, see Marie Houllemare, *Justices d'empire: La répression dans les colonies françaises au XVIIIᵉ siècle* (Paris: Presses universitaires de France, 2024). I am grateful to Marie Houllemare for sharing her manuscript in advance of her book's publication.

38 David Geggus, "The French Slave Trade: An Overview," *William and Mary Quarterly* 58, no. 1 (2001); Laure Pineau-Defois, "Un modèle d'expansion économique à Nantes de 1763 à 1792: Louis Drouin, négociant et armateur," *Histoire, économie et sociale* 23, no. 3 (2004): 367–395; Michèle Daget, Serge Daget, and Jean Mettas, *Répertoire des expéditions négrières françaises au XXVIIIᵉ siècle,* 2 vols. (Paris: Société française d'histoire d'outre-mer, 1984); Robert Louis Stein, *The French Slave Trade: An Old Régime Business* (Madison: University of Wisconsin Press, 1979); Herbert Klein and Stanley Engerman, "Facteurs de mortalité dans le trafic français d'esclaves au XXVIIIᵉ siècle," *Annales* (1976): 1213–1224; Jean-Claude Nardin, "Encore des chiffres, la traite négrière pendant la première moitié du XXVIIIᵉ siècle," *Outre-Mers: Revue d'histoire* (1970): 421–446. On the Indian Ocean trade, see Richard Allen, "The Constant Demand of the French: The Mascarene Slave Trade and the Worlds of the Atlantic during the Eighteenth and Nineteenth Centuries," *Journal of African History* 49, no. 1 (2008): 43–72.

39 Robin Blackburn, *The Making of New World Slavery: From the Baroque to the Modern, 1492–1800* (London: Verso 1997), 433–439.

40 On opposition to global approaches to French history, see Cécile Vidal, "The Reluctance of French Historians to Address Atlantic History," *Southern Quarterly* 43, no. 4 (2006): 153–189; Vidal, "Pour une histoire globale du monde atlantique ou des histoires connectées dans et au-delà du monde atlantique," *Annales: Histoires, sciences sociales* 67, no. 2 (2012): 391–413. On Atlantic ports, see Jean Meyer, *L'armement nantais dans la deuxième moitié du XVIIIᵉ siècle* (Paris: Éditions de l'École des hautes études en sciences sociales, 2013); Gaston Martin, *Nantes au XXVIIIᵉ siècle: L'ère des négriers (1714–1774) d'après des documents inédits* (Paris:

178 **Notes to Pages 15–16**

Alcan, 1931); Paul Butel, *Les négociants Bordelais, L'Europe et les îles au XVIIIe siècle* (Paris: Aubier, 1974); Butel, *Les dynasties Bordelaises: De Colbert à Chaban* (Paris: Perrin, 1991); Silvia Marzagalli and Hubert Bonin, *Négoce, ports et océans: XVIe–XXe siècles: Mélanges offerts à Paul Butel, La mer au fil des temps* (Bordeaux: Presses universitaires de Bordeaux, 2000); Olivier Pétré-Grenouilleau, *Nantes et la traite négrière* (Nantes: Château des ducs de Bretagne-Musée d'histoire de Nantes, 2007); Éric Saunier, "Financer et armer pour la traite au Havre et à Nantes au XXVIIIe siècle: Maîtres accusés et accusateurs," in *Revue du philanthrope: Histoire et mémoires de la traite négrière, de l'esclavage et de leurs abolitions en Normandie* (Mont-Saint-Aignan: Presses universitaires de Rouen et du Havre, 2016); Éric Saugera, *Bordeaux: Port négrier: Chronologie, économie, idéologie, XVIIe–XIXe siècles* (Paris: Karthala, 1995); Robert Richard, "Financement des armements maritimes du Havre au XVIIIe siècle (position de problèmes)," *Revue d'histoire économique et sociale* 47, no. 1 (1969): 5–31; Edouard Delobette, *Ces messieurs du Havre: Négociants, commissionnaires et armateurs de 1680 à 1830* (Caen: Université de Caen, 2005); Delobette, "Négociants et traite des noirs au XXVIIIe siècle," *Annales de Normandie* (1998): 259–295; *Bordeaux, La Rochelle, Rochefort, Bayonne: Mémoire noire, histoire de l'esclavage,* ed. Caroline Le Mao (Abbeville: Mollat, 2020).

41 François Regourd, "Les lieux de savoir et d'expertise coloniale à Paris au XVIIIe siècle: Institutions et enjeux savants," in *Les mondes coloniaux à Paris au XVIIIe siècle: Circulation et enchevêtrement des savoir,* ed. Anja Banau, Marcel Dorigny, and Rebekka von Mallinckrodt (Paris: Karthala, 2010), 31–48. See also *Connaissances et pouvoir: Les espaces impériaux (XVIe–XVIIIe siècles): France, Espagne, Portugal,* ed. Charlotte de Castelnau-L'Estoile and François Regourd (Pessac: Presses universitaires de Bordeaux, 2005).

42 Marcel Dorigny, "Avant-propos," in Banau et al., *Les mondes coloniaux,* 7–9.

43 For a comparative look at the words *colonies* and *empire* in French political thought, see François-Joseph Ruggiu, "Des nouvelles France aux colonies: Une approche comparée de l'histoire impériale de la France de l'époque moderne," *Nuevo Mundo Mundos Nuevos [En línea], Débats,* published 14 June 2018. Literary scholars and art historians have done innovative work in integrating the slave empire into Enlightenment culture, though not within a specifically Parisian framework. See Madeline Dobie, *Trading Places: Colonization and Slavery in Eighteenth-Century French Culture* (Ithaca, NY: Cornell University Press, 2010). Christopher L. Miller evokes a literary geography focused on port cities when discussing literary works set in Paris and plays staged there. See Miller, *The French Atlantic Triangle: Literature and Culture of the Slave Trade* (Durham, NC: Duke University Press, 2008).

44 Fredrik Barth, "The Analysis of Culture in Complex Societies," *Ethos: Journal of Anthropology* 54, no. 3–4 (1989), 124, 134.

45 On the difficulty of determining people's status in European records, see Simon P. Newman, *Freedom Seekers: Escaping from Slavery in Restoration London* (London: Institute for Historical Research, University of London Press, 2022), 43.

Notes to Pages 17–20 179

1. JEAN

1 Rouillé to Dubois de la Motte, 11 May 1752, B 95, fol. 35, AN.

2 Gwendolyn Midlo Hall, *Slavery and the African Ethnicities in the Americas: Restoring the Links* (Chapel Hill: University of North Carolina Press, 2005), 111–125; Robin Law, "Ethnicities of Enslaved Africans in the Diaspora: On the Meanings of 'Mina' (Again)," *History in Africa* 32 (2005): 247–267.

3 AB mss. 11,807, 11,788.

4 Departure 4 July 1752 aboard *La Paix Couronnée*. Colonies F^{5B} 57, cited in Erick Noël, ed., *Dictionnaire des gens de couleur dans la France moderne*, vol. 3, Le Midi (Geneva: Droz, 2017), 830.

5 See Gilles d'Ambrières, *Les Rameaux parisiens de la famille Coustard de Nerbonne* (G. d'Ambrières, 2008).

6 There is a 1754 legal document about the inheritance of Guy Coustard's grandchildren, signed in Paris by the judge Jean-Jacques Coustard and by three of his children, suggesting that he might have been providing legal advice to the family about an ongoing inheritance dispute. See Registres des Tutelles, 13 February 1754, Y 4740A, AN (digi). On the inheritance dispute, see "Coustard, Guy, né en 1695, major des milices de Léogane, ses démêlés avec Buteaut (Pierre), capitaine de cavalerie des milices du quartier de Léogane, son gendre et Hais (Georges Louis), conseiller au Conseil supérieur de Port-au-Prince, au sujet de la tutelle des enfants de sa fille, Coustard (Marie Louise), veuve de La Buissonnière (Louis Marie de), en son vivant major du Petit-Goave, à Saint-Domingue," Colonies E 97, ANOM (digi).

7 "Mémoire au sujet du nègre détenu au For l'Évêque et que Madame la Princesse de Nassau réclame," AB ms. 11,788, fol. 72.

8 Jean-Baptiste Labat, *Voyage aux îles françaises de l'Amérique: Nouv. édit. d'après celle de 1722* (Paris: Lefebvre, 1831), 237. Where Labat mentions the castle of a Spanish princess, Moreau de Saint-Méry writes of the preconquest kingdom of Xaragua. See Moreau de Saint-Méry, *Description topographique, physique, civile, politique et historique de la partie française de l'isle Saint-Domingue* (Philadelphia, chez l'Auteur, 1797–1798), 443.

9 Paul Cheney, *Cul de Sac: Patrimony, Capitalism, and Slavery in French Saint-Domingue* (Chicago: University of Chicago Press, 2019), 4–5. See also, Gabriel Debien, "Aux origines de quelques plantations des quartiers de Léogane et du Cul-de-Sac (1680–1715)," *Notes d'histoire coloniale* 14 (n.p., 1947).

10 Marriage contract, Jean-Baptiste Merger and Marie-Madeleine Boisgautier Desperrières, 22 September 1751, MC/ET/XII/520, AN.

11 Louis-Philippe de Ségur, *Souvenirs et anecdotes sur le règne de Louis XVI* (Paris: Fayard, 1909); Marriage contract, Henri-Philippe de Ségur and Louis-Anne-Madeleine de Vernon, 13 January 1749, MC/RS/1354, AN (digi).

12 Jean-Nicolas Dufort de Cheverny, *Mémoires sur les règnes de Louis XV et Louis XVI et sur la Révolution par J. N. Dufort, Comte de Cheverny (1731–1802)* (Paris: E. Plon, 1886), 43–44.

180   *Notes to Pages 20-25*

13   Vaudreuil to Min., 9 August 1748, Au Cap, Colonies C^{9A} 74, ANOM.

14   *L'habitant de la Guadeloupe, comédie en quatre actes, par M. Mercier* (Neuchâtel: Imprimerie de la Société typographique, 1782), 104.

15   Both Antoine Watteau and the artist Charles de la Fosse lived in Crozat's house. See Michael Levey, "A Watteau Rediscovered: 'Le Printems' for Crozat," *Burlington Magazine,* February 1964, 53–59; Cordélia Hattori, "Contemporary Drawings in the Collection of Pierre Crozat," *Master Drawings* 45, no. 1 (2007): 38–53. The house was inherited by the Duc de Choiseul—from a family with extensive sugar and plantation connections—and is represented on a famous snuffbox at the Louvre. Darin Bloomquist, "The Choiseul Box: A Study of the Duc de Choiseul's Furniture," *Furniture History* 40 (2004): 53–72.

16   Philippe Haudrère, *La Compagnie française des Indes au XVIIIe siècle (1719–1795)* (Paris: Les Indes Savantes, 2005); Léonce Jore, *Les établissements français sur la côte occidentale d'Afrique de 1758 à 1809* (Paris: Maisonneuve et Larose, 1965); Jean-Bernard Lacroix, *Les Français au Sénégal au temps de la Compagnie des Indes* (Vincennes: Service historique de la Marine, 1986); André Delcourt, *La France et les établissements français au Sénégal entre 1713 et 1763: La Compagnie des Indes et le Sénégal; la guerre de la gomme,* Mémoires de l'Institut français d'Afrique noire, No. 17 ([Dakar]: [IFAN], 1952); Albert Girard, "La réorganisation de la Compagnie des Indes (1719–1723) (1er Article)," *Revue d'histoire moderne et contemporaine* (1908). On the participation of financiers in slaving ventures, see Delcourt, *La France,* 74–77.

17   Despite downplaying the extent of links between Parisian finance and the slave trade in glaring cases like those of the Magon de la Balue and La Borde families, Yves Durand does provide a few details about colonial connections in *Les fermiers généraux aux XVIIIe siècle* (1971) (Paris: Maisonneuve et Larose, 1996), 156–158. For a digitized document about the financier Dupleix de Bacquencourt's shared ownership of the slave ship *Le Pacifique,* see Consentement, 10 March 1761, ET / CVIII / 542, AN.

18   See vente d'une place située rue et porte de Richelieu à Monsieur Michel, 2 September 1751, and transport by the Marquise de Vaudreuil to Gabriel Michel, 14 September 1751, in MC / ET / XCV / 211, AN. See also Quittance, 30 October 1766, MC / ET / XCIV / 335, AN.

19   Document marked "20e pièce," 12 October 1750, Colonies C^6 12, ANOM.

20   On the meaning of "India piece," see Ana Lucia Araujo, *The Gift: How Objects of Prestige Shaped the Atlantic Slave Trade and Colonialism* (Cambridge: Cambridge University Press, 2023), 39.

21   Lordelot, officier de monseigneur le duc d'Orléans, to LGP, Paris, 13 January 1751, AB ms. 11,745, fol. 235v.

22   Mustapha (1–27 July 1755), AB ms. 11,909, fol. 224–232.

23   Sarah C. Maza, *Servants and Masters in Eighteenth-Century France: The Uses of Loyalty* (Princeton, NJ: Princeton University Press, 1984), 122.

24   Beaumarchais to LGP, 1 March 1766, AB ms. 12,228, fol. 73.

25 David Bindman and Helen Weston, "Court and City: Fantasies of Domination," in *The Image of the Black in Western Culture*, vol. 3, *From the "Age of Discovery" to the Age of Abolition*, pt. 3, *The Eighteenth Century*, ed. David Bindman and Henry Louis Gates (Cambridge, MA: Harvard University Press, 2011), 125–170.

26 Scholars of Beaumarchais have long noted the disconnect between his rhetoric of liberty and his commercial ventures. In 1765, one year before the arrest of Lucas, Beaumarchais spent time in Madrid negotiating on behalf of the financier Joseph Pâris-Duverney and the Company of the Indies, who hoped to obtain the *asiento*—the exclusive privilege to sell African slaves in Spanish colonies. See Hugh Thomas, in *Beaumarchais in Seville: An Intermezzo* (New Haven, CT: Yale University Press, 2006), 14.

27 See Admiralty sentence of 6 July and 1 September 1775 and undated petition, Z^{1D} 134, AN.

28 Guillaume-François-Louis Joly de Fleury, *Mémoire pour le vicomte de Besse, mestre-de-camp des dragons, appellant et défendeur; contre Louis-Camille Crispin, nègre, procédant sous l'autorité de Louis-Antoine-Jacques de Junquières, procureur en la Cour, son curateur ad hoc, intimé et demandeur* (Paris: Didot, 1776), Bibliothèque Municipal de Bordeaux (digi).

29 On the policing of foreigners or outsiders, see Vincent Milliot, "La surveillance des migrants et des lieux d'accueil à Paris du XVIᵉ siècle aux années 1830," in *La ville promise: Mobilité et accueil à Paris (fin XVIᵉ–début XIXᵉ siècle)*, ed. Daniel Roche (Paris: Fayard, 2000), 21–76. *Métiers de police: Être policier en Europe, XVIIIᵉ–XXᵉ siècle*, ed. Jean-Marc Berlière, Catherine Denys, et al. (Rennes: Presses universitaires de Rennes, 2008); Vincent Milliot, *Un policier des lumières suivi de mémoires de J. C. P. Lenoir, ancien lieutenant général de police de Paris, écrits en pays étrangers dans les années 1790 et suivantes* (Seyssel: Champ vallon, 2011); Fayçal El Ghoul, *La police parisienne dans la seconde moitié du XVIIIᵉ siècle*, 2 vols., Publications de la Faculté des sciences humaines et sociales, ser. 4, vol. 27 (Tunis: University of Tunis, 1995); Catherine Denys, Brigitte Marin, and Vincent Milliot, eds., *Réformer la police: Les mémoires policiers en Europe au XVIIIᵉ siècle* (Rennes: Presses universitaires de Rennes, 2009); Justine Berlière, *Policer Paris au siècle des Lumières: Les commissaires du quartier du Louvre dans la seconde moitié du XVIIIᵉ siècle* (Paris: École des Chartes, 2012). On the invention of inspectors, see Rachel Couture, "Inspirer la crainte, le respect, et l'amour du public: Les inspecteurs de police parisiens" (PhD diss., University of Quebec and University of Caen, 2013). On the policing of specific urban zones, see Camille Sallé, "Constitution de lieu et mise en ordre: Le boulevard du Temple, un espace policé (1750–1788)," in *Ordonner et régénérer la ville: Entre modernités et révolutions*, Actes du 137ᵉ Congrès national des sociétés historiques et scientifiques, Tours, 2012 (Paris: Éditions du CTHS, 2014), 93–101; J. C. Hervé, "L'ordre à Paris au XVIIIᵉ siècle: les enseignements du 'Recueil de règlements de police,'" *Revue d'histoire moderne et contemporaine*, no. 34 (1987): 185–214; Nicolas Vidoni, "Les 'officiers de police' à Paris (milieu

XVIIe–XVIIIe siècle)," *Rives méditerranéennes,* published online 15 February 2010; Vidoni, "Une 'police des Lumières'?," *Rives méditerranéennes* 40 (2011), published online October 15, 2012. On police commissioners, see Steven L. Kaplan, "Note sur les commissaires de police de Paris au XVIIIe siècle," *Revue d'histoire moderne et contemporaine* 28, no. 4 (October–December 1981): 669–686. On police administration in Paris, see J. Chagniot, "La lieutenance générale de police à la fin de l'ancien régime," in *Les Institutions parisiennes à la fin de l'ancien régime et sous la Révolution: Actes du colloque tenu à l'Hôtel de ville de Paris, 13 Oct. 1989* (Paris: CREPIF, 1990), 13–28; see also Marc Chassaigne, *La lieutenance générale de police de Paris* (Paris: Rousseau, 1906). For an English-language account of changes to the eighteenth-century police, see Alan Williams, *The Police of Paris, 1718–1789* (Baton Rouge: Louisiana State University, 1979).

30 Arlette Farge, "La guerre n'existe pas sur la terre de France au XVIIIe siècle," *Politix: Revue des sciences sociales du politique,* no. 58 (2002): 83–88.

31 Flights recorded by the Admiralty before 1750 include Charlot (9 August 1734, Z^{1D} 127); Pierrot, 23 May 1742, Z^{1D} 139), AN; Gracien (29 December 1746, Z^{1D} 139, AN); Pierre Lorient (6 February 1745, Z^{1D} 139, AN); Marc (28 January 1747, Z^{1D} 139, AN); Jeanne (28 August 1749, Z^{1D} 139, AN); Jean-Baptiste (9 December 1749, Z^{1D} 139, AN).

32 See statements by Dame Marie-Joseph Sorel, 23 May 1742, and Jacques-Pierre Colin, 28 August 1749, premier régistre, Z^{1D} 139, AN.

33 Stéphane Castellucio, *La noblesse et ses domestiques au XVIIIe siècle* (Saint-Remy-en-l'Eau: Monelle Hayot, 2021), 23–29.

34 Signalement, Figueret (ordre du 13 mars 1751), AB ms. 11,746, fol. 43.

35 Figueret, AB ms. 11,746, fol. 44.

36 Aubin, AB ms. 11,735, fol. 170v.

37 Invoice of 20 April 1786 from Raymond (the shop owner) to the Baron Kaguenek, T 1295–1297, AN.

38 Famin to LGP, 12 October 1756, Noel dit Polidor (17 October 1756), AB ms. 11,941, fols. 54v–55.

39 Interrogation of 15 January 1762, Y 11,346, AN.

40 Yvan Debbasch, "Le marronnage: Essai sur la désertion de l'esclave antillais," *L'année sociologique* 12 (1961): 1–112; Debbasch, "Le marronnage: Essai sur la désertion de l'esclave antillais: La société coloniale contre le marronnage," *L'année sociologique* 13 (1962): 117–195; Gérard Barthélémy, "Le rôle des bossales dans l'émergence d'une culture de marronnage en Haïti," *Cahiers d'études africaines* 37, no. 148 (1997): 839–862.

41 Alain J. Lemaître, *Le monde parlementaire au XVIIIe siècle: L'invention d'un discours politique* (Rennes: Presses universitaires de Rennes, 2010), 57–88; Jules Flammermont, *Remontrances du Parlement de Paris au XVIIIe siècle,* 3 vols. (Paris: Imprimerie nationale, 1888–1898).

42 *Déclaration du roi concernant la Guinée, qui ordonne que trois négrillons ne seront payés que sur le pied de deux nègres, et deux négrittes pour un nègre, donné*

à Paris le 14 décembre 1716 (Paris: Imprimerie royale, 1717), registered by Parlement on 9 January 1717.

43 Maurepas to Hérault, 22 December 1739, Colonies B 69, fol. 150, ANOM.

44 Joly de Fleury, De la Roue (avocat), Collet (procureur), *Mémoire signifié pour le nommé Francisque, indien de nation, néophyte de l'église romaine, intimé, contre le Sieur Allain François Ignace Brignon, se disant écuyer, appellant* (Paris: Imprimeur du Parlement, 1759), 24, in Collection Joly de Fleury, ms. 1833 (Parlement 1759, January–April), Département des Manuscrits, Bibliothèque nationale de France (Paris).

45 Augustin Chambon, *Le commerce de l'Amérique par Marseille, ou, Explication des lettres patentes du roi, portant règlement pour le commerce qui se fait de Marseille aux isle françoise de l'Amérique données au mois de février* (Avignon, 1764), 2:225.

46 "Déclaration du roi qui règle la manière d'élire des tuteurs et des curateurs aux enfants dont les pères possédaient des biens tant dans le royaume que dans les colonies et qui défend à ceux qui seront émancipés de vendre leurs nègres, donnée à Paris le 15 décembre 1721," in Meslé, *Traité des minorités, tutelles et curatelles* (Paris, 1752), 732.

47 Maurepas to Hérault, 22 December 1739, Colonies B 69, fol. 150, ANOM.

48 On lawyers and their relationship to the Crown, see David Bell, "Des stratégies d'opposition sous Louis XV: L'affaire des avocats 1730–1731," *Histoire, économie, et société* 9, no. 4 (1990): 567–590; Bell, "Lawyers into Demagogues: Chancellor Maupeou and the Transformation of Legal Practice in France, 1771–1789," *Past & Present* 130 (February 1991): 107–141.

49 AB ms. 12,137 (Télémaque, 23 April 1761). On Marville, see Suzanne Pillorget, *Claude-Henri Feydeau de Marville: Lieutenant-général de police de Paris (1740–1747) et choix de lettres inédites* (Paris: Pedone, 1987).

50 For statistics, see Jeffry Kaplow, "La population flottante de Paris à la fin de l'Ancien Régime," *Annales historiques de la Révolution française* 187 (1967): 1–14. On master-servant interactions in this period, see Cissie Fairchilds, *Domestic Enemies: Servants and Their Masters in Old Regime France* (Baltimore: Johns Hopkins University Press, 1984); Jacqueline Sabbatier, *Figaro et son maître: Maîtres et domestiques à Paris au XVIIIᵉ siècle* (Paris: Perrin, 1984); Maza, *Servants and Masters;* Jean-Pierre Gutton, *Domestiques et serviteurs dans la France de l'ancien régime* (Paris: Aubier Montaigne, 1981); see also Claude Fleury, *Les devoirs des maîtres et des domestiques,* reprinted in Alfred Franklin, ed., *La vie privée d'autrefois,* vol. 23 (Paris: Plon, 1898).

51 For a denunciation to the police of violence against a servant, see François-René Boucher, bourgeois de Paris, to Guillaume-Louis de la Fleutrie, 4 June 1762, Y 15,460, AN.

52 Letter from Famin to LGP, 12 October 1756, AB ms. 11,941, fol. 56.

53 Letter of 29 May 1745, in Claude-Henri Feydeau de Marville, *Lettres de Monsieur de Marville, lieutenant général de police au ministre Maurepas (1742–1747),* vol. 2, *1745–1746,* ed. A. de Boislisle (Paris: H. Champion, 1903), 86–87.

184 *Notes to Pages 33–35*

54 AB ms. 11,788, fol. 64.

55 Charlotte de Mailly de Nesle, Princesse de Nassau-Siegen, *Mémoire* (7 April 1752), AB ms. 11,788, fol. 72v.

56 Jean-Baptiste Laporte de Lalanne to Min., 1 June 1752, Colonies C^{9A} 90, AN.

57 Chevallier de Conflans to Min., 22 November and 26 December 1748, Colonies C^{9A} 72, ANOM.

58 On Guyot de Mongeot, see Colonies E 216, ANOM (digi).

59 Min. to Gov., Versailles, 6 April 1759, Colonies B 109, ANOM.

60 Ribon de la Poterie is named as the owner of the soldier, who was staying in Nantes with la dame Coquelin. "De par le roi," 24 December 1739, Colonies B 69, fol. 150, ANOM.

61 AD Charente-Maritime, B229, cited in Noël, *Dictionnaire des gens de couleur,* 3:826.

62 Régiment d'infanterie de Penthièvre, Colonies GR 1 YC 657, ANOM (digi). André Corvisier, "Les soldats noirs du Maréchal de Saxe: Le problème des antillais et africains sous les armes en France au XXVIIIe siècle," *Outre-Mers: Revue d'histoire* (1968): 367–413; see also Boris Lesueur, "Le soldat de couleur dans la société d'ancien régime et durant la période révolutionnaire," in *Les traites et esclavages: Perspectives historiques et contemporaines,* ed. Myriam Cottias, Elisabeth Cunin, and Antonio de Almeida Mendes (Paris: Karthala, 2010), 137–151. For general works on Maurice de Saxe, see Jean-Pierre Bois, *Maurice de Saxe* (Paris: Fayard, 1992); Saint-René Taillandier, *Maurice de Saxe: Étude historique d'après les documents des archives de Dresde* (Paris: Michel-Lévy frères, 1865); Jacques Soyer, "Les Uhlans du Maréchal de Saxe au château de Chambord," *Bulletin de la Société d'architecture et histoire de l'Orléanais* 240 (1940): 70–76; J. Mathorez, *Les étrangers en France sous l'ancien régime: Histoire de la formation de la population français* (Paris: E. Champion, 1919–1921), 403. Long before the Saxe regiment, a police chronicle ("on dit") dated 31 August 1742, by the Chevalier de Mouhy, reported gossip about the creation of a special regiment of black infantrymen for dangerous missions— known as a forlorn hope, or *les enfants perdus.* See AB ms. 15,883, published in the nineteenth century as "Chronique du règne de Louis XV," *Revue rétrospective ou Bibliothèque historique: Contenant des mémoires et documens authentiques, inédits et originaux, pour servir à l'histoire proprement dite, à la biographie, à l'histoire de la littérature et des arts* 5 (1834): 37–38. On this source, see Gilles Malandain, "Les mouches de la police et le vol des mots: Les gazetins de la police secrète et la surveillance de l'expression publique à Paris au deuxième quart du XVIIIe siècle," *Revue d'histoire moderne et contemporaine* (1954–) 42, no. 3 (1995): 376–404; Robert Darnton, "An Early Information Society: News and the Media in Eighteenth-Century Paris," *American Historical Review* 105, no. 1 (2000): 1–35.

63 Antoine-Léonard Thomas, *Œuvres complètes,* vol. 1 (Paris: Desessarts, 1802), 42. Biographers of Saxe who mention this plan relating to Jews do so without documentary support. Bois, *Maurice de Saxe,* 446; Céline Fallet, *Le Maréchal de*

Saxe (Rouen: Mégard, 1866), 240; Henri Malo, *La vie ardente du Maréchal de Saxe* (Paris: Hachette, 1928), 176. An incautious reading of the funeral oration by the Lutheran pastor Jean-Michel Lorenz for Maurice de Saxe may be the source of this rumor. See Jean-Michel Lorenz, *Oraison funèbre de très haut et très excellent seigneur monseigneur Maurice de Saxe* (Strasbourg, 1751). On Saxe and the rise of a new model of officer—as freemason, impresario, humanitarian, and philosopher—see Christy Pichichero, *The Military Enlightenment: War and Culture in the French Empire from Louis XIV to Napoleon* (Ithaca, NY: Cornell University Press, 2017), esp. 41–42, 90–97, 115–119.

64 "De l'habillement," in Maréchal de Saxe, *Mes rêveries: Ouvrage posthume de Maurice comte de Saxe, duc de Curlande et de Sémigalle, maréchal général des armées de Sa Majesté Très-Chrétienne: augmenté d'une histoire abrégée de sa vie, & de différentes pièces qui y ont rapport, par monsieur l'abbé Pérau* (Paris: Desaint & Saillant/Durand, 1757), 15.

65 Maurepas to d'Argenson, 15 February 1745, Colonies B 82, fol. 24, ANOM.

66 Maurepas to d'Argenson, 13 April 1745, Colonies B 82, fol. 67, ANOM.

67 On the slave of Nugent, the Earl of Westmeath, see Maurepas, 3 January 1747, Colonies B 86, fol. 2; and 18 December 1749, Colonies B 90, ANOM.

68 On Thélémaque, 23 March 1747, Colonies B 86, fol. 44; and 19 May 1747, Colonies B 86, fol. 71, ANOM.

69 On the fate of Phaeton and Scipion, see letters to Tourny and d'Argenson, 8 May 1747, Colonies B 86, fol. 64; and 21 July 1747, Colonies B 86, fol. 101; and Colonies B 86, fol. 107, ANOM.

70 Maurepas to Saxe, 14 February 1749, Colonies B 90, ANOM.

71 André Corvisier, "Les soldats noirs du Maréchal de Saxe," 409.

72 Maurepas to Romieu, 27 August 1746, Colonies B 84, fol. 111, ANOM.

73 Maurepas to de Sauvage, 20 October 1747, Colonies B 86, fol. 155, ANOM.

74 Maurepas to Tourneur, 12 February 1748, Colonies B 88, fol. 23, ANOM.

75 Corvisier, "Les soldats noirs du Maréchal de Saxe," 407.

76 Of these Bordeaux captives, see "Aux officiers de l'Amirauté de Bayonne," 16 January 1747, fol. 8; Maurepas to Rostand, Colonies B 86, fol. 47; De Par le Roi, 20 July 1747, Colonies B 86, fol. 109, ANOM.

77 In the enlistment role, Cyrus appears as Tyrsis. There is no Philippe. The person in question seems to have enlisted under the name Baptiste Alexis in the register. All these men entered the regiment on 2 December 1747. For lettres de cachet, see Colonies B 86, fol. 165, ANOM; for the register, see 3 Yc 278, SHD (digi). For documents about fugitives from La Rochelle, see Barentin to Maurepas, 18 May 1747, Marine B³ 461, fols. 176–181 (François Dénis, slave of Sombrun), AN; Barentin to Maurepas, 22 May 1747, Marine B³ 461, fols. 184–187 (François Dubois, slave of Moizeau), AN. Of the eight fugitives captured in La Rochelle, see Barentin to Maurepas, 28 September 1747, Marine B³ 461, fols. 198–199, AN.

78 Barentin to Maurepas, 28 September 1747, Marine B³ 461, fol. 198, AN.

186 *Notes to Pages 39–43*

79 Maurepas to Saxe, 3 November 1747, Colonies B 86, fol. 161, ANOM.

80 Barbara Klamon Kopytoff, "The Early Political Development of Jamaican Maroon Societies," *William and Mary Quarterly* 35, no. 2 (1978): 287–307; Orlando Patterson, "Slavery and Slave Revolts: A Socio-Historical Analysis of the First Maroon War, Jamaica 1655–1740," *Social and Economic Studies* 19, no. 3 (1970): 289–325; Kathleen Wilson, "The Performance of Freedom: Maroons and the Colonial Order in Eighteenth-Century Jamaica and the Atlantic Sound," *William and Mary Quarterly* 66, no. 1 (2009): 45–86.

81 Circulaire aux intendants et commissaires des ports où se fait des armements pour les colonies, 10 December 1750, Colonies B 92, fol. 267, ANOM.

82 On Charles Bouchaud, the husband of Françoise-Marthe Achard, see Colonies E43, ANOM (digi). Of her death in Paris on 28 December 1755, when her slaves remained imprisoned in Le Havre, see Y 12, AN ("scellés apposes par des commissaires au Châtelet"). On this affair, see Léo Elisabeth, *La Société martiniquaise au XVIIe et XVIIIe siècles, 1664–1789* (Paris: Karthala, 2003), 344; see also Sue Peabody, *"There Are No Slaves in France": The Political Culture of Race and Slavery in the Ancien Régime* (New York: Oxford University Press, 2002), 53–55.

83 See order of the king dated 22 July 1756 and covering letter (of the same date) from Machault to LGP (Berryer), Colonies B 104, fol. 110v, ANOM. See order of the king for "les négresses de la succession de la Dame Bouchaud," Colonies B 104, fol. 152. See also Dumée to LGP, letters of 5 August 1756 and 25 September 1756, fols.297 and 301; Bouchaud to LGP, Paris, 24 September and 9 November 1756, fols. 295 and 313. These documents can all be found in AB ms. 11,941.

84 Machault to Joly de Fleury (fils), Versailles, 18 January 1756, Colonies B 104, ANOM.

85 Ripart de Montclar to Etienne-Français, César-Gabriel, Duc de Praslin, Min. Navy, 9 May 1766, Marine B^3 571, AN.

86 Rouillé to Berryer, 10 March 1752, AB ms. 11,807, fol. 289.

87 There were abortive schemes in the 1760s aimed at banning both free and enslaved people of African and Asian descent from the country at the instigation of Choiseul (which I discuss in Chapter 2). See Choiseul to Joly de Fleury, 31 January 1763; Choiseul to Sartine, 24 May 1763 and 29 August 1763; and two separate letters from Choiseul to Hurson and Védier, 31 July 1763, all in Colonies B 117, ANOM.

88 Sources about Pèdre / Peidre include registration notices dated 17 March 1760 and 19 May 1762, Z^{1D} 139, AN; see also court appearance on 28 June 1765, Z^{1D} 132; and AB ms. 12,230.

89 Affidavit of 7 April 1752, 2 P.M., at the request of SAS Madame Charlotte de Mailly née Marquise de Nesle, by the clerk at For L'Évêque, AB ms. 11,788, fol. 65.

90 Report by Sainte-Croix, sergeant of the watch at the Place Royale, 25 April 1715, AB ms. 10,621, fol. 186.

91 She was incarcerated in the Bastille on 4 May 1714 and later transferred to a convent in Rethel (probably Ursuline) according to the file; see letter of 8

May 1715 from Comte de Pontchartrain to d'Argenson and order of release signed *Louis* of 15 August 1715, AB ms. 10,621, fols. 174, 186.

92 On gambling, see dossier of L'abbé Lelarge (3 February 1732), AB ms. 11,195, fol. 6.

93 *L'imposture de la Marquise de Mailly de Nesle et de son fils adultérin Maximilien Guillaume Adolphe exposée aux yeux du public par un grand nombre de pièces authentiques auxquelles on a joint la sentence définitive du suprême conseil aulique de sa majesté impériale rendu le V Oct. 1746* (Herborn, 1746), AN Bibliothèque, K^{II} 60.

94 Marie-Henri d'Arbois de Jubainville, *Inventaire sommaire des archives départementales antérieures à 1790: Aube, archives civils, séries C et D* (Troyes: Brunard, 1864), I: 271. "Huit fauconneaux ou petits canons saisis sur la princesse de Nassau, dame de l'isle sous Montréal (aujourd'hui Isle sur le Serein, Yonne) qui assiégée dans son château par quarante cavaliers de maréchaussées, vers la fin de l'année 1743, avait fait tirer un de ces fauconneaux sur les assaillants." Liasse C 1833, Archives départementales de l'Aube.

95 Louis III Mailly de Nesle, *Mémoire signifié pour Madame la Princesse Douairière de Nassau, née Marquise de Mailly de Neelle, contre Monsieur le Mailly de Néelle, son frère, les syndics de ses créanciers, et le tuteur à la substitution des biens de la Maison de Mailly* (Paris: Delormel, 1740).

96 *Arrêt du parlement qui déclare le prince Maximilien de Nassau Siegen fils légitime du prince Emmanuel de Nassau Siegen et de Charlotte Mailly, son épouse, ordonnent au Marquis de Nesle de le reconnaître* (Paris: P.-G. Simon, 1756).

97 Mailly de Nesle to LGP, 7 April 1752, AB ms. 11,788, fol. 64r.

98 Thierry Bressan, *Serfs et mainmortables en France au XVIIIe siècle: La fin d'un archaïsme seigneurial* (Paris: L'Harmattan, 2007), 73–75. Bressan includes an appendix about Mailly de Nesle's estate; see "La plus polémique des coutumes mainmortables du XVIIIe siècle: La coutume locale non homologuée de la châtellenie de l'Isle-sous-Montréal," 295. See also Mary Ann Quinn, "Pratiques et théories de la coutume: Allodialité et conflits de droits dans la seigneurie de L'Isle-sous-Montréal au XVIIIe siècle," *Études rurales* nos. 103–104, *Droit et paysans* (1986): 71–104.

99 Folarin Olawale Shyllon, *Black People in Britain, 1555–1833* (London: Oxford University Press, 1977), 41; Gretchen Gerzina, *Black England: A Forgotten Georgian History* (London: John Murray, 1995), 61.

100 Mailly de Nesle may have come across Adonis by way of Ovid's *Metamorphosis,* either in written form or as a popular topic of illustrations and tapestries; through Jean de La Fontaine's tragic poem "Adonis" (ca. 1671); in theatrical adaptations such as Jean-Baptiste Rousseau, *Vénus et Adonis* (1697); in the music of Lully (1669) and Scarlatti (1700); in sketches or paintings by artists including Titian (mid-1550s in multiple versions), Veronese (ca. 1580), Tintoretto (1580–1590), Rubens (1608, 1610–1611, 1614, 1630s), Poussin (1624–1625, 1630), Boucher (1720s)—or in prints based on those works. The ceiling of the Fontainebleau Palace features a portrait of wounded Adonis with Venus by Rosso Fiorentino (1530). A cheerful retelling of the Adonis story by Jean-Joseph de Mondonville debuted at the Château

188   *Notes to Pages 45–48*

de Bellevue in April 1752 starring Madame de Pompadour as Venus; this *opéra-ballet,* performed for the king, coincided with Jean's capture and imprisonment. See Rahul Markovits, *Staging Civilization: A Transnational History of French Theater in Eighteenth-Century Europe* (Charlottesville: University of Virginia Press, 2021), 110. On Adonis and the baroque esthetic, see Roger Freitas, "The Eroticism of Emasculation: Confronting the Baroque Body of the Castrato," *Journal of Musicology* 20, no. 2 (2003): 196–249; David Rosand, "The Passion of Adonis," *Arion: A Journal of Humanities and the Classics* 21, no. 3 (2014): 5–27. On the diffusion of Adonis images, see, for instance, Matthias Wivel, "Titian's 'Venus and Adonis' in Sixteenth-Century Prints," *Marburger Jahrbuch für Kunstwissenschaft* 40 (2013): 113–127; Donald M. Poduska, "Classical Myth in Music: A Selective List," *Classical World* 92, no. 3 (1999): 195–276.

101   Marie-Thérèse (11 February, 26 February, 5 May 1752), AB ms. 11,793.

102   René-Louis de Voyer, Marquis d'Argenson, *Mémoires et journal inédit du marquis d'Argenson, ministre des Affaires étrangères sous Louis XV,* vol. 2 (Paris: Nendeln, 1857), 344–346.

103   "Adrien, Maurice de, duc, propriétaire à Saint-Domingue," Colonies E 322, ANOM (digi). See also Charles François Hesse, *Plan de la plaine de Cul-de-Sac du Port au Prince, isle de Saint-Domingue* (1780).

104   David Hume, *An Enquiry concerning the Principles of Morals* (1751), sec. II, chap. 1.

2. PAULINE

1   Parish records from Saint-Dénis, the capital of Bourbon (now Réunion), provide clues about the earlier lives of Pierre and L'Empereur, Bouvet's male slaves. See baptism of Romaine Adelaide, daughter of Claire, Indienne, on May 15, 1760, where Pierre is the godfather; see baptism of Marcelin, daughter of Cécile, Creole slave, on November 16, 1760, where L'Empereur is listed as the father. Parish records for Isle de France and Bourbon that are mentioned in this chapter are digitized at www.anom.archivesnationales.culture.gouv.fr, except where noted. All other digitized records are indicated with the parenthetical abbreviation "(digi)."

2   Bouvet and his slaves are not on the passenger list of the ship *Le Vaillant*—see 2P 39-I.8, Services aistoriques de la Défense, Lorient (hereafter SHDL). Documents on this and other ships mentioned in this chapter are digitized at www .memoiresdeshommes.sga.defense.gouv.fr. Of Bouvet's presence on the ship, see letter to Company Directors of 8 September 1763, Isle de Bourbon, C° 645, Archives départementales de la Réunion (hereafter ADR). Of the slaves who accompanied him, see Admiralty declarations of 9 and 27 February 1765 by René-Julien Bouvet, Z^{1D} 139, AN. Pierre was still Bouvet's domestic on 14 October 1786. See Z^{1D} 139, AN.

3   Of the Bouvet family, see Bourde de la Rogerie, *Les Bretons aux îles de France et de Bourbon (Maurice et la Réunion au XXVIIe et au XVIIIe siècle* (Rennes:

Imprimeries Oberthur, 1934), 186–192; see also Philippe Haudrère, "Les officiers des vaisseaux de la Compagnie des Indes: Un corps d'élite dans la Marine française," *Histoire, économie et société* 1 (1997): 124.

4 Bouvet and his wife, Pauline David, traveled from Lorient to the Mascarene Islands aboard the *Auguste,* which departed from Lorient on 4 March 1750 and arrived in Isle de France on 15 August 1750. For the passenger list, see Rôle de *l'Auguste* (1750–1752), 2 P 34-II.1, SHDL.

5 Baptism of Marie-Antoinette de Lozier Bouvet (*sic*), born 20 December 1750, Births Marriages Deaths, 1750, Saint-Suzanne (Réunion); baptism of Ursule-Pauline de Lozier Bouvet, born 21 January 1752, Births Marriages Deaths 1752, Saint-Denis (Réunion). Marie-Antoinette was embarked with her aunt and uncle, Pierre-Félix-Barthélemy David, outgoing governor-general, aboard the *Centaure* from Isle de France on 9 February 1753; see Rôle du *Centaure* (1752–1753), 2P 35-4, SHDL. Ursule-Pauline was embarked aboard the *Duc de Chartres* on 18 March 1754, captained by her uncle, Joseph Bouvet. See Rôle au désarmement, 2P 36-16, SHDL.

6 Death of Pauline David on 12 December 1757, Births Marriages Deaths 1757, Saint-Dénis (Réunion). On epidemic of 1758, see Hubert Gerbeau, "Maladie et santé aux Mascareignes: Une histoire aux prises avec l'idéologie," in *Au Visiteur lumineux: Des îles créoles aux sociétés plurielles, mélanges offerts à Jean Benoist*, ed. Jean Barnabé et al. (Petit-Bourg, Guadeloupe: Ibis Rouge Éditions, 2000), 738.

7 Bouvet to Sartine, 27 November 1764, AB ms. 12,252, fol. 362.

8 The two lettres de cachet for Pauline are from 14 December 1764 (from the police) and 11 March 1765 (from the navy). See Pauline file, AB ms. 12,252, fols. 364, 367, 369. For documents relating to her Admiralty trial, see 9 January, 27 February, and 18 March 1765 in Z^{1D} 132, AN.

9 Trevor Burnard and John Garrigus, "The Seven Years' War in the West Indies," in *The Plantation Machine: Atlantic Capitalism in French Saint-Domingue and British Jamaica* (Philadelphia: University of Pennsylvania Press, 2016), 82–100. As a world war, see Daniel A. Baugh, *The Global Seven Years War, 1754–1763: Britain and France in a Great Power Contest,* 2nd ed. (London: Routledge, 2021); Edmond Dziembowski, *La Guerre de Sept Ans: 1756–1763* (Quebec: Septentrion, 2015). On British-French rivalry, see Hamish Scott, "The Decline of France and the Transformation of the European State System, 1756–1792," in *The Transformation of European Politics, 1763–1848: Episode or Model in Modern History?,* ed. Peter Krüger, Paul W. Schroeder, and Katja Wüstenbecker (Munster: Lit Verlag, 2002); Jonathan R. Dull, *The French Navy and the Seven Years' War* (Lincoln: University of Nebraska Press, 2005); Lee B. Kennett, *The French Armies in the Seven Years' War: A Study in Military Organization and Administration* (Durham, NC: Duke University Press, 1967).

10 See "État des prisonniers de guerre faits sur l'Isle de Gorée," Marine F^2 83, AN. Men of color who identified themselves to the Admiralty as soldiers displaced by war included Jean-Baptiste (27 July 1763), André Bordenave (21 November 1763), and Louis (3 December 1763), in Z^{1D} 132, AN. Renaud Morieux, "French

190   *Notes to Pages 50–52*

Prisoners of War, Conflicts of Honour, and Social Inversions in England, 1744–1783," *Historical Journal* 56, no. 1 (2013): 55–88. On maritime prisoners of war, see Alain Cabatou, "Gens de mer, guerre et prison: La captivité des gens de mer au XVIIIᵉ siècle," *Revue d'histoire moderne et contemporaine* 28, no. 2 (April–June 1981): 246–267; see also Reginald Savary, "The Convention of Écluse, 1759–1762: The Treatment of the Sick and Wounded, Prisoners of War and Deserters of the British and French Armies during the Seven Years War," *Journal of the Society for Army Historical Research* 42, no. 170 (1964): 68–77.

11   Correspondance d'arrivée, Colonies C¹⁴ 25, fol. 318, ANOM.

12   Miranda Spieler, "Slave Voice and the Legal Archive: The Case of Freedom Suits before the Paris Admiralty Court," in *Hearing Enslaved Voices: African and Indian Slave Testimony in British and French America, 1700–1848,* ed. Sophie White and Trevor Burnard (New York: Routledge, 2020), 165–183.

13   Choiseul to LGP (Sartine), 31 January 1763, Colonies B 117, fol. 28, ANOM.

14   Letters by Choiseul to Hurson and Vedier, 31 July 1763, Colonies B 117, ANOM. More than a year earlier, the prosecutor-general of the Paris Court of Admiralty proposed to draft legislation in concert with Antoine de Sartine, lieutenant-general of police, relating to black people in France; he asked Sartine to draw the matter to Choiseul's attention. See Poncet de la Grave to Sartine, 24 April 1762, Louis file, AB ms. 12,160, fol. 281.

15   Hearing of 18 March 1765, Z¹ᴰ 132, AN.

16   Enclosed with Muron letter of 3 April 1765, Pauline file, AB ms. 12,252, fol. 380.

17   On the ancient practice, see Ulrike Roth, "'Peculium,' Freedom, Citizenship: Golden Triangle or Vicious Circle? An Act in Two Parts," *Bulletin of the Institute of Classical Studies,* suppl. no. 109 (2010): 91–120. In other New World slave societies influenced by Roman law, slave self-purchase was commonplace. See Claudia Varella and Manuel Barcia, *Wage-Earning Slaves: Coartación in Nineteenth-Century Cuba* (Gainesville: University of Florida Press, 2020); Aline Helg, *Slave No More: Self-Liberation before Abolitionism in the Americas,* trans. Lara Vergnaud (Chapel Hill: University of North Carolina Press, 2019), 64–81; Alejandro de la Fuente, "Slaves and the Creation of Legal Rights in Cuba: Coartación and Papel," in *Slavery and Antislavery in Spain's Atlantic Empire,* ed. Josep M. Fradera and Christopher Schmidt-Nowara (New York: Berghahn Books, 2013), 101–133.

18   A decision of the Council of Léogane of 14 May 1751 enabled a slave called Petit-Baptiste, who belonged to a branch of the Coustard family (see Chapter 1), to farm out his labor to buy himself and his daughter after the death of their master. Arrêt du Conseil de Léogane, 14 May, 18 September, and 15 November 1751, Colonies F³ 79, fols. 38–39, ANOM. On self-purchase and the *libres de fait* (those who are free in fact), see Dominique Rogers and Boris Lesueur, eds., *Sortir de l'esclavage: Europe du sud et Amériques (XIVᵉ–XIXᵉ siècle)* (Paris: Karthala, 2018); Bernard Moitt, "In the Shadow of the Plantation: Women of Color and the *Libres de fait* of Martinique and Guadeloupe, 1685–1848," in *Beyond Bondage: Free Women of Color in the Amer-*

icas, ed. David Barry Gaspar and Darlene Clark Hine (Urbana: University of Illinois Press, 2004), 37–59; Dominique-Aimé Mignot, "Le droit romain aux Antilles: La pratique des affranchissements," *Revue historique de droit français et étranger (1922–)* 79, no. 3 (2001): 347–360. Alessandro de la Fuente and Ariela Gross are more skeptical about self-purchase in the French context. See Alejandro de la Fuente and Ariela Gross, "Manumission and Freedom in the Americas: Cuba, Virginia and Louisiana, 1500s–1700s," *Quaderni Storici* 50, no. 148 (1) (2015): 15–48.

19   One person, Pierre dit Durieu, who does not have a Bastille file, probably eluded the police. See Pierre dit Durieu, slave of Lussy, Colonies B 122, fols. 14, 346, 461, ANOM; complaint and reports relating to Louis Masclary mulâtre libre of 24 January, 7 February, and 11 February 1765, Y 11,355, AN.

20   Megan Vaughan, *Creating the Creole Island: Slavery in Eighteenth-Century Mauritius* (Durham, NC: Duke University Press, 2005), 14–18.

21   On the Indian Ocean slave trade, see Richard B. Allen, "Exporting the Unfortunate: The European Slave Trade from India, 1500–1800," *Slavery & Abolition* 43, no. 3 (2022): 533–552; Richard Blair Allen, *European Slave Trading in the Indian Ocean, 1500–1850* (Athens, OH: Ohio University Press, 2014); Rafaël Thiébaut, "Some Thoughts concerning the Effects of the European Slave Trade on the Dynamics of Slavery in Madagascar in the Seventeenth and Eighteenth Centuries," in *Slaving Zones: Cultural Identities, Ideologies, and Institutions in the Evolution of Global Slavery,* ed. Damian Alan Pargas and Jeff Fynn-Paul, vol. 4 of *Studies in Global Slavery* (Leiden: Brill, 2018), 169–204; Edward Alpers, "The Other Middle Passage: The African Slave Trade in the Indian Ocean," in *Many Middle Passages: Forced Migration and the Making of the Modern World,* ed. Emma Christopher, Cassandra Pybus, and Marcus Rediker (Berkeley: University of California Press, 2007), 20–38.

22   For documents about early French colonial society in the Mascarenes, see Jean Barassin, *La vie quotidienne des colons de l'île Bourbon à la fin du règne de Louis XIV, 1700–1715* (Saint-Clotilde: Nouvelle Imprimerie dionysienne, 1989). On the dominance of Malagasies in colonial Bourbon and Isle de France, see Pier Martin Larson, *Ocean of Letters: Language and Creolization in an Indian Ocean Diaspora* (Cambridge: Cambridge University Press, 2009), 101–105. On South Asians, see Marina Carter, "Slavery, Ethnicity, and Identity in the Indian Ocean Colonial World: A Case Study of 'Indian' Slaves on Mauritius," in *Being a Slave: Histories and Legacies of European Slavery in the Indian Ocean,* ed. Alicia Schrikker and Nira Wickramasinghe (Leiden: Leiden University Press, 2020), 43–60; Prosper Eve, "Les Indiens à Bourbon au temps de l'esclavage ou l'histoire d'une dissonance," in *La diaspora indienne dans l'histoire des îles et pays de L'Océan indien: Actes du colloque international organisé du 20 au 22 janvier 2010 par l'Université de Pondichéry et la Chaire UNESCO de l'Université de la Réunion,* ed. Sudel Fuma and Dr. Pannirselvame (Saint-Denis: Université de la Réunion, 2010).

23   Vaughan, *Creating the Creole Island,* 40.

24   Vaughan, *Creating the Creole Island,* 105.

192　*Notes to Pages 53–55*

25　Letter from Conseil de la Direction (Delacombe, Aussenac), "Pour copie Villecollet," Gorée, 4 March 1744, Colonies C^6 12, ANOM.

26　Nathan Marvin, "Instructions du Ministère de la Marine, concernant la tolérance envers l'islam et l'hindouisme dans les colonies françaises de l'Océan indien sous l'ancien régime," *Outre-Mers* 102, nos. 388–389 (2015): 285–290; Pier M. Larson, *Ocean of Letters: Language and Creolization in an Indian Ocean Diaspora* (New York: Cambridge University Press, 2009), 362–408.

27　The 1685 code for the Atlantic prohibited masters "de tenir la marché des nègres & de tous autres marchés lesdits jours, sur pareilles peines et de confiscation des marchandises" (art. 7) and also announced that non-Catholics were "incapables de contracter à l'avenir aucun marriage valable" and declared anyone born of those unions to be bastards (art. 8). These articles did not appear in either the code that applied to the Mascarenes or that for Louisiana. See *Le Code noir ou l'Édit du roy servant de règlement pour le gouvernement et l'administration de justice et la police des isles françoises de l'Amérique, et pour la discipline et le commerce des nègres et esclaves dans le pays, donnée à Versailles au mois de mars 1685* (Paris: Claude Girard dans la Grande Salle, 1735); compare wth Edit de 1723 concernant les esclaves, O^A 96, NAM.

28　Janet J. Ewald, "African Bondsmen, Freedmen, and the Maritime Proletariats of the Northwestern Indian Ocean World, c. 1500–1900," in *Indian Ocean Slavery in the Age of Abolition,* ed. Robert Harmes, Bernard K. Freamon, and David W. Blight (New Haven, CT: Yale University Press, 2013), 200–215.

29　Lettre du curé du Port Louis (Isle de France) au sujet des cultes non-catholiques, 26 March 1742, Colonies F^{5A} 32 / 5, ANOM (digi).

30　Auguste Toussaint, *Port Louis: Deux siècles de l'histoire (1735–1935)* (Port Louis: Visavi, 2013). For everyday life in neighboring Isle de Bourbon, see Albert Jauze, *Vivre à l'île de Bourbon au XVIIIe siècle* (Paris: Riveneuve, 2017).

31　Megan Vaughn emphasizes the Creole nature of Malagasy culture and notes the distorting effect of ethnic categories (Malagasy, Indian, and Bambara) in colonial documents. See Vaughn, *Creating the Creole Island,* esp. 120–122, 202–208. On the multilingual character of the Isle de Bourbon, see Pier Larson, *Ocean of Letters,* 112–113.

32　Sépulture d'une négresse de Monsieur M. Picault, 13 June 1746, KA 12, Baptêmes, mariages, décès, Port Louis 1746, fol. 13, National Archives of Mauritius (hereafter NAM).

33　Sépulture d'un enfant anonyme et d'un esclave, 1 May 1760, KA 35, Sépultures blancs, libres, esclaves, Port Louis, 1760, NAM.

34　Prosper Eve, *Le corps de l'esclave à l'île Bourbon* (Paris: Presses universitaires de la Sorbonne, 2013), 42.

35　Baptême de Pauline esclave de Broens, 15 April 1753, KA 20 P: Baptêmes, mariages, blancs, libres et esclaves, 2 January–30 December 1753, NAM.

36　Rôle du *Comte d'Artois* (1765–1767), 2P 41-1.3, SHDL.

37　Edward Duyker, *An Officer of the Blue: Marc-Joseph Marion Dufresne, South Sea Explorer, 1724–1772* (Melbourne: Melbourne University Press, 1994); Gananath Obeyesekere, *Cannibal Talk: The Man-Eating Myth and Human Sacrifice in the South Seas* (Berkeley: University of California Press, 2005), 57–87.

38 The Pauline who is most plausible of these three women is the spouse of the soldier, Jean-Jacques Morel. See Affaire de parents, nomination tuteurs, mineurs Morel, 5 September 1781, and inventaire de la communauté des biens de Jean-Jacques Morel et la défunte Pauline, Extrait des minutes du greffe de la juridiction royale de l'Isle de France, NA6 / 1, NAM. The 1776 census (KK / 47, NAM) describes Jacques-Morel as an *archer de la Marine,* age 46, born in Paris, who arrived in Mauritius aboard *Le Content* in 1748.

39 See articles 14–16 of the 1723 Code Noir as applied to the Mascarenes, which appear in the 1685 Code Noir under different numbers. There are two manuscript copies of this document in the National Archives of Mauritius; see Edit de 1723 concernant les esclaves, O^A 96 and Z^{SA} 1, NAM. The latter copy is marked "18 7bre 1724" at the top, which is the date of its local enactment.

40 On the company's bankruptcy and ensuing debate about the future of privileged firms in France, see Georges Dulac, "Les gens de lettres, le banquier et l'opinion: Diderot et la polémique sur la Compagnie des Indes," *Dix-huitième siècle* 26 (1994): 177–199.

41 Saisie de plusieurs comestibles sur des esclaves regrattiers (21 July 1785), OA 58, *Journal de police,* NAM. On the police archives of Mauritius, see Catherine Denys, "Écritures policières coloniales et circulations impériales: Le bureau de police de Port-Louis à l'Isle de France (Maurice), 1766–1788," *Revue d'histoire moderne et contemporaine* 66, no. 4 (2019): 32–52.

42 See *Defense à Mlle Gassin de faire faire de la pâtisserie,* 20 August 1785, OA 58, fol. 98, NAM; *Noirs recelés aux casernes,* 15 April 1785, OA 58, fol. 4, NAM; on the bakeshop, see entry of 26 November 1780, 9:30 A.M.; on the speakeasy, see 14 October 1784, 5 P.M. In *Journal de police,* 1779–1784, Z^{2B} 3, NAM.

43 Antoine Boucher, "Mémoire d'Antoine Boucher sur l'Île de Bourbon," *Recueil trimestriel de documents inédits pour servir à l'histoire des Mascareignes françaises,* no. 4 (January–March 1941): 300.

44 On the piastre in the Mascarenes, Madagascar, and East Africa, see Gwyn Campbell, "The Structure of Trade in Madagascar, 1750–1810," *International Journal of African Historical Studies* 26, no. 1 (1993): 111–114; Edward A. Alpers, "The French Slave Trade in East Africa (1721–1810)," *Cahiers d'études africaines* 10, no. 37 (1970): 80–124 ; on the colonial circulation of the piastre, see Carlos Marichal, "La piastre ou le real de huit en Espagne et en Amérique: Une monnaie universelle (XVIe–XVIIIe siècles)," *Revue européenne des sciences sociales* 45, no. 137 (2007): 107–121; see also Marichal, "Réflexions sur le problème des monnaies et des métaux précieux en Méditerranée Orientale, au XVIIIe siècle," Actes des journées d'études Bendor, 25–26 April 1975, *Cahiers de la Méditerranée* 1 (1976): 4–5. Albert Jauze, "Les campagnes du *Ruby* en 1763 et 1764 : Étude des colonies françaises des Mascareignes, de Madagascar et de la côte orientale de l'Afrique: Contribution à la connaissance de la traite indien-océanique au XVIIIe siècle," *Outre-mers* 99 (2012): 119–189. For

194   **Notes to Pages 58–59**

a basic summary of monetary terms and usage, see E. Wesley O'Neill, "French Coinage in History and Literature," *French Review* 39, no. 1 (1965): 1–14; on the livre as "fictitious currency," see Thomas M. Luckett, "Imaginary Currency and Real Guillotines: The Intellectual Origins of the Financial Terror in France," *Historical Reflections/Réflexions Historiques* 31, no. 1 (2005): 117–139; see also François Crouzet, *La grande inflation: La monnaie en France de Louis XVI à Napoléon* (Paris: Fayard, 1993). On French colonial money, see Jean Mazard, *Histoire monétaire et numismatique des colonies et de l'Union française, 1670–1952* (Paris: E. Bourgey, 1953).

45   See Testament de la Dame Marie-Geneviève Gruel, 25 January 1751, MC/ET/LXXXV/527, AN; unnotarized receipt of sale by Jean-Antoine Choppy Desgranges-Delaravine and Marie Cadet to Chevalier Banks, arpenteur du roi, 7 August 1774; notarized sale of Luce by Pierre Maillot, habitant, to "la nommée Dauphine, négresse libre" (June 1776), in file marked "ventes volontaires des noirs"; the 2000 livres paid for Luce's liberty are specified as having come from Luce's earnings; both in 10C, ADR. On Banks's love affair with his slave, see Hervé Perret, "De l'amour impossible d'un franc-maçon pour une esclave à l'Ile Bourbon ou le procès d'un transgresseur," *Dix-huitième siècle* 36 (2004): 405–433.

46   Aubert de la Rue, "Les îles dans la géographie," *Bulletin de la Société de géographie de Lille* 78, no. 1 (1936): 3. On Bouvet and French exploration in the Pacific, see Noelene Bloomfield, "Overview—France's Quest for Terra Australis: Strategies, Maladies and Triumphs," *The Great Circle* 39, no. 2 (2017): 8–24; John Gascoigne, "The Globe Encompassed: France and Pacific Convergences in the Age of Enlightenment," in *Discovery and Empire: The French in the South Seas,* ed. John West-Sooby (Adelaide: University of Adelaide Press, 2013), 17–40; see also O. H. K. Spate, "De Lozier Bouvet and Mercantilist Expansion in the Pacific in 1740," in *Merchants and Scholars: Essays in the History of Exploration and Trade,* ed. John Parker (Minneapolis: University of Minnesota Press, 1965). Even the location Bouvet provided for the island was erroneous, as Cook later discovered; see Louis-Marie Bajot, *Abrégé historique et chronologique des principaux voyages de découvertes par mer depuis l'an 2000 avant Jésus Christ jusqu'au commencement du XIXe siècle* (Paris: Imprimerie royale, 1829), 57.

47   See René Estienne, *Les compagnies des Indes* (Paris: Gallimard and Ministre des armées, 2017); Philippe Haudrère, *La Compagnie française des Indes au XVIIIe siècle (1719–1795)* (Paris: Les Indes savantes, 2005); Haudrère, "Les officiers des vaisseaux de la Compagnie des Indes," *Histoire, économie et société* 16, no. 1 (1997): 117–124; Haudrère, "L'origine du personnel de direction général de la Compagnie des Indes, 1719–1794," *Revue française d'histoire d'outre-mer* 67, no. 248–249 (1980): 339–371.

48   1723 Code noir concernant les esclaves, OA 96, NAM. This article did not appear in the 1685 code but does appear in the 1724 version for Louisiana.

49   Louis-Charles Grant, Baron de Vaux, *Letters from Mauritius in the Eighteenth Century by Grant, Baron de Vaux: Including an Account of Labourdonnais's Capture of Madras, with an Introduction by Sir John Pope Hennesy* (printed for private circulation, 1886), letter of 1 June 1743, 38; letter of June 1749, 165.

Notes to Pages 60–64 195

50 Certificat délivré à Henry Hoareau, 14 février 1753, C° 996, ADR.

51 Bernardin de Saint-Pierre, *Voyage à l'Isle de France, à l'Isle de Bourbon, au Cap de Bonne Espérance, &c avec observations nouvelles sur la nature et sur les hommes, par un officier du roi*, vol. 1 (Paris: Chez Merlin, 1773), 195–196.

52 Marco Cicchini, "La désertion: Mobilité, territoire, contrôles; enjeux sociaux et politiques au siècle des Lumières," *Dix-huitième siècle*, no. 37 (2005): 101–115.

53 Two men in Léogane (Saint-Domingue) were condemned for marronnage in March 1752, with one sentenced to the slicing of his Achilles tendon, another to death. The death penalty was converted to forced labor because the condemned man was young, strong, and able to work. Jean Laporte de Lalanne to Min., 18 March 1752, Port au Prince, Colonies C⁹ᴬ 91, ANOM.

54 Extrait du registre de marronnage du greffe de Saint Paul, 7 August 1752, Destruction des noirs marrons, C° 948, ADR.

55 Angela Redish, "Why Was Specie Scarce in Colonial Economies? An Analysis of the Canadian Currency, 1796–1830," *Journal of Economic History* 44, no. 3 (1984): 713–728.

56 Art. 3, letter of 12 January 1737 from Conseil supérieur de l'Île de Bourbon to Compagnie des Indes, in Albert Lougnon, *Correspondance du Conseil supérieur de Bourbon et de la Compagnie des Indes, 23 janvier 1736–9 mai 1741, ensemble trois lettres de la Compagnie au Conseil supérieur de l'Ile-de-France, 17 février–29 décembre 1738*, vol. 3, *Correspondance du Conseil supérieur de Bourbon et de la Compagnie des Indes* (Paris: E. Leroux, 1935), 76.

57 See letter of 24 February 1738, art. 6, in Lougnon, *Correspondance du Conseil supérieur de Bourbon* (1935), 36; see also Baron de Vaux, *Letters from Mauritius*, 192.

58 See Bouvet's comments enclosed with a note from Muron to Sartine, 3 April 1765, AB ms. 12,252, fols. 384–385.

59 AB ms. 12,252, fol. 380.

60 On Madame Dupleix, see Yvonne Robert Gaebele, *Créole et grande dame: Johanna Bégum, Marquise Dupleix, 1706–1756* (Paris: Éditions Leroux, 1934).

61 Salaberry's comments appear in a memoir with facing comments by Bouvet enclosed with a note from Muron to Sartine of 3 April 1765; AB ms. 12,252, fol. 380v.

62 Muron to Sartine, 3 December 1764, AB ms. 12,252, fol. 365.

63 Admiralty declarations of 9 and 27 February 1765 by René-Julien Bouvet, Z¹ᴰ 139, AN.

64 AB ms. 12,252, fol. 365.

65 See Robert Darnton, "A Police Inspector Sorts His Files: An Anatomy of the Republic of Letters," in *The Great Cat Massacre and Other Episodes in French Cultural History* (New York: Vintage; 1984), 185.

66 s.v. libertin, jurisprudence, *Encyclopédie ou Dictionnaire raisonné des sciences, des arts, et des métiers par une société de gens de lettres*, vol. 9 (Paris, 1765),

196 *Notes to Pages 64–67*

476–477; on ancient usages of this term, see Lily Ross Taylor, "Freedmen and Freeborn in the Epitaphs of Imperial Rome," *American Journal of Philology* 82, no. 2 (1961): 113–132.

67 Jean-Pierre Carrez, *Femmes opprimées à la Salpêtrière de Paris (1656–1791)* (Paris: Éditions connaissances et savoirs, 2005); Henry Légier Desgranges, *Hospitaliers d'autrefois: Hôpital Général de Paris, 1656–1790* (Paris: Hachette, 1952); on organization and sources, see Nicolas Sainte Fare Garnot, "L'Hôpital Général de Paris, institution d'assistance, de police ou de soins?," *Histoire, économie et société* 3, no. 4 (1984): 535–542. On the roundup and punishment of streetwalkers during the Old Regime, see Erica-Marie Benabou, *La prostitution et la police des mœurs au XVIIIᵉ siècle* (Paris: Perrin, 1987).

68 On Marie Stuart, see "Femmes évadées de la Salpêtrière au mois de juillet 1758," "État des femmes détenues à l'Hôpital pour lesquelles Mme de Moysan demande la liberté," and "Note des femmes retenues à l'Hôpital auxquelles on ne croit pas devoir accorder la liberté," AB ms. 12,695, fols. 114, 251, 274.S.

69 "Annonces & avis divers," *Annonces, affiches, et avis divers,* 19 June 1760, 378.

70 Jean Duma, *Les Bourbon-Penthièvre (1678–1793): Une nébuleuse aristocratique au XVIIIᵉ siècle* (Paris: Publications de la Sorbonne, 1995), 24, 36–38, 538.

71 A. B. Duhamel, *Homme en grand deuil,* engraving for *Cabinet des Modes* (Paris: Buisson, 1786); Lou Taylor, *Mourning Dress: A Costume and Social History* (London: Allen and Unwin, 1983).

72 George Latimer Bates, *Handbook of Birds of West Africa* (London: John Bales and Son, 1930); Gabriel A. Jamie et al., "Multimodal Mimicry of Hosts in a Radiation of Parasitic Finches," *Evolution* 74, no. 11 (2020): 2526–2538; Todd Windquist and Robert E. Lemon, "Sexual Selection and Exaggerated Male Tail Length in Birds," *American Naturalist* 143, no. 1 (1994): 95–116; Robert B. Payne, "Behavior and Songs of Hybrid Parasitic Finches," *The Auk* 97, no. 1 (1980): 118–134. On the appellations "widow" and "veuve," see Georges-Louis Leclerc, Comte de Buffon, and Gabriel Léopold Charles Amé Bexon, *Histoire naturelle des oiseaux,* vol. 4 (Paris: Imprimerie royale, 1786), 334–336.

73 During the period 1700–1791, 54 percent or 143,373 of the 264,503 captives sold out of Whydah in the eighteenth century were transported to the New World aboard French ships (the remaining 121,130 people were embarked on ships belonging to merchants in Great Britain, Portugal, and the Netherlands combined). Statistics from Trans-Atlantic Slave Trade Database. See Robin R. Law, *Ouidah: The Social History of a West-African Slaving Port, 1727–1892* (Athens, OH: Ohio University Press, 2004).

74 See Henrik Ziegler, "Le demi-dieu des païens: La critique contemporaine de la statue pédestre de Louis XIV," in Isabelle Dubois, Alexandre Gady, and Henrik Ziegler, *Place des Victoires: Histoires, architecture, société* (Paris: Fondation Maison des sciences de l'homme, 2003), 43–65; Edouard Fournier, *Chroniques et légendes des rues de Paris* (Paris: Dentu, 1864), 184–185.

75 The architect Robert de Cotte designed many *hôtels particuliers* in this neighborhood. See François Fossier, *Les dessins du fonds Robert de Cotte de la Bibliothèque nationale de France* (Paris: Bibliothèque nationale de France / École française de Rome, 1997).

76 Duma, *Les Bourbon-Penthièvre,* 280, 413.

77 Xavier Fournier, Marquis de Bellevue, *Généalogie de la maison Fournier actuellement représentée par Les Fournier de Bellevue* (Rennes: Imprimerie Francis Simon, 1909).

78 Pierre Bardin, "Déclaration des hommes de couleur, colons americains (1789)," *Généalogie et histoire de la Caraïbe* 179 (2005): 4454–4459.

79 Frédéric Durand, *Balthazar: Un prince de Timor en Chine, en Amérique, et en Europe au XVIIIᵉ siècle* (Paris: Les Indes savantes, 2015), 111–113.

80 Interrogation of Marie-Françoise Laperle, 12 December 1777, Police des noirs, F^{1B} 4, fols. 190–192, ANOM.

81 On the Ferronaye-Fournier family as a model for social fusion between nobles and Creole heiresses, see Paul Cheney, *Cul de Sac: Patrimony, Capitalism, and Slavery in French Saint-Domingue* (Chicago: University of Chicago Press, 2017), esp. 27–29, 133, 141, 155.

82 From a petition to the king by the Marquis de Gouy d'Arsy, deputy for Saint-Domingue to the National Assembly. Quoted in Pierre de Vaissière, *Saint-Domingue: La société et la vie des créoles sous l'ancien régime* (Paris: Perrin, 1909), 355.

83 *Copie de lettre de M. de Castellane à Madame de Saint-Vincent au Pressoir, près Fontainebleau, le 26 juillet 1773* (Paris: L. Cellot, 1776).

84 Honoré Bonhomme, *Le duc de Penthièvre Louis-Jean-Marie de Bourbon, sa vie, sa mort (1725–1793)* (Paris: Firmin Didot frères, 1869), 62.

85 Declaration of 18 July 1789 by Fournier and Bellevue, Archives de l'Assemblée générale des électeurs de Paris (July 1789), C 134, dossier VI, AN (Pierrefitte).

86 On Malouet's opposition to the "domestic sovereignty" of masters in Saint-Domingue and resulting memoir of 1779, see Yvan Debbasch, "Au cœur du 'gouvernement des esclaves,' la domestique aux Antilles françaises (XVIIᵉ–XVIIIᵉ siècles)," *Revue française d'histoire d'outre-mer* 72, no. 266 (1985): 39–42; on reform ideas, see also Michèle Duchet, *Anthropologie et histoire au siècle des Lumières* (Paris: F. Maspero, 1971), 134–135, 156–157. For a legal historical treatment of "domestic sovereignty" in relation to slave abuse, see Malick W. Ghachem, *The Old Regime and the Haitian Revolution* (Cambridge: Cambridge University Press, 2012), 62–63, 167–210, 154–155. On Malouet and the Abbé Raynal as friends and coauthors, see Carminella Biondi, "L'apport antiesclavagiste de Pechméja et de Diderot à *l'Histoire des deux Indes*," *Outre-mers* 102, no. 386 (2015): 49–64; David Diop, "Raynal, les colonies, la Révolution française et l'esclavage," *Outre-mers* 103, no. 386 (2015): 218–221.

87 On his advocacy for white planters during the 1790s, see Gabriel Debien, "Gens de couleur libres et colons de Saint-Domingue devant la Constituante," *Revue*

198   Notes to Page 71

d'histoire de l'Amérique française 4, no. 2–4 (1950–1951): 362–408; Debien, *Les Colons de Saint-Domingue et la Révolution: Essai sur le Club Massiac (août 1789–août 1792)* (Paris: Armand Colin, 1953).

88 Antoine Lilti, *Le monde des salons: Sociabilité et mondanité à Paris au XVIIIᵉ siècle* (Paris: Fayard, 2013), 94–95. On the *noyau ploutocratique*, see Guy Chaussinand-Nogaret, *La noblesse au XVIIIᵉ siècle: De la féodalité au lumières* (Paris: Hachette, 1976), 77.

89 Émile Laurent, *Ruelles, salons et cabarets: Histoire anecdotique de la littérature française*, vol. 2 (Paris: Dentu, 1892), 180.

90 See Francis Steegmuller, *A Man, a Woman, and Two Kingdoms: The Story of Madame d'Épinay and the Abbé Galiani* (Princeton, NJ: Princeton University Press, 1991); Cécile Cavaillac, "Audaces et inhibitions d'une romancière au XVIIIᵉ siècle: Le cas de Madame d'Épinay," *Revue d'histoire littéraire de la France* 104, no. 4 (2004): 887–904; for her semi-biographical novel, see Louise d'Épinay, *Les contre-confessions: Histoire de Madame de Montbrillant* (Paris: Mercure de France, 2000); Robert Perroud, *Madame d'Houdetot* (Milan: Malfasi, 1952); Jean Ritter, "J. J. Rousseau et Madame d'Houdetot," *Annales de la Société Jean-Jacques Rousseau*, vol. 2 (Geneva: Julien, 1906); and Hippolyte Buffenoir, *La Comtesse d'Houdetot, une amie de J.-J. Rousseau* (Paris: Calmann Lévy, 1901). On both women, see Rousseau, *Confessions* (1758) vol. 2, bk. 10. See also Dena Goodman, "Enlightenment Salons: The Convergence of Female and Philosophic Ambitions," *Eighteenth-Century Studies* 22, no. 3 (1989): 329–350.

91 On John Law, see John Shovlin, *Trading with the Enemy: Britain, France, and the 18th-Century Quest for a Peaceful World Order* (New Haven, CT: Yale University Press), 115–145; Antoin E. Murphy, *John Law: Economic Theorist and Policy Maker* (Oxford: Clarendon Press, 1997); on Law's long shadow in French history, see Rebecca L Spang, "The Ghost of Law: Speculating on Money, Memory and Mississippi in the French Constituent Assembly," *Historical Reflections / Réflexions historiques* 31, no. 1 (2005): 3–25.

92 On Laborde slaves, see Yves-René Durand, "Mémoires de Jean-Joseph de Laborde, fermier général et banquier de la cour," *Annuaire-Bulletin de la Société de l'histoire de France* (1968–1969): 106; see also Bernard Foubert, "Les habitations Laborde à Saint-Domingue dans la seconde moitié du dix-huitième siècle: Contribution à l'histoire d'Haiti, plaine des Cayes" (doctoral diss., Université Paris-Sorbonne, 1990). For sources on Laborde's plantations, see Papiers saisis sur François Lavignolle, régisseur de la première habitation du banquier Laborde, plaine des Cayes, Haiti, HCA 30 / 381, Prize Papers, UK National Archives (Kew). On Laborde as an Enlightenment arts patron, see François d'Ormesson and Jean-Pierre Thomas, *Jean-Joseph de la Borde: Banquier de Louis XVI, mécène des Lumières et inventeur des jardins de Méréville* (Paris: Taillandier, 2021).

93 Lilti, *Le monde des salons*, 129–131.

94 Pierre Ménard, *Le français qui possédait l'Amérique: La vie extraordinaire d'Antoine Crozat, milliardaire sous Louis XIV* (Paris: Cherche Midi, 2017); beyond

Crozat's privilege to trade with Louisiana, see, for instance, "Aux directeurs de la compagnie de l'Assiento au sujet de propositions présentées par le Sieur Crozat pour la fourniture des nègres sur le pied de 400 livres pièces d'Inde," 26 August 1705, Colonies B 26, fol. 155, ANOM; see also Colonies B 28, fol. 219.

95   The ceremony at Morne-Rouge launching the Haitian Revolution occurred near "an uncultivated section of the Choiseul plantation called 'le Caïman.'" See Marlene L. Daute, *An Intellectual History of the Haitian Revolution* (Chapel Hill: University of North Carolina Press, 2023), 112; on the Vicomte de Choiseul in Saint-Domingue, see M. L. E. Moreau de Saint-Méry, *Description topographique, physique, civile, politique et historique de la partie française de l'isle Saint-Domingue,* 2d ed., vol. 1 (Paris: T. Mongand, 1875), 169, 175; on slave trading and the Choiseul family, see François-Pierre Guillaudeu Duplessis, *Mémoire pour le Sieur Gillaudeu Duplessis, appellant, intimé, demandeur & défendeur, contre Demoiselle de Beauval, veuve du Marquis de Choiseul-Beaupré, intimée et défenderesse* (Paris: P. G. Simon, 1779); François-Joseph de Beaupré, Comte de Choiseul, was governor of Saint-Domingue from 1707 to 1710.

96   Gontaut-Biron participated in the recapture of French forts in Senegal during the War of American Independence. See "Gontaut-Biron, Armand Louis de, colonel des volontaires étrangers de la Marine, brigadier des troupes des colonies, gouverneur des pays et Ports du Sénégal," Colonies E 261, ANOM (digi).

97   The financial involvement of Amélie Boufflers in Pierre-Félix-Barthélemy David's slave-trading activities together with the Duchesse de Montmorency, her husband the Duc de Boufflers (then deceased), and the Comte and Comtesse de Châtelet is revealed in documents relating to the liquidation of David's assets in 1780 following the catastrophic failure of the Compagnie de la Guyane; the failure stemmed from the loss of many slave ships to the British. See printed document of 19 April 1780, Fonds de la Compagnie des Indes, Papiers de Barthélemy David, carton 1, NAF 28258, Manuscripts Department, Bibliothèque nationale de France.

98   On Brancas, see Bonnet Natacha Bonnet, "Les pay de Lathan: Histoire d'une famille angevine implantée à Saint-Domingue au XVIIIᵉ siècle," *Annales de Bretagne et des pays de l'Ouest* 107, no. 4 (2000): 51, 55–57. For digitized files relating to the Brancas family's estates in Saint-Domingue, see Colonies E 50 and Colonies E 67, ANOM (digi).

99   For colonial documents relating to Charles de Salaberry's perquisites in the colonies, see Colonies B 18, fol. 301 (dead colonists' property, 1691–1696); Colonies B 24, fol. 226 (Compagnie de Guinée, 1701); Colonies B 26, fol. 147, and B 28, fol. 211 (tax-free sugar shipped to France, 1705–1706), ANOM. On Charles de Salaberry's work in the department of the navy under Pontchartrain, see Jörg Ulbert, "Les bureaux du secrétariat d'État de la Marine sous Louis XIV (1669–1715)," in *La liasse et la plume,* ed. Jörg Ulbert and Sylviane Linares (Rennes: Presses universitaires de Rennes, 2017), 17–31; Didier Neuville, *État sommaire des Archives de la Marine antérieures à la Révolution* (Paris: L. Baudoin, 1898), xxix, n1.

200   *Notes to Pages 72–75*

100   Jean-Nicolas Dufort de Cheverny, *Mémoires sur les règnes de Louis XV et Louis XVI et sur la Révolution,* vol. 1 (Paris: E. Plon, Nourrit, 1886), 328; Antoine de Sartine, *Journal des Inspecteurs de Monsieur de Sartine, première série: 1761–1766, Documents inédits sur le règne de Louis XV* (Paris: Dentu, 1863). On Brissault's, see Gaston Capon, *Les maisons closes au XVIIIᵉ siècle: Académies de filles et courtières d'amour, maisons clandestines, matrones, mères-abbesses, appareilleuses et proxénètes: Rapports de police, documents secrets, notes personnelles des tenancières* (Paris: H. Daragon, 1903), 162–171.

101   Jean-Nicolas Dufort de Cheverny, *Mémoires sur les règnes de Louis XV et Louis XVI et sur la Révolution,* 2:75.

102   Examples of slave owners include the three Lameth brothers, Coustard de Saint-Lô (grandson of Jean's master in Chapter 1), and Gouvernet de la Tour du Pin, former governor of Tobago. Marcel Dorigny and Bernard Gainot reproduce the annotated list of attendees for each club session along with the minutes in *La Société des Amis des Noirs, 1788–1799: Contribution à l'histoire de l'abolition de l'esclavage* (Paris: UNESCO, 1998).

103   Antoine Lilti, "1769: The World's a Conversation," in *France in the World: A New Global History,* ed. Patrick Boucheron (New York: Other Press, 2019), 415–421. For a longer discussion of verbal communication, see Lilti, *Le monde des salons,* esp. 273–284, 401–405. Lilti's history of the salon opposes the depiction, by Jürgen Habermas and Dena Goodman, of the salon as an egalitarian sphere of enlightened exchange. See Dena Goodman, *The Republic of Letters: A Cultural History of the French Enlightenment* (Ithaca, NY: Cornell University Press, 1994); on applying Habermas to eighteenth-century France, see Keith Michael Baker, "Defining the Public Sphere in Eighteenth-Century France: Variations on a Theme by Habermas," in *Habermas and the Public Sphere,* ed. Craig Calhoun (Cambridge, MA: MIT Press, 1992), 181–211.

104   Judith N. Shklar, *The Faces of Injustice,* Storrs Lectures on Jurisprudence, Yale Law School, 1988 (New Haven, CT: Yale University Press, 1990), 51–53.

105   Jèze, *État ou tableau de la ville de Paris,* new ed. (Paris: Prault père, 1765), 339–341.

106   All details recounted here are from Muron's report to Sartine, Rapport concernant la nommée Pauline négresse (missing) June 1765, marked 6 June 1765 with initials MR, AB ms. 12,252, fol. 389.

107   For Gracis, see Jèze, *Tableau de Paris pour l'année 1759* (Paris: Hérissant, 1759), 190. For Sauvel, distiller, see *L'avant-coureur,* 28 November 1763, 764. For the caterer Mongenot, see Louis Mannory, *Plaidoyers et mémoires,* vol. 10 (Paris: Hérissant, 1764), 310. For the wine merchant on Rue du Mail, see *Annonces, affiches et avis divers,* 24 October 1765, 765. For Pierre Jelyotte, see Contre lettre faisant état d'une obligation de 20000 livres due par Pierre Jelyotte, chanteur de l'Opéra, haute-contre, pensionnaire du roi, demeurant place des Victoires, 2 August 1763, MC / ET / XXX / 380; for Labille, fashion merchant, see *Mercure de France* 1 August 1751, 194. On the cabinetmaker Erstet, see François de Salvert, *Les ébénistes*

du XVIIIe siècle (Paris: Van Oest, 1923), 109; Dame Martin, éventailliste, rue de la Vrillière, *Annonces, affiches, et avis divers,* 1 September 1763. Lacking information for 1765 alone, I have also incorporated information from years that immediately preceded and succeeded her arrival. For Louis Martin (fan maker), Gerard (carpenter), Edme Cottin (wine merchant) Quillain (barman, Café de Toulouse), and saddlers (Fourier, Ferierre, Temoigt), see Roze de Chantoiseau, *Essai sur l'almanach général d'indication d'adresse personnelle et domicile fixe, des six corps arts et métiers* (Paris: Veuve Duchesne, 1769).

108   Natacha Coquery, *L'hôtel aristocratique: Le marché du luxe à Paris au XVIIIe siècle,* vol. 39 of *Histoire Moderne* (Paris: Publications de la Sorbonne, 1998), 15; also Coquery, *Tenir boutique à Paris au XVIIIe siècle: Luxe et demi-luxe* (Paris: CTHS, 2011); Duma, *Les Bourbon-Penthièvre,* 514.

109   For statistics on violent confrontations with the police in 1765, see Arlette Farge and André Zysberg, "Les théâtres de la violence à Paris au XVIIIe siècle," *Annales: Économies, Sociétés, Civilisations* 5 (1979): 984–1015, esp. 986.

110   Jean Duma, *Les Bourbon-Penthièvre,* 191–194; for a partial list of people with apartments in the Hôtel de Toulouse, see appendix 75, p. 712. It is not clear why the Castellanes are missing from the above list. In the body of the work Duma says they lived there.

111   On Joseph Aza (Prince de Colonna), see AB ms. 12,230, and Colonies B 122, fol. 146, ANOM; Charles-Dominique Lazy (de Chambault), AB ms. 12,247 and Colonies B 122, fols. 161, 314; Pedre Alengin (Guer), AB ms. 12,230 and Colonies B 122, fol. 147; Hector (Rocques), AB ms. 12,245 and Colonies B 122, fol. 183; Charles-Auguste (Verdière), AB ms. 12,230 and Colonies B 122, fol. 216; Hélène (Ronseray), AB ms. 12,245 and Colonies B 122, fols. 232, 263, 316, 350, 401, 403; Cézar (Chevalier de Roy), AB ms. 12,235; Papillon (Loubois), AB ms. 12,252; François (Saige), AB mss. 10,748, 12,241, and Colonies B 122, fol. 315.

112   Durand, "Mémoires de Jean-Joseph de Laborde," 120. For an example of Colabau's activities as a slave trader, see Procuration générale: Gestion de la compagnie de la traite des nègres, 5 May 1761, MC / ET / LIX / 268, AN.

113   Martial Delpit, *Journal et correspondance* (Paris: Firmin Didot, 1897), 352.

3. LUCIDOR

1   For the list of members, see Jèze, *Tableau de Paris pour l'année 1759, formé d'après les antiquités, l'histoire, la description de cette ville* (Paris: C. Hérissant, 1759), 182–183. Also see *Statuts et règlemens, déclaration du Roy, lettres patentes [de septembre 1643, mai 1656 et décembre 1758] et arrêts du Parlement, sentence de la prévôté de l'Hôtel et arrêt du Grand Conseil confirmatif de ladite sentence, concernant l'exercice, les fonctions, la discipline et les privilèges des maîtres en fait d'armes des Académies du Roi, de la ville . . . de Paris* (Paris: Veuve Lamesle, 1760). On the guild, see Pascal Brioist, Hervé Drévillon, and Pierre Serna, *Croiser le fer: Violence et culture de l'épée*

202   *Notes to Pages 77–79*

dans la France moderne (Paris: Champvallon, 2002); Claudius Wackermann, *Histoire des maîtres d'armes* (Stockholm: Académie d'armes de Suède, Plein Chant, 2009); Pierre Serna, "Le manuel d'escrime: Science du savoir-vivre élégant ou 'art de tuer son homme proprement'?," *Dix-huitième siècle* 34 (2002): 349–370; Nick Evangelista, *The Encyclopedia of the Sword* (Westport, CT: Greenwood, 1995); Philippe Macquer, *Dictionnaire portatif des arts et métiers,* vol. 2 (Amsterdam: Rey, 1767), 122–124.

2   *Déclaration du roy, concernant le port d'armes, donnée à Versailles le 25 août 1737* (Paris: Simon, 1737).

3   Ordonnance du roi qui défend le port d'armes et les épaulettes à tous domestiques, et nommément à ceux appelés chasseurs, heiduques et aux nègres, Signed Louis and Amelot (1779); reprinted 1781 and 1785.

4   Prost de Royer and Pierre-Jacques Brillon, *Dictionnaire de jurisprudence et des arrêts, ou nouvelle édition du Dictionnaire de Brillon,* vol. 6 (Lyon: de la Roche, 1781–1784), s.v. "armes," esp. 475.

5   Stephen L. Kaplan, "Social Classification and Representation in the Corporate World of Eighteenth-Century France: Turgot's Carnival," in *Work in France: Representations, Meaning, Organization, and Practice,* ed. Steven Laurence Kaplan and Cynthia J. Koepp (Ithaca, NY: Cornell University Press, 2018), 176–228, esp. 182–183, 185, 192–194.

6   Kaplan, "Social Classification," 219; Kaplan, *La fin des corporations* (Paris: Fayard, 2001), 317–318; see, Journal Hardy, entry for 28 November 1777, 421.

7   Michael Sonenscher, *Work and Wages: Natural Law, Politics, and the Eighteenth-Century French Trades* (Cambridge: Cambridge University Press, 2012), 104.

8   These privileged places included the Faubourg Saint-Antoine, the cloister of Notre Dame, the courtyard of Saint-Benoit ou de la Trinité, and enclosures at Saint-Germain-des-Près, the Temple, Saint-Denis de la Chartre, Saint-Jean de Latran, Saint-Martin des Champs, and the Rue l'Oursine. There were also privileges for people who taught the poor at the Hôpital de la Trinité, the Hôpital Général, and the Hôpital de Notre Dame de la Miséricorde. On privileged places, see J. P. Mazaroz, *Histoire des corporations françaises d'arts et métiers* (Paris: Librairie Germer Ballière, 1878), 176; Etienne Martin Saint-Léon, *Histoire des corporations de métiers depuis leurs origines jusqu'à leur suppression en 1791* (Paris: Librairie Félix Alcan, 1922), 442, 509, 550–551. In his magnificent book on the Faubourg Saint-Antoine—a guild-free enclave outside the city's center—Alain Thillay chronicles efforts by the guilds to suppress all special zones, including the famous faubourg. Alain Thillay, *Le Faubourg Saint-Antoine et ses faux ouvriers: La liberté du travail à Paris au XVIIe et XVIIIe siècles* (Paris: Champ Vallon, 2002), 114.

9   *De Par le Roi S.A.S. Le duc de Penthièvre, amiral de France, et nosseigneurs de l'Amirauté de France, ordonnance portant injonction à toutes personnes demeurantes dans l'étendue de l'Amirauté particulières de son ressort qui ont à leur services des nègres ou mulâtres de l'un ou de l'autre sexe, d'en faire leur déclaration, en personne ou par*

procureur, aux greffes de l'Amirauté de la France, ou aux Greffes des amirautés par-
ticuliers de son ressort, sous telles peines qu'il appartiendra, 31 March and 3 April 1762,
AB ms. 12,160 (Louis, 1762).

10 Entry for 25 May 1762, Z^{1D} 139, AN.

11 Jean-Joseph Amat has a vast personnel file as agent of the navy in Pondicherry, the Cape of Good Hope, and Mauritius. See Colonies E 4, ANOM (digi).

12 On Allada, see especially Robin Law, *The Kingdom of Allada* (Leiden:
Research School CNWS, School of Asian, African, and Amerindian Studies,
1997); Law, "The Fall of Allada, 1724: An Ideological Revolution?," *Journal of the
Historical Society of Nigeria* 5, no. 1 (December 1969): 157–163; Law, "Dahomey and
the Slave Trade: Reflections on the Historiography of the Rise of Dahomey,"
Journal of African History 27, no. 2 (1986): 237–267; Law, "Jean Barbot as a Source
for the Slave Coast of West Africa," *History in Africa* 9 (1982): 155–173; Jacques
Lombard, "Contribution à l'histoire d'une ancienne société politique du Da-
homey: La royauté d'Allada," *Bulletin de l'Institut fondamental d'Afrique noire* 29,
no. 1–2 (1967): 40–66; David Ross, "Robert Norris, Agaja, and the Dahomean
Conquest of Allada and Whydah," *History in Africa* 16 (1989): 311–324. On the
Dahomeyan military state and its formation, see J. Cameron Monroe, *The Pre-
Colonial State in West Africa: Building Power in Dahomey* (New York: Cambridge
University Press, 2014); Monroe, "Building the State in Dahomey: Power and
Landscape on the Bight of Benin," in *Power and Landscape in Atlantic West Africa:
Archeological Perspectives,* ed. J. Cameron Monroe and Akinwumi Ogundiran
(New York: Cambridge University Press, 2012). On Whydah, see Robin Law, *Ouidah:
The Social History of a West African Slaving "Port," 1727–1892* (repr., Athens, OH:
Ohio University Press, 2015); Simone Berbain, *Le comptoir français de Juda (Ouidah)
au XVIIIe siècle* (Amsterdam: Swets & Zeitlinger, 1968); Elisabeth Heijmans, *The
Agency of Empire: Connections and Strategies in French Overseas Expansion (1686–1746)*
(Leiden: Brill, 2020).

13 Voyage ID 32894, *Junon,* Compagnie des Indes, Trans-Atlantic Slave Trade
Database, www.slavevoyages.org.

14 For an overview, see Koen Impens, "Essai de bibliographie des Azande,"
Annales Aequatoria 22 (2001): 449–514. On the uncertainties of early Zande history, see Emeka Onwubuemeli, "Early Zande History," *Sudan Notes and Records*
53 (1972): 36–66. On the making of the Azande, see Edward Evans Evans-Pritchard,
"The Ethnic Composition of the Azande of Central Africa," *Anthropological Quarterly* 31(October 1958): 95–118.

15 On Asante expansion, see Randy Sparks, *Where the Negroes Are Masters:
An African Port in the Era of the Slave Trade* (Cambridge, MA: Harvard University
Press, 2014).

16 Pierre-Philibert Blancheton and Catherine de Salins, marriage contract,
22 February 1728, in "Blancheton 1692–1756: Liasse 4–68," E89, Archives départementales de la Côte d'Or (Dijon) (hereafter ADCO). See also her petition of
separation to the lieutenant civil of Paris, 52 F 40, Fonds Blancheton, ADCO.

204 **Notes to Page 83**

Blancheton died on 6 March 1756 at the Château de Meursault in Burgundy. See inventory of family townhouse in Beaune, 13 July 1756, and of Paris townhouse, 6 September 1756, in 52 F 44, Fonds Blancheton, ADCO; testament of his mother, Henriette Broussard, 27 April 1757, and posthumous inventory of Chévry château, 27 August 1757, both in 52 F 27, Fonds Blancheton, ADCO.

17   Chenaye-Desbois, *Dictionnaire de la noblesse,* vol. 11 (Paris: 1786), s.v. "Prévost de la Croix"; Etienne Broglin, "Dictionnaire biographique sur les pensionnaires de l'académie royale de Juilly," s.v. "de Salins," unpublished manuscript, Centre Roland Mousnier.

18   Robert Prévost (1654–1712) is from a peasant family in Montreuil. For the document of his appointment as stockbroker, see Réception à l'office d'agent de change et banque à Paris, 20 September 1678, Y 3982A, AN. His marriage contract (26 April 1676) with Catherine Pézant describes him as the son of "defunct Robert Prévost, laboreur," MC/ET/LXIX/83, AN. In 1705 Prévost becomes a financial advisor to the Crown. See Provision d'office, 30 April 1705, V^2 38, AN. For his testament, which lists his many debts to the financier Samuel Bernard, see 20 September 1712, MC/ET/LII/175, AN.

19   On the Lestobec family, see Philippe Haudrère, "L'origine du personnel de direction général de la Compagnie des Indes, 1719–1794," *Revue française d'histoire d'outre-mer* 67, no. 248–249 (1980): 354. Jean-François Lestobec has two personnel files in the colonial archives. See "Lestobec directeur de la compagnie des Indes à Lorient," Colonies E 282 (1730), ANOM (digi). See also "Saint-Catherine, directeur de la Compagnie des Indes, à Port Louis, simple avis de sa mort et demande du sieur de Lestobec pour remplir sa place demeurée vacante" (1731), Colonies E 354, ANOM (digi).

20   Marc Perrichet, "Plume ou épée: Problèmes de carrières dans quelques familles d'officiers d'administration de la marine au XVIIIe siècle," *Actes du quatre-vingt-onzième congrès national des Sociétés savantes* (Rennes, 1966), 145–166.

21   See Pierre H. Boulle, "Slave Trade, Commercial Organization and Industrial Growth in Eighteenth-Century Nantes," *Revue française d'histoire d'outre-mer* 59, no. 214 (1972): 70–112; Olivier Pétré Grenouilleau, *Nantes au temps de la traite des noirs* (Paris: Hachette, 2007); Gaston Martin, *Nantes au XVIIIe siècle: L'ère des négriers* (1931; repr., Paris: Karthala, 1993); Robert Louis Stein, "The Profitability of the Nantes Slave Trade, 1783–1792," *Journal of Economic History* 35, no. 4 (1975): 779–793.

22   The pioneer on this topic in Old Regime France is Jeffrey Merrick, *Sodomy in Eighteenth-Century France* (Newcastle-upon-Tyne: Cambridge Scholars, 2020); for a useful comparative perspective in the early modern context, see Kent Gerard, Hekma Gert, and James W. Jones, eds., *The Pursuit of Male Homosexuality in Renaissance and Enlightenment Europe,* special issue, *Journal of Homosexuality* 16, no. 1/2 (1989). The document I cite here results in imprisonment without trial. On the legal dimension of sexual deviance in Old Regime France, see Ludovico Hernandez, *Les procès de sodomie aux XVIe, XVIIe et XVIIIe*

Notes to Pages 84–89   205

siècles: Publiés d'après les documents judiciaires conservés à la Bibliothèque nationale (Paris: Bibliothèque des Curieux, 1920); see also F. Carlier, *Les deux prostitutions* (Paris: E. Dentu, 1888).

23   8 September 1733, André Lucidor (1733), AB ms. 11,231.

24   On Capolin and Rama, see Y 11,356, AN, and AB ms. 12,234, which both concern their theft and fencing of stolen goods in August 1765. Rama (but not Capolin) was declared to the Admiralty. See declaration by the Comte d'Estaing of 3 March, 1763, Z^{1d} 139, AN. On Capolin, see Jeffrey S. Ravel, "The Coachman's Bare Rump: An Eighteenth-Century French Cover-up," *Eighteenth-Century Studies* 40, no. 2 (2007): 279–308.

25   Louis-Sébastien Mercier, "Chapitre 604: Bicêtre," in *Le Tableau de Paris,* vol. 8, new ed. (Amsterdam, 1782–1788), 1–2.

26   André Lucidor (1733), AB ms. 11,231.

27   Examples include Girod (21 May 1727), Duhamel (1 April 1728), Fleury, Jean Dumont (5 May 1729), Michel Gautier (14 August 1730), Jean Gallé (12 September 1735), AB ms. 10,257, fols. 15, 121, 176, 189, 227, 339; Jean Fournier (18 April 1727), fol. 102. Fleury (fol. 176) seeks a valet with whom he can have sex. Sting operations of 3 May and 22 September 1737 involved people identified as lackeys and unemployed domestic servants; see AB ms. 10,258, fols. 151, 241. Louis-Caesar Rolland was said to be cohabiting sinfully with his lackey (20 August 1733), AB ms. 10,258, fol. 223.

28   Comte de Lisle (21 June 1728), AB ms. 10,257.

29   Desjardins (4 August 1730), AB ms. 10,257, fol. 263.

30   File of Robert dit Lacroix (13 June 1736), AB ms. 10,258, fol. 66.

31   Signed affidavit of 12 February 1737, AB ms. 1131, fol. 143.

32   The ceremony took place on 12 January 1745 in the Church of Saint-Séverin (Paris). See Mariages à Paris (1613–1805), Fonds Andriveau. The previous husband of Lucidor's wife, François Bourval, died at the Hôtel des Invalides in 1743, where he was admitted on 6 December 1731 after losing a hand in a fall from his horse. He is described in French records as a Portuguese-speaking Moor from Lisbon who served as a drummer in the Rosen cavalry, a German regiment. See GR 2Xy25, act 046868, Services historiques de la Défense, Vincennes (hereafter SHD).

33   Registre paroissial de Rueil-la-Gadelière, 3 E 322 / 05, p. 170, Archives départementales de L'Eure et Loir (digi).

34   André Corvisier, "Les soldats noirs du Maréchal de Saxe: Le problème des antillais et africains sous les armes en France au XVIIIe siècle," *Outre-Mers: Revue d'histoire* (1968): 408.

35   Preuve de majorité, 12 August 1754, Z^{1o} 205B, AN. The formulaic language in these sources required all foreigners without baptism certificates to prove that they were adults, Catholic, and free. This formula might suggest that the curate refused to marry Lircot because he suspected the man was a slave. In fact, every single document in this overlooked series, which overwhelmingly concerns Frenchmen, uses the same formula.

206 *Notes to Pages 90–92*

36   La Curne de Sainte-Palaye, *Dictionnaire historique de la langue française ou Glossaire de la langue française depuis son origine jusqu'au siècle de Louis XIV,* vol. 6 (Paris: H. Champion, 1879), s.v. "ferrailleur"; Furétière, *Dictionnaire universel,* 3rd ed. (1708); Denis Diderot et Jean d'Alembert, eds., *L'Encyclopédie,* vol. 6 (1756); *Dictionnaire de l'Académie française* (1718, 1740, 1762, 1798).

37   For a later raid and sentence against ferrailleurs, see Henri Daressy, *Archives des maîtres d'armes* (Paris: Maison Quantin, 1888), 18–19; for an early history of fencing, see Anglo Sydney, *The Martial Arts of Renaissance Europe* (New Haven, CT: Yale, 2000).

38   Noblemen who chose to buy commissions as officers without first attending military academies needed this instruction. See Jean Chagniot, "La formation des officiers à la fin de l'ancien régime," *Revue historique des armées* 228 (2002): 3–10. Fencing also became part of gentlemanly education for people outside the nobility. For England, see Robert B. Shoemaker, "The Taming of the Duel: Masculinity, Honour and Ritual Violence in London, 1660–1800," *Historical Journal* 45, no. 3 (2002): 525–545; Ashley L. Cohen, "Fencing and the Market in Aristocratic Masculinity," in *Sporting Cultures, 1650–1850,* ed. Daniel O'Quinn and Alexis Tadié (University of Toronto Press, 2018), 66–90. Recreational dueling became popular among French soldiers during the Revolution—expanding in popularity in the nineteenth century. Drawing blood in recreational duels was thought to cement male friendship. Laurence Montroussier, "La pratique du duel dans l'armée du premier XIXème siècle au travers des mémoires," *Revue historique des armées* 230 (2003): 77–86, esp. 80. On women and fencing, see Dominique Godineau, "De la guerrière à la citoyenne: Porter les armes pendant l'ancien régime et la Révolution française," *Clio: Femmes, genre, histoire,* no. 20 (2004): 43–69; Arsène Vigieant, *La bibliographie de l'escrime ancienne et moderne* (Paris: Motteroz, 1882); see also Alexandre Dumas, *Le maître d'armes* (1840), about a fencing master in Russia. On the popularity of fencing in France during the late nineteenth century (in an account that ignores the eighteenth-century sport), see Robert A. Nye, "Fencing, the Duel and Republican Manhood in the Third Republic," *Journal of Contemporary History* 25, no. 2/3 (1990): 365–377. On modern duels of honor (not sport), see Mika Lavaque-Monty, "Dueling for Equality: Masculine Honor and the Modern Politics of Dignity," *Political Theory* 34, no. 6 (2006): 715–740.

39   Bail, 8 January 1702, Henry-François Rousseau maître en fait d'armes des pages de la grande et petite écuries et provôt d'armes Estienne Lebreton, ET / VII / 168, AN.

40   Letter of Hyacinth Serval to LGP, 2 December 1787, and voluminous court case, in T/1294/4, AN.

41   On Marteau, and the insignia of the guild, see the Henri Paressy, *Archives des maîtres d'armes de Paris,* 20–21; see also Brioist et al., *Croiser le fer,* 89. On Gardinier, see "Permission de poser un enseigne," 11 August 1731, Minutes, Z^2 3724, AN.

42   Alain Mercier, *La deuxième fille de Cluny: Grandeurs et misères de Saint-Martin des Champs* (Paris: Glénat, 2021); Camille Pascal, "Politique immobilière

Notes to Pages 92–93   207

et esprit de quartier: L'exemple de Saint-Martin-des-Champs au XVIIIe siècle," *Cahiers du CREPIF* 38 (March 1992): 78–85. See also Marie-Odile Perulli, "Un enclos privilégié à Paris au XVIIIe siècle: Saint-Martin-des-Champs d'après les archives de baillage," Mémoire de maîtrise (1968), Bibliothèque historique de la ville de Paris.

43   See, for instance, the suit between Monsieur Daniel and Monsieur Levi in Référés et enquêtes, Z^2 3728, AN.

44   See request of the fiscal prosecutor of 2 October 1754 relating to Ulrick dit Saxe, Gotlib, Mathieu, Leinitz, and Duchesnay, Minutes, Z^2 3725B, AN; and of 17 July 1755 about Michel, cabinetmaker, in Régistre audiences, Z^2 3719–3721, AN.

45   See affair involving Sieur Sabot, Marchand Boucher, 6 May 1762, in Minutes, Z^2 3725A, AN.

46   The ordinance appears under the date 6 June 1755 (repeating previous regulations of other years), in Régistre audiences du 29 January 1727–7 August 1755, Z^2 3719–3721, AN.

47   Natalie Zemon Davis, "The Reasons of Misrule: Youth Groups and Charivaris in Sixteenth-Century France," *Past & Present,* no. 50 (1971): 41–75.

48   Pierre-Jacques Brillon, *Dictionnaire des arrests ou jurisprudence universelle des parlements de France et autres tribunaux,* vol. 1 (Paris: Cavelier, 1711), s.v. "charivari." See also *Dictionnaire de jurisprudence et des arrêts, ou nouvelle édition du Dictionnaire de Brillon,* vol. 1 (Lyon: Imprimerie de la Roche, 1781–1788), 726.

49   See transcript of the affair involving Gagneux of 2 September 1756 in Z^2 3719–3721, AN.

50   Of the Prévost residence on the Rue Saint-Martin, see Transport de bail, 11 October 1712, MC/ET/LII/175, AN.

51   See *Dépôt au greffe d'une feuille à éventail représentant le marché de Saint Martin trouvée chez le Sieur Barbe,* minutes, 29 July 1764, with fan painting enclosed, Z^2 3742, AN.

52   Vente Estienne Jean Jacques Pry à André Lucidor et sa femme, 29 October 1756, MC/ET/LXXIX/94, AN.

53   I am basing this depiction of Ménilmontant on the registers of the tax attorney, which include references to Belleville. Proprietors mentioned there include Pierre Lemoine, master luthier in Paris (23 November 1767); Jacques Philibert, master caterer in Paris and wife Marie-Genevieve Baudin (20 July 1761), who inherited the property from her parents; Pierre Galoppin dit Dubois, another master caterer from Paris (9 June 1787). On grocers, see unpaid rent by Germain Lienard, fruit merchant in Paris (17 May 1756). Drinking: Parisian bourgeois at cabaret Ste. Geneviève complains of rough treatment (29 July 1776); jewelry workers Alexis Drumont, Jacques Oudart, and Georges Blanquet refresh themselves at Legrand's cabaret (6 July 1781); bourgeois strollers fall in a ditch near the Cabaret Bel Air (24 July 1778); Parisian dancing master rents house to hold large party in Belleville (21 June 1775), Z^2 1328–1329, AN.

208   *Notes to Pages 94–97*

54   Anne Conchon, Hélène Noizet, et Michel Ollion, *Les limites de Paris (XIIᵉ–XVIIIᵉ siècles)* (Villeneuve d'Ascq: Presses universitaires du Septentrion, 2017), 45–46. Alain Thilay dates the creation of Faubourg Saint-Antoine—a privileged enclave—to the 1630s. He notes that Chaillot, which became a faubourg in 1707, was exempted from being patrolled by the Paris arts and crafts police, whereas no such exemption applied to the newly created Faubourg de la Roule (1722). See Thilay, *Le Faubourg Saint-Antoine et ses faux ouvriers: La liberté du travail à Paris au XVIIᵉ et XVIIIᵉ siècles* (Paris: Champ Vallon, 2002), 19, 121.

55   Ménilmontant looks bucolic in Rousseau's writings, but less so in the village archives. See Denis Goguet, "De la rue Platrière à la haute borne: Sur les pas de Rousseau l'avant dernier jeudi du mois d'octobre 1776," in *L'accident de Ménilmontant,* ed. Anouchka Vasak (Paris: Classiques Garnier, 2015), 23–40. Compare regulations of 3 June 1749 *qui font deffences à tous particuliers mêmes aux boueurs de Paris de décharger sur le grand chemin pavée qui conduit de ce lieu à Paris des tas de boues, matière foecales, fumiers, et autres immondices,* Z² 1324, AN.

56   See 11 July 1766, 3 March 1768, 26 January 1769, and 19 July 1770, Registres d'audience du baillage de Saint-Martin-des-Champs à Paris, 1755–1770, Z² 3719–3721, AN.

57   Erick Noël, ed., *Dictionnaire des gens de couleur dans la France moderne,* vol. 1, *Paris et son bassin* (Geneva: Droz, 2011), 27–28. See also Pierre Bardin, "Lucidor, ancien esclave et sa fille Marie-Thérèse, à Paris," *Généalogie et histoire de la Caraïbe,* 227 (July–August 2009): 5982–5985.

58   These details are all from the same source, Brioist et al., *Croiser le fer,* 100.

59   See arrangements for the payment of arrears in *titre nouvelle,* 26 January 1761, MC / ET / 4278 / XLIII; inventory of 12 December 1771, MC / ET / XXXVII / 109, AN; for the report by mason, see Z¹ʲ 961, dossier 9, AN.

60   See tweet by Julie Duprat for Black History Month in 2021 and https://tanlistwa.com/2018/08/25/andre-dit-lucidor-v-1718-1771-a-life-between-3-continents/.

61   George Sand, *Histoire de ma vie* (Paris: Quarto Gallimard, 2004), 77–78.

62   Joseph-Marie-Jacques-Ambroise de Bonald, *Samuel Bernard: Banquier du Trésor royal et de sa descendance* (Rodez: Imprimerie Carrère, 1912), xl–xli; Yves Durand, *Les Fermiers généraux au XVIIIᵉ siècle* (Paris: Maisonneuve et Larose, 1996), 157.

63   On the Hermitage, see Jean-Jacques Rousseau, *Confessions,* trans. J. M. Cohen (London: Penguin, 1953), bk. 8 (1754–1756), 369. See also *Mémoires de Madame d'Épinay* (Paris: Bibliothèque Charpentier, 1863), 2:114–117.

64   Prévost, *Mémoire pour les enfants et héritiers du feu Sieur Prevôt (Prevost), secrétaire du roi, payeur des rentes de l'hôtel de ville de Paris, banquier et agent de change, appelants, contre le sieur Samuel Barnard, banquier à Paris, intimé* (Paris: Veuve Le Mercier, 1739).

65   François Lesure, "The Music Department of the Bibliothèque nationale," *Notes* 35, no. 2 (1978): 251–268; Lionel de La Laurencie, *Inventaire critique du fonds*

Notes to Pages 98–103   209

Blancheton de la Bibliothèque du Conservatoire de Paris (Paris: Société française de musicologie, 1931).

66   Georges Cucuel, *La Pouplinière et la musique de chambre au XVIIIe siècle* (Paris: Librairie Fischbacher, 1913), 332–333; Gaston de Villeneuve-Guibert, *La portefeuille de Madame Dupin, dame de Chenonceaux: Lettres et œuvres inédites de Madame Dupin, l'abbé de Saint-Pierre, Voltaire, Jean-Jacques Rousseau, Montesquieu, Mably, &c.* (Paris: Lévy, 1884), 11–12.

67   De par le roi, ordonnance portant injonction à toute personnes demeurantes dans l'étendue de l'Amirauté . . . qui ont à leur service des nègres ou mulâtres de l'un ou de l'autre sexe, 5 April 1765, see Louis file, AB ms. 12,160.

68   On Pharaon, Corinne, Fanchon, and Marie Jeanne, see Sue Peabody, *"There Are No Slaves in France": The Culture of Race and Slavery in the Ancien Régime* (New York: Oxford University Press, 1996), 53–55; Noël, *Dictionnaire des gens de couleur*, for Corinne (no. 136), AB ms. 11,941 (1756); for the convocation of the case to the royal council, see report of 17 January 1756, Colonies A6, ANOM.

69   See letter from Sartine to Commissioner Delafleutrie and the minutes of the same day, 13 October 1762, in Y 15,4651, AN.

70   François-Saige dossier, AB ms. 10,748.

71   Plainte du 9 décembre 1767, le Sieur Lucidor contre le nommé Chemitz et sa femme, la femme Roché, et autres, Z² 3744–3745, AN.

72   Appendix to statement of 9 December 1767, Z² 3744–3745, AN.

73   Signed affidavit, Docteur Regent de la Faculté de Médecine de Paris (illegible signature), 18 January 1768, Z² 3744–3745, AN.

74   Appendix to statement of 9 December 1767, Z² 3744–3745, AN.

75   The word *morisco,* absent from all eighteenth-century French dictionaries, is defined in a French-English dictionary from this period as the name of a Moorish dance. In Spanish, *morisco* referred to one of the Christianized Muslims who remained in Spain until their expulsion in 1609. See, for instance, Mercedes García-Arenal, "Religious Dissent and Minorities: The Morisco Age," *Journal of Modern History* 81, no. 4 (2009): 888–920. The word also had a distinct meaning in Spanish colonial taxonomies of racial mixture. The Morisco was "the fifteenth race, from a Spaniard and a *Mulata*." See Richard Twiss, *Voyage en Portugal et en Espagne par Richard Twiss, gentilhomme anglais* (Berne: 1776), 373.

76   Note dated 18 July 1767, the date of the door incident. The note was written afterward. "Le dit Lucidor nous a appris cela à la fin du mois d'octobre 1767." See Z² 3744–3745, AN.

4. JULIEN

1   Sources consulted for this paragraph include *L'arracheur de dents sur le Pont-Neuf* (print, seventeenth century); Claude-Stephen Le Paulmier, *L'Orviétan, histoire d'une famille de charlatans du Pont-Neuf aux XVIIe et XVIIIe siècles* (Paris:

210 *Notes to Pages 103–110*

Librairie illustrée, 1893); Liliane Korb, *Le Pont-Neuf à travers les siècles* (Paris: Flammarion, 1997); *Almanach de la Samaritaine avec ses prédictions pour l'année 1787* (Paris, 1787); *Le Voisin de la Samaritaine, étrennes du Pont-Neuf . . . avec les numéros qu'il faut prendre pour gagner à la loterie royale de France* (Paris: à la descente du Pont-Neuf, 1787).

2 *Mémoire pour Julien Baudelle, Américain, Contre le Sieur Ruste de Rezeville, Négociant de la Martinique, et Demoiselle Reine Baudelle, son épouse, appelllans, en présence du Procureur Général, plaignant et accusateur, contre la Dame Ruste et Sieur Ozenne* (Paris: Nyon, 1787). The author of this text was Jean-Pierre-Louis Delaval (1744–1813), who served as Julien's legal representative (*procureur*). All parenthetical page numbers that I provide in this chapter refer to this text.

3 Jacques Michel, *Du Paris de Louis XV à la marine de Louis XVI: L'œuvre de Monsieur de Sartine* (Paris: Éditions de l'érudit, 1983), 141; François-Fortuné Fernand-Michel, *Histoire philosophique et anecdotique du bâton depuis les temps les plus reculés jusqu'à nos jours* (Paris: Librairie de la Société des gens de lettres, 1873).

4 Louis Sébastien Mercier, *Tableau de Paris,* new ed., vol. 1 (Amsterdam, 1783), 172–173.

5 Pierre Chenon, Interrogation of Louis-Pierre Hazard, 15 January 1762, Grand Châtelet Prison, Y 11346, AN.

6 Note of 30 March 1787, "Ruste de Rezeville, commissaire du commerce pour les intérêts de la métropole à la Martinique et Baudelle sa femme, 1787 / 1789," 575, Colonies E 360, ANOM (digi).

7 Louis-Petit de Bachaumont et al., *Mémoires secrets pour server à l'histoire de la République des lettres en France* (London chez John Adamson, 1789), 35:57–58 ("to be false"), 35:180–181 ("applause"), 35:295 ("so-called negro"), 36:3 ("become free").

8 *Mémoires secrets,* 35:181 ("adversaires"), 35:185 ("back to the colonies").

9 Pierre-Ferdinand Ozenne to Castries, 16 April 1787, in Ruste de Rezevelle personnel file, Colonies E 360, pp. 579–581, ANOM (digi).

10 Entry for 17 January 1790, in *Arthur Young's Travels in France for the Years 1787, 1788, 1789,* ed. Mathilda Betham-Edwards (London: G. Bell and Sons, 1906), 303–304 (digi).

11 Unsigned précis of Julien case dated 30 March 1787 in Ruste de Rezeville personnel file, Colonies E 360, p. 29, ANOM (digi).

12 Claude-Nicolas Le Cat, *Traité de la couleur de la peau humaine en général, de celle des nègres en particulier, et de la métamorphose d'une de ces couleurs en l'autre, soit de naissance, soit accidentellement* (Amsterdam: n.p., 1765), 10.

13 David A. Bell, *The Cult of the Nation in France: Inventing Nationalism, 1680–1800* (Cambridge, MA: Harvard University Press, 2003); see also William H. Sewell Jr., *A Rhetoric of Bourgeois Revolution: The Abbé Sieyès and What Is the Third Estate? Bicentennial Reflections on the French Revolution* (Durham, NC: Duke University Press, 1994).

Notes to Pages 110–115   211

14   Louis-Félix Guinement Keralio, *Encyclopédie méthodique,* vol. 3 (Paris: Pancoucke, 1787), s.v. "art militaire," 14 (digi).

15   For Godard's text, see "Réclamation de liberté," in *Causes célèbres, curieuses et intéressantes de toutes les cours souveraines du royaume, avec les jugements qui les ont décidées,* ed. Nicolas-Toussaint Des Essarts, vol. 168 (Paris: 1788), 3–74. I am grateful to Gerard Leval for sharing his unpublished manuscript, "Lobbying for Equality: Jacques Godard and the Struggle for Jewish Equality during the French Revolution."

16   Dominique Rogers, "De l'origine du préjugé de couleur en Haïti," *Outre-Mers* 90, no. 340–341 (2003): 83–101, esp. 86–88.

17   Doris Garraway, "Race, Reproduction, and Family Romance in Moreau de Saint-Méry's Description de la partie française de l'isle Saint-Domingue," *Eighteenth-Century Studies* 38, no. 2 (Winter 2005): 227–246. On Moreau de Saint-Méry in wider context, see Sara E. Johnson, *Encyclopédie noire: The Making of Moreau de Saint-Méry's Intellectual World* (Chapel Hill: University of North Carolina Press, 2023).

18   Dominique Rogers, "Raciser la sociéé: Un projet administratif pour une société domingoise complexe (1760–1791)," *Journal de la Société des américanistes* 95, no. 2 (2009).

19   "Delpech, Antoine, habitant de Sainte Lucie," Colonies E 117, ANOM (digi).

20   Henri de la Perrière, *Une vieille famille malouine: Les Magon* (Paris: Bibliothèque d'Héraldica, 1911); L. Vignols, "La campagne négrière de *La Perle* et sa réussite extraordinaire," *Revue historique* 163, no. 1 (1930); Léon Vignols, "Le commerce maritime et les aspects du capitalisme commercial à Saint-Malo de 1680 à 1792: Simples aperçus d'après des textes inédits," *Revue d'histoire économique et sociale* 19, no. 1 (1931).

21   Johan-Casper Lavater to Marie-Jean Hérault de Séchelles, 19 August 1784, FA Lavater, ms. 564.112, Zentralbibliothek Zürich (digi).

22   Émile Dard, *Un épicurien sous la Terreur: Hérault de Séchelles (1759–1794) d'après les documents inédits* (Paris: Librairie académique, 1907), 25–29.

23   See perquisition chez la Dame Van Fleury (6 August 1787) and perquisition avec Monsieur Henri chez la Veuve Dubois (17 July 1787), Y 11,430, AN.

24   *Phénomènes extraordinaires vivants,* printed advertisement in octavo (Paris: Cailleau, January 1787), Bibliothèque nationale de France (digi).

25   Anne Lafont, *L'art et la race: L'Africain (tout) contre l'œil des Lumières: Oeuvres en sociétés* (Dijon: Les Presses du réel, 2019), esp. chap. 1, which Lafont devotes to the white monstrosity obsession in visual culture.

26   Dorvigny, *Le nègre blanc: Comédie en un acte et en prose par Monsieur Dorvigny représentée à Versailles devant leurs majestés et à Paris sur le Théâtre des variétés amusantes, le 28 juin 1780* (Paris: Chez Cailleau, 1780).

27   Andrew Curran, *The Anatomy of Blackness: Sciences and Slavery in the Age of Enlightenment* (Baltimore: Johns Hopkins University Press, 2011), 171. Curran

212 Notes to Pages 115–117

treats the theme of albinism extensively; see esp. 89–105. On degeneration, see also Henry Louis Gates and Andrew S. Curran, *Who's Black and Why? A Hidden Chapter from the Eighteenth-Century Invention of Race* (Cambridge MA: Harvard University Press, 2022), 3–43.

28 Henry Skipworth to Thomas Jefferson, 20 January 1784, *The Papers of Thomas Jefferson* (Princeton, NJ: Princeton University Press, 2020), 6:472.

29 Natasha Trethewey, "The Americans," *Callaloo* 35, no. 4 (2012): 845.

30 Léo Elisabeth, *La société martiniquaise aux XVII* et XVIII* siècles, 1664–1789* (Paris: Karthala, 2003), 290–292, 315–317; on the Louisianan text, see Guillaume Aubert, "'To Establish One Law and Definite Rules': Race, Religion, and the Transatlantic Origins of the Louisiana Code Noir," in *Louisiana: Crossroads of the Atlantic World,* ed. Cécile Vidal (Philadelphia: University of Pennsylvania Press, 2014), 21–43.

31 The classic work on French colonial race law is Yvan Debbasch, *Couleur et liberté: Le jeu du critère ethnique dans un ordre juridique esclavagiste,* 2 vols. (Paris: Dalloz, 1967); for a broad look at French colonial law relating to interracial sex and marriage, see Mélanie Lamotte, "Beyond the Atlantic: Unifying Racial Policies across the Early French Empire," *William and Mary Quarterly* 81, no. 1 (2024): 3–36; on interracial intimacy and the Code Noir in Louisiana, see Cécile Vidal, *Empire, Race, and the Making of a Slave Society* (Williamsburg: Omohundro Institute of Early American History and Culture; Chapel Hill: University of North Carolina Press, 2019); on the color line and interracial sex in Saint-Domingue, see Doris Garraway, "The Libertine Colony: Desire, Miscegenation, and the Law," in *The Libertine Colony: Creolization in the Early French Caribbean* (Durham, NC: Duke University Press, 2005), 194–239.

32 *Annales du conseil souverain de la Martinique ou tableau historique du gouvernement de cette colonie depuis son premier établissement jusqu'à nos jours auquel on a joint l'analyse raisonnée des loix qui y ont été publiées avec des réflexions sur l'utilité ou l'insuffisance de chacune de ces loix en particulier* (Bergerac: B. Puynesge, 1786), 103–104.

33 Mémoire particulier de M. Hurson au sujet des registres de paroisses et baptêmes des mulâtres et mestifs, 22 August 1752, Colonies C^{8A} 59, fol. 304, ANOM. See Guillaume Aubert, "Kinship, Blood, and the Emergence of the Racial Nation in the French Atlantic World, 1600–1789," in *Blood and Kinship: Matter for Metaphor from Ancient Rome to the Present,* ed. Christopher H. Johnson et al. (New York: Berghan Books, 2013), 175–195.

34 For examples of Parisian pregnancy announcements at the time of the Julien affair, see, for instance, Déclaration par la fille Briand au sujet de sa grossesse (24 March 1787), Déclaration de grossesse Delarue (19 January 1787), and déclaration de grossesse Deviterne (29 April 1787), Y 11,430, AN. Julie Hardwick challenges traditional top-down understandings of these announcements to reframe them as demands for redress actuated by women and families, rather than regulatory obligations. See Julie Hardwick, *Sex in an Old Regime City: Young*

Workers and Intimacy in France, 1660–1789 (New York: Oxford University Press, 2020), esp. 41–49.

35 No. 472, Ordonnance de MM les général et intendant faisant défenses aux gens de couleur de porter les noms des blancs, 6 January 1773, in *Code de la Martinique,* ed. Martin Durand-Molard (Saint-Pierre, Martinique: J. B. Thounens, 1807–1814), 3:151–153.

36 No. 484, Ordonnance de MM. Les général et intendant, concernant les gens de couleur libres, qui prennent les noms des blancs leurs anciens maîtres ou protecteurs, 4 March 1774, in Durand-Molard, *Code de la Martinique,* 168.

37 Petition, Louis-Joseph Anson to Cambacérès, 8 fructidor an V (25 August 1797), D/III 240, AN (Pierrefitte).

38 Unsigned letter of 24 May 1771 from an official in the navy at the time when Fontenelle sought letters of nobility. He was ennobled seven years later, on 24 April 1778. See "Saillenfest de Fontenelles, Charles François Antoine, sénéchal de la juridiction et lieutenant-général de l'amirauté de Port-au-Prince à Saint-Domingue 1746–1830," Colonies E187, ANOM (digi).

39 Plainte du Sieur de Grouchet, 13 juillet 1792, Sections de Paris: Procès-verbaux des commissaires de police, Museum (August 1791–July 1792), A[A] 183, Archives de la Préfecture de Police (Pré-Saint-Gervais).

40 AB ms. 12,230 (Pèdre Alengin, 1765).

41 AB ms. 12,245 (Hélène, 1765).

42 Poncet de la Grave to Antoine de Sartine, 16 June 1763, AB ms. 12,196 (Pierre Scipion).

43 For Hélène, see belated registration on 18 July 1765, Z[1D] 139, AN; see also AB ms. 12,245; for the quarrel between Hélène's master and Poncet de la Grave, the prosecutor for the Admiralty Court, see *Mémoire pour M. Claude-Denis de Ron-ceray, ci-devant substitute du procureur du roi au siège royal de Saint Louis . . . contre Monsieur le Procureur Général, intimé,* Colonies E 357, ANOM (digi).

44 Déclaration du roy pour la police des noirs, 9 August 1777, in *Recueil des déclarations, édits, lettres patentes, et arrêts du Conseil d'état du Roi, enregistrés au parlement de Dijon* (Dijon: Imprimerie du Roy, 1777), 94–98 (digi).

45 Arrêt du Conseil d'état pour la police des noirs mulâtres ou autres gens de couleur, qui sont dans la ville de Paris (11 January 1778), in *Le Code noir ou recueil des règlements rendus jusqu'à présent concernant le gouvernement, l'administration de la justice, la police, la discipline et le commerce des nègres dans les colonies françaises, et les conseils et compagnies établis à ce sujet* (Paris: L. F. Prault, Imprimeur du roi, 1783), 510–513 (digi).

46 Arrêt du Conseil d'état du roi concernant les mariages des noirs mulâtres et autres gens de couleur (5 April 1778), in *Le Code noir,* 518–520 (digi).

47 Joly de Fleury, Mémoire signifié pour le nommé Francisque, Indien de nation, néophyte de l'Église romaine, intimé, contre le sieur Allain-François Ignace Brignon, se disant écuyer, appellant (Paris: Simon, Imprimeur du Parlement, 1759), esp. 25.

214   *Notes to Pages 120–125*

48   Déclaration de 30 August 1791, Sections de Paris, Fontaine de Grenelle, A^A148, Archives de la Préfecture de Police (Pré Saint-Gervais).

49   6P612: disarmament at Le Havre (1783), 260 (*Aimable Françoise*), registres matricules des gens de mer, rôles des bâtiments de commerce, Inscription maritime, Archives départementales de Seine maritime (digi).

50   AB ms. 1027, Collection Joly de Fleury, fols. 234–236.

51   On these unions, see marriage contract between Jean-François Corbin dit Desjardins and Marie-Thérèse Lucidor, 27 August 1785, MC/ET/CXV/945, AN. For the dissolution of their household and of her stake in his business a few months later, see Convention Le Sieur Corbin dit Desjardin et La Dame Lucidor, 15 December 1785, MC/ET/XXI/534, AN. On the marriage of her sister, see contract of Jean-François Maillard and Marie-Louise Lucidor, 4 April 1780, MC/ET/CXV/914, AN. On the violent revelry of Corbin prior to his marriage to Marie-Thérèse, see Procès-verbal fait contre Bonnefans et Corbin, 4 July 1777, Z² 3742, AN.

52   Marriage contract Fusée and Armille Conan, 28 April 1775, MC/ET/XXIX/552, AN.

53   Collection Malesherbes, 399/AP/571, AN (Pierrefitte).

54   André Corvisier, "Les soldats noirs du Maréchal de Saxe: Le problème des antillais et africains sous les armes en France au XVIIIᵉ siècle," *Outre-Mers: Revue d'histoire* (1968): 367–418. See Chapter 1.

55   "Almanzor Charles Louis, noir, autorisation de mariage sollicitée en 1785," Colonies E 396, ANOM (digi).

56   "Tassime-Didier, Antoine, nègre esclave de Marguerite Guyomar de Saint-Laurent, veuve de Anne Antoine, Comte d'Aché, Vice-Amiral, on demande pour lui l'autorisation d'épouser Ansquer (Perrine Françoise) blanche, dont il a plusieurs enfants (1786)," E 375bis, ANOM (digi). A later petition was also refused by the Maréchal de Castries, despite her pregnancy. See note of 29 September 1787 in "Frédéric (le nommé), mulâtre libre, demande l'autorisation de se marier avec une fille de Maubeuge, blanche, mariage contraire à l'arrêt du Conseil du 5 avril 1778," Colonies E 194, ANOM (digi).

57   "Demoiselle Baudelle épouse de Ruste de Rezeville, négociant à la Martinique, et le Sieur Ozenne, à l'occasion du nommé Julien, mulâtre, demande en cassation de décrets du Parlement de Paris en évocation et d'un sauf conduit," report of 30 March 1787; and blank *ordre du roi* granting protection and legal immunity in "Ruste de Rezeville, commissaire de commerce pour les intérêts de la métropole et Baudelle sa femme, 1787/1789," Colonies E 360, ANOM (digi).

58   Jacques-Pierre Brissot de Warville, *Mémoires,* vol. 3 (Paris: A. Picard et fils), 55–57.

59   Alphonse Aulard, *Le culte de la raison et le culte de l'être suprême (1793–1794): Essai historique* (Paris: Félix Alcan, 1904).

60   "Convention Nationale," *Journal historique et politique,* 6 February, 1794 (18 pluviôse II), cited in Yves Bénot, "Comment la Convention a-t-elle voté l'abo-

lition de l'esclavage en l'an II?," *Annales historiques de la Révolution française* 65, no. 293 (1993).

61 J.-F. Landolphe, *Mémoires du Capitaine Landolphe contenant l'histoire de ses voyages pendant trente-six ans aux côtes d'Afrique et aux deux Amériques, rédigés sur son manuscrit par J. S. Quesné* (Paris: Bertrand, 1823), 1:147, 159.

62 Inventaire après décès, Jean-François Landolphe, 18 July 1825, MC/ET/XLIX/1075, AN.

63 Landolphe, vol. 1, 105 (king), 109 (elders, fabric list).

64 Alun Withey, *Technology, Self-Fashioning, and Politeness in Eighteenth-Century Britain: Refined Bodies* (New York: Palgrave Macmillan, 2016).

65 Landolphe, *Mémoires*, 1:129.

66 On the steelworks at Essonne, see Chopitel, *Mémoire sur les ouvrages en fer et en acier, qui se fabriquent dans la manufacture royale d'Essonne par le moyen du laminage et qui se vendent à Paris chez le Sr Bullot, rue des Bourdonnois vis-à-vis la rue des Mauvaises-Paroles* (Paris: Duran, 1753).

67 See notices in *Gazette de France*, 17 March 1786, 94; and *Feuille du Cap français, supplément aux affiches américaines*, 8 December 1787, 974.

68 François-Alphonse Aulard, ed., *Recueil des actes du Comité de Salut Public*, vol. 17 (Paris : Imprimerie nationale, 1906), 260. Ozenne's tenure as arms specialist began on 28 floréal year II (12 May 1794).

69 Decree of 23 September 1794. Aulard, *Recueil des Actes du Comité de Salut Public*, 17:35.

70 Jean-Baptiste Nairac to La Rochelle Chamber of Commerce, 23 February 1790, in Jean-Michel Deveau, *Le commerce rochelais face à la Révolution: Correspondance de Jean-Baptiste Nairac* (La Rochelle: La rumeur des âges, 1989), 192.

71 2 August 1791, report by Nicolas Chepy, police commissioner, Section du Museum, AA183, Archives de la Préfecture de Paris. Vincent Denis, "Police et ordre public dans les rues du Paris révolutionnaire: Les sections des Arcis et du Louvre en 1791," *Crime, histoire & sociétés/Crime, History & Societies* 20, no. 1 (2016): 73–74.

72 Archives parlementaires (1st ser.), 31:431–433.

73 Déclaration du S. Pascal homme de couleur qui a demandé sa liberté, Section du Temple, AA239, Archives de la Préfecture de Paris.

74 *Collection des lois et décrets approuvée et encouragée par le Comité de Salut Public de la Convention nationale*, vol. 1 (Douia: Lagarde, n.d.), 371.

75 Act of 10 May 1815, St-Germain-de-l 'Auxerrois, dépouillements effectués d'après les registres paroissiaux et d'état civil.

76 *Le télégraphe: Gazette officielle*, Port au Prince, 16 July 1820, 4 (watchmaker's estate); 2 June 1822, 4 (salvage); 9 June 1822, 4 (luxury goods and fabrics).

77 Inventaire après décès, 6 June 1837, MC/ET/LXXIX/643, AN. A dispute would ensue over this inheritance between two of Julien's children—with different women. See *Gazette des tribunaux*, 11 December 1842, 1.

216 *Notes to Pages 130–131*

5. OURIKA

1 Here I differ with Roger Little, who claims that the name "Ourika" reveals this girl to be a Peul speaker from a region to the south of the Senegal River, in Fouta Jallon. The children Boufflers collected all received names in Paris from fables, a practice that was consistent with slave-naming practices at this time. Such names included Vendredi (Friday, from *Robinson Crusoe*) and Zimeo (from an eponymous story by Saint-Lambert, who lived in the Hotel Beauvau). Amilcar, a third child Boufflers brought to France, bore the name of a character in the famous novel *Clélie* by Madame de Scudéry. Madame de Staël wrote *Mirza* in 1786, with characters named Ximeo and Ourika. She and her parents, the Neckers, socialized with the Beauvau family. Roger Little, "Le nom et les origines d'Ourika," *Revue d'histoire littéraire de la France* 98, no. 4 (1998): 633–637.

2 On Boufflers's brief appearance at the Society of the Friends of the Blacks, and later proslavery writing, see Marcel Dorigny and Bernard Gainot, *La Société des amis des noir, 1788–1799: Contribution à l'histoire de l'abolition de l'esclavage* (Paris: Éditions UNESCO, 1998), 174–178.

3 Documents relating to her estate indicate that Ourika received an allowance from Beauvau's daughter at her father's instructions, and a second allowance arranged by two couples on behalf of an unknown party on 3 floréal year III (22 April, 1795). They included Antoine-Arnoult Lavallard from Versailles, former palace kitchen manager or cook, his wife, her brother, the lawyer Pierre Chambert (son of a goldsmith from Versailles), and Chambert's wife, Geneviève-Marguerite Joly (or Jolly), who descended from the Jolly and Bonnel families of Saint-Domingue. For documents relating to Ourika's pensions at the time of her death, see "État des pièces remises au directeur des domaines nationaux de l'intérieur de Paris formant la totalité de celles déposées aux archives de domaines nationales du département de la Seine provenant de la succession en déshérence de Charlotte Catherine Benezet Ourika négresse qui demeure chez la citoyenne Beauvau rue du Faubourg Honorée No. 44 division du Roule dépôt No. 3685," dossier marked récépissés de pluviose, carton DQ10/461, Archives de Paris. See also "Ourika Charlotte Catherine Benezet décédée sans héritiers connus à Paris," Archives de Paris, série DQ10, carton 1443; and Régie nationale de l'enregistrement et des domaines, Archives de Paris, DQ8/12, fol. 16. Jean-Nicolas Deal is listed as a valet several years earlier, at the time of the Prince de Beauvau's death, in the transcript of the state seizure and sealing of the Hôtel Beauvau. See "Scellé Beauvau," 22 May 1793, carton D/1U^1 0018, Archives de Paris. On the donor Lavallard, see death certificate of 29 September 1816, which lists his former profession: Versailles, État civil (décès), 1816, Cote 1112520 ADY (digi). The Saint-Domingue parentage of Geneviève Joly is described in a pre-Revolution custodial document. See Act of 28 November 1728, Registre des tutelles, Y 50,99B, AN (digi).

4 État civil Saint-Germain-en-Laye, D 1798–1799, 4^E 2826, ADY.

5 Lucien Scheler, "Un best-seller sous Louis XVIII, *Ourika* par Mme de Duras," *Bulletin du bibliophile* 1 (1988): 11–28. For texts inspired by the novel, including translations, see Doris Y. Kadish and Françoise Massardier-Kenney, eds., *Translating Slavery*, vol. 2, *Ourika and Its Progeny*, 2nd ed. (Kent, OH: Kent State University Press, 2010); Sylvie Chalaye, ed., *Les "Ourika" du boulevard* (Paris: L'Harmattan, 2004); and Marie-Bénédicte Diethelm and Roger Little, eds., *La Nouvelle Ourika ou les avantages de l'éducation; suivi de La Négresse* (Paris: 2021).

6 Maréchal de Castries aux administrateurs des colonies, 22 March 1783, in "Correspondance ministérielle adressée aux administrateurs des îles de France et de Bourbon (1783)," 22C, ADR.

7 Boubacar Barry, "The Slave Trade in the Eighteenth Century," in *Senegambia and the Atlantic Slave Trade*, trans. Ayi Kwei Armah (Cambridge: Cambridge University Press), 61–80; Ibrahima Seck, "Les français et la traite des esclaves en Sénégambie," *Société française d'étude du dix-huitième siècle* 44 (2012): 49–66; Paul Lovejoy, "Islam, Slavery, and Political Transformation in West Africa: Constraints on the Trans-Atlantic Slave Trade," *Outre-Mers: Revue d'histoire* (2002).

8 Oumar Kane, "Les Maures et le Futa Toro au XVIIIe siècles," *Cahiers d'études africaines* 14, no. 54 (1974): 237–252.

9 Dorrit van Dalen, *Gum Arabic: The Golden Tears of the Acacia Tree* ([S.l.]: Leiden University Press, 2019), 77–94; Margaret O. McLane, "Commercial Rivalries and French Policy on the Senegal River, 1831–1858," *African Economic History*, no. 15 (1986): 39–67; James L. A. Webb Jr., "The Trade in Gum Arabic: Prelude to French Conquest in Senegal," *Journal of African History* 26, no. 2 (1985): 149–168.

10 Richard B. Allen, "The Constant Demand of the French: The Mascarene Slave Trade and the Worlds of the Indian Ocean and Atlantic during the Eighteenth and Nineteenth Centuries," *Journal of African History* 49, no. 1 (2008): 43–72, esp. table on 61.

11 "Pourquoi a-t-il envoyé à Paris un négrillon enlevé de ses parents?," C^{14} 29, fol. 125, ANOM.

12 See Bentalou to Jefferson, 9 August 1786, and Jefferson's response of 25 August 1786, *Correspondence*, 10:205, 296.

13 Gaston Maugras, *La Marquise de Boufflers et son fils le Chevalier de Boufflers* (Paris: Librairie Plon, 1907), 484.

14 Maugras, *La Marquise de Boufflers*, 478.

15 Carline Stéphanie Félicie de Ducrest de Genlis, *Souvenirs de Félicie* (Brussels: De Mat, 1828), 285.

16 Boufflers to Sabran, 19 July 1786, in *La Comtesse de Sabran et le Chevalier de Boufflers: La promesse, correspondance, 1786–1787*, ed. Sue Carrell (Paris: Tallandier, 2010), 218.

17 He considers purchasing "une petite Mauresse de vingt mois, qu'on dit charmante" (for whom he must wait), in a letter to his sister, 27 May 1786; E. de Magnieu and Henri Prat, eds., *Correspondance inédite de la comtesse de Sabran et du Chevalier de Boufflers, 1778–1788* (Paris: E. Plon, 1875), 190. Of another girl,

218 *Notes to Pages 137–138*

"qui a l'air d'être la continuation de la belle Hourica," whom he purchased on the Sierra Leone River, see entry for 5 April 1787 in *Journal inédit du second séjour au Sénégal, 3 décembre 1786–25 Décembre 1787* (Paris: Éditions de la Revue politique et littéraire (Revue bleue), 1905), 71.

18 See Thomas M. Kavanagh, "Boufflers's La Reine de Golconde and the Conte Philosophique as an Enlightenment Form," *French Forum* 23, no. 1 (1998): 5–21. Boufflers's tale inspired a 1766 opera-ballet with music by Pierre-Alexandre Monsigny and a libretto by Michel-Jean Sedaine. See Manuel Couvreur, "Aline, Reine de Golconde," in *Michel-Jean Sedaine (1719–1797): Theater, Opera, and Art,* ed. David Charlton and Mark Ledbury (Aldershot: Ashgate, 2000), 71–96.

19 Maugras, *La Marquise de Boufflers*, 130.

20 Boufflers service file, GR 4 YD 2982, SHD.

21 "Vol d'une veste de drap écarlate (galonné)," 1 January 1774, Y 9813 A–B, AN.

22 Boufflers to Madame de Boisgelin, 22 April 1786, in Prat, *Correspondance inédite, 1778–1788,* 185–186. A French silver sword, which a slave trader bestowed on a Woyo ruler in Cabinda, is the topic of an excellent recent study. See Ana Lucia Araujo, *The Gift: How Objects of Prestige Shaped the Atlantic Slave Trade and Colonialism* (New York; Cambridge University Press, 2024), esp. chap. 4.

23 See *La Lorraine dans l'Europe des Lumières: Actes du colloque organisé par la Faculté des lettres et des sciences humaines de l'Université de Nancy,* Nancy, 24–27 October 1966 (Nancy: Presses universitaires de Nancy, 1968); and Gaston Maugras, *La cour de Lunéville au XVIIIe siècle* (Paris: Librairie Plon, 1904).

24 Maugras, *La Marquise de Boufflers,* 132.

25 Boufflers to Beauvau, 10 January 1771, quoted Maugras, *La Marquise de Boufflers,* 136–137.

26 Boufflers to Beauvau, 6 March 1771, quoted in Maugras, *La Marquise de Boufflers,* 140.

27 Boufflers to Beauvau, 14 May 1771, quoted in Maugras, *La Marquise de Boufflers,* 145.

28 See Philippe-Auguste de Sainte-Foy d'Arcq and Gabriel-François Coyer, *Noblesse commerçante contre noblesse militaire: Une querelle des Lumières (1756–1759),* ed. Christian Cheminade (Paris: Classiques Garnier, 2021); Leonard Adams, *Coyer and the Enlightenment* (Oxford: Voltaire Foundation, 2017); Jay M. Smith, *The French Nobility in the Eighteenth Century: Reassessments and New Approaches* (University Park: Pennsylvania State University Press, 2006); Smith, *Nobility Reimagined: The Patriotic Nation in Eighteenth-Century France* (Ithaca, NY: Cornell University Press, 2005); Pierre Chaunu and Guy Richard, *Noblesse d'affaires au XVIIIe siècle* (Paris: Armand Colin, 1974); Guy Chaussinand-Nogaret, "Aux origines de la Révolution: Noblesse et bourgeoisie," *Annales: Histoire, sciences sociales* 30, no. 2 / 3 (1975): 265–278; Henri Lévy-Bruhl, "La noblesse de France et le commerce à la fin de l'ancien régime," *Revue d'histoire moderne et contemporaine* (1933): 209–236.

29 *Imputations de Monsieur Dumontet contre Monsieur D'Aigrement et les autres officiers d'administration* (1783), in "Du Montet Aimé Guillin . . . gouver-

Notes to Pages 139–141   219

neur du Sénégal, son remplacement par le Gardeur de Repentigny (Louis)," Colonies E 155, fols. 563v–566, ANOM (digi), images 481–486.

30 "Précis pour le Sieur Cornet, capitaine au corps royal de l'artillerie, contre Monsieur Dumontet, colonel d'infanterie," Colonies E 155, pt. II, fols. 217–223, images 408–420, ANOM (digi).

31 Léon-Louis Crespy, chirurgien du roi au Sénégal 1778–1786, Letter of 5 June 1784, Colonies E 155, pt. III, image 9, ANOM (digi).

32 See Léon-Pierre Raybaud, "L'administration du Sénégal de 1781–1784: L'affaire Dumontet," *Annales africaines* (1968): 113–172. The son of Le Normant de Flaghac, a Parisian financier, was aide-de-camp to Governor du Montet. For this scandal, see his personnel file (Colonies E 184), that of Du Montet (Colonies E 155), and that of the governor's second aide-de camp, Louis-Aimé de la Ferière, Colonies E 245, ANOM (digi).

33 L. Jore, "Un Canadien gouverneur du Sénégal: Louis Le Gardeur De Repentigny, 1721–1786," *Revue d'histoire de l'Amérique française* 15, no. 1 (1961): 64–89; no. 2 (1961): 256–276; no. 3 (1961): 396–418.

34 On Repentigny's slave trading, see Boufflers to Sabran, 20 January 1786, in Carrell, *La Promesse*, 87.

35 Stanislas-Jean de Boufflers 1785-an IX, Colonies E 44, ANOM.

36 Boufflers to Sabran, 20 January 1786, in Carrell, *La Promesse*, 87.

37 On Boufflers's pension, see Ségur to Boufflers, Versailles, 20 May 1785, GR 4 YD 2982, fol. 22, SHD.

38 See personnel file for the Comte and Vicomte de Ségur (1783), Colonies E 368bis, ANOM (digi).

39 Boufflers to Sabran, 4 February 1786, in Carrell, *La Promesse*, 57.

40 Raymond Douville, "Officiers canadiens dans la marine de la révolution et de l'empire," *Les cahiers des dix* 27 (1962): 107–133. For Jacques Bedout's Legion of Honor file, which contains a chronology of his service record, see LH / /163/16, AN (Pierrefitte) (digi). For his brother Michel-Antoine Bedout, see Secours au Colon de Saint-Domingue, F^{12} 2747, AN (Pierrefitte). On the Leclerc mission, see Philippe R. Girard, *The Slaves Who Defeated Napoleon: Toussaint Louverture and the Haitian War of Independence, 1801–1804* (Tuscaloosa: University of Alabama Press, 2011); Henri Mesière, *Le Général Leclerc: 1772–1802, et l'expédition de Saint-Domingue* (Paris: Tallandier, 1990); and Jean-Pierre Le Glaunec, *L'Armée indigène: Le défaite de Napoléon en Haïti* (Quebec: Lux Éditeur, 2020).

41 Alain Demerliac, *La marine de Louis XVI: Nomenclature des navires français de 1774* (Nice: Éditions Omega, 1996), 22.

42 Min. Navy to Grand Chancellor of the Legion of Honor, 19 December 1803 (27 frimaire year XII), LH / /163/16, AN (Pierrefitte) (digi).

43 Boufflers to Sabran, 8 February 1786, in Carrell, *La Promesse*, 100–101.

44 Golbery, *Fragments d'un voyage en Afrique: Fait pendant les années 1785, 1786 et 1787, dans les contrées occidentales de ce continent*, vol. 2 (Paris: Treuttel & Würtz, 1802), 331. On French Senegal in this period, see Marie-Hélène Knight-Baylac, "Gorée au XVIIIe siècle du sol," *Outre-Mers: Revue d'histoire* (1977): 33–54;

Knight-Baylac, "La vie à Gorée de 1677 à 1789," *Outre-Mers: Revue d'histoire* (1970): 377–420; Bronwen Everill, "'All the Baubles That They Needed': 'Industriousness' and Slavery in Saint-Louis and Gorée," *Early American Studies* 15, no. 4 (2017): 714–739; Mark Hinchman, *Portrait of an Island: The Architecture and Material Culture of Gorée, Sénégal, 1758–1837* (Lincoln: University of Nebraska Press, 2015); see also Guillaume Vial, *Femmes d'influence: Les signares de Saint-Louis de Sénégal et de Gorée, XVIIIᵉ–XIXᵉ siècle: Étude critique d'une identité métisse* (Paris: Hémisphères, 2018).

45   My rendering of this phrase is based on the concurrence of three Wolof speakers. I wish to thank Professor Amy Niang at the University of Witwatersand. I am equally indebted to Konstantin Pozdniakov, Stéphane Robert, and Marc van de Velde at LLACAN (Langages, Langues et Cultures d'Afrique).

46   Boufflers to Sabran, 14 February 1786, in Carrell, *La Promesse,* 104.

47   Boufflers de Sabran, 22 January 1786, in Carrell, *La Promesse,* 89–90.

48   Boufflers to Sabran, Rochefort, 11 December 1785, in *Le lit bleu: La Comtesse de Sabran et le Chevalier de Boufflers, Correspondance, 1777–1785,* ed. Sue Carrell (Paris: Taillandier, 2009), 336.

49   Boufflers, *Journal inédit du second séjour au Sénégal, 3 Dec. 1786–25 Dec. 1787,* ed. Paul Bonnefon (Paris: Éditions politique et littéraire, 1905), 137.

50   Boufflers to Sabran, 1 October 1787, in *Journal inédit* (1905), 156.

51   Société de Gens de Lettres, *Le mercure du dix-neuvième siècle rédigé par une société de gens de lettres* (Paris: Baudouin frères, 1823), 486–487.

52   "Nouvelles des Théâtres," *Le Constitutionnel: Journal du commerce politique et littéraire,* 29 March 1824, 4.

53   C. A. Sainte Beuve, *Portrait des femmes* (Paris: Garnier frères, 1845), 70. See also G. Pailhès, *La Duchesse de Duras et Chateaubriand d'après les documents inédits* (Paris: Librairie académique Perrin, 1910).

54   Adeline Koh, "Marriage, 'Métissage,' and Women's Citizenship: Revisiting Race and Gender in Claire de Duras's 'Ourika,'" *French Forum* 38, no. 3 (2013): 16. The publication of a translation of *Ourika* by the Modern Language Association helped to inaugurate the book's canonical status at the turn of the twenty-first century. See Claire de Duras, *Ourika,* trans. with a foreword by John Fowles, ed. Joan Dejean and Margaret Waller (New York: Modern Language Association, 1994). Christopher Miller and Robin Mitchell, whose scholarship I address later in this chapter, do not embrace this anticolonial reading of the text.

55   Carol Sherman, "Race, Melancholy, and Therapeutic Narrative in *Ourika,*" *Journal for Early Modern Cultural Studies,* no. 1 (2001): 89; see also Susan Castillo Street, "Writing Race and Slavery in the Francophone Atlantic: Transatlantic Connections and Contradictions in Claire de Duras's Ourika and Victor Hugo's Bug-Jargal," in *The Edinburgh Companion to Atlantic Literary Studies,* ed. Leslie Elizabeth Eckel and Clare Frances Elliott (Edinburgh: Edinburgh University Press, 2016), 119–130.

56   Doris Y. Kadish, "Voices of Daughters and Slaves: Claire de Duras," in *Fathers, Daughters, and Slaves: Women Writers and French Colonial Slavery,* ed. Doris Y. Kadish (Cambridge: Liverpool University Press, 2013), 113; Chantal Bertrand-

Jennings, "Condition féminine et impuissance sociale: Les romans de la duchesse de Duras," *Romantisme* 63 (1989): 43. Leon Hoffmann takes the same view as these critics in his classic work *Le nègre romantique* (Paris: Éditions Payot, 1973), 322.

57 Claire de Duras, *Ourika,* ed. Virginie Belzgao and Alain Jaubert (Paris: Gallimard, 2007). For Anglophones, see *Approaches to Teaching Duras's Ourika,* ed. Mary Ellen Birkett and Christopher Rivers (New York: Modern Language Association, 2009).

58 Claire de Duras, *Ourika,* ed. Rachel Boucobza, Folio+Lycée (Paris: Gallimard, 2022).

59 Madame de Duras, *Ourika,* ed. Benedetta Craveri, trans. Isabel Violante (Paris: Flammarion, 2010), 86. All further page references are to this edition. Translations are mine.

60 Léontine de Noailles, *Vie de la princesse de Poix, née Beauvau, par la vicomtesse de Noailles* (Paris: Lahure, 1855), 4, 42, 45.

61 For receipts from the festival, which took place on 21 frimaire year II (11 December 1793), see VD*9, Archives de Paris; for the speech by the section orator, see "Nouvelles des départements: Paris," *Journal de la Montagne* 47 (18 July 1793): 270. On the Maratiste reputation of the section, see Louis Adolphe Thiers, *Histoire de la Révolution française,* vol. 5 (Paris: Lecointe, 1834), 86. On the cult of martyrs to liberty, see *La mort de Marat,* ed. Jean-Claude Bonnet (Paris: 1986).

62 Marie-Charlotte de Beauvau, *Souvenirs de la Maréchale princesse de Beauvau, née Rohan-Chabot, suivis des Mémoires du Maréchal prince de Beauvau, recueillis et mis en ordre par Madame Standish, née Noailles, son arrière-petite-fille* (Paris: Techener, 1872), 149.

63 Rapports de la Préfecture de police, 22 ventôse year X (13 March 1802) and 28 ventôse year X (19 March 1802). Alphonse Aulard, *Paris sous le consulat: Recueil de documents pour l'histoire de l'esprit public à Paris (1 frimaire an IX au 30 germinal an X)* (Paris: Cerf, Quantin, Noblet, 1904), 781, 789–790.

64 Jennifer Heuer, "The One-Drop Rule in Reverse? Interracial Marriages in Napoleonic and Restoration France," *Law and History Review* 27, no. 3 (2009): 515–548; *Rétablissement de l'esclavage dans les colonies françaises, 1802: Ruptures et continuités de la politique coloniale française (1800–1830): Aux origines d'Haïti: Actes du colloque international tenu à l'Université de Paris VIII les 20, 21 et 22 juin 2002,* ed. Yves Bénot and Marcel Dorigny (Paris: Maisonneuve et Larose, 2003).

65 Éléonore-Adèle d'Osmond, Comtesse de Boigne, *Récits d'une tante: Mémoires de la comtesse de Boigne, née Osmond,* vol. 1 (Paris: Émile Paul, 1921), 275.

66 See London contract of 25 November 1797 transcribed under "inventorié des papiers, première parti, " in Inventaire après le décès de Madame la Duchesse de Duras, 23 April 1828, MC / ET / I / 831, AN.

67 The extent of Duras's father's property, lost during the Revolution, was later catalogued. See Inventaire après le décès de Monseigneur le Duc de Duras, 30 April 1828, MC / ET / I / 831, AN.

68 Inventaire après le décès de Madame la Duchesse de Duras, 23 April 1828, MC / ET / I / 831, AN.

222 **Notes to Pages 148–153**

69 Mariage, le citoyen de Duras à la demoiselle de Kersaint, 3 floréal year X (23 April 1802), MC / ET / XXVIII / 603, AN.

70 Pierre-Félix-Barthélemy David to Kersaint, 29 August 1748, Correspondance de M David et M de Kersaint, 1748–1749, NAF 28258 (1), Département des manuscrits, Bibliothèque nationale de France.

71 Edouard Delobette, "Les mutations du commerce du Havre (1680–1763)," *Annales de Normandie* (2003): 19–68; Delobette, "Négociants et traite des noirs au Havre au XVIIIe siècle," *Annales de Normandie* 48, no. 3 (1998): 259–295; Richard Robert, "Le financement des armements maritimes du Havre au XXVIIIe siècle (position de problèmes)," *Revue d'histoire économique et sociale* 47, no. 1 (1969): 5–31.

72 M. (Pierre) Bart, 21 December 1756, Marine B^2 353, AN.

73 Capt. Kersaint, 1 January 1757, "joint à la lettre de Monsieur de Neviere du 1 juin 1757," Marine B^4 77, AN.

74 Marriage Armand-Simon-Guy Coëtnempren, chevalier Seigneur de Kersaint & Louise-Claire Françoise de Paul d'Alesso Desragny, 7 January 1772, État civil Martinique, Paroisse des Trois Ilets, tous actes (1771), fol. 3, ANOM (digi).

75 "Lettres Eustache," Kersaint Papers, E-1430, ADY.

76 Certificat de vente et de livraison d'un nègre et d'une négresse à M. de Kersaint par Ruste de Rezeville frères, à raison de 1650 livres chacun, provenant de la cargaison du navire danois *Le Baron de Schimelman*, au Fort-Royal, le 7 août 1782. Kersaint Papers, E-1429, ADY.

77 Kersaint Papers, E-1428, ADY; on Loff, see Carrère to Kersaint, Saint-Pierre de la Martinique, 30 May 1785, E-1430, ADY.

78 Orlando Patterson, *Slavery and Social Death: A Comparative Study* (Cambridge, MA: Harvard University Press, 1982), 55–62.

79 Vente des terres et domaine d'Ussé, 29 octobre 1807, le fondé de pouvoir de M. de Chalabre à Madame Veuve de Duras, à Madame veuve de Kersaint, et à Madame de Duras, MC / ET / XXVIII / 639, AN. Papers relating to the purchase of this château are also transcribed in the posthumous inventory of Duras's property in 1828. On the Martinican plantation, see "5ème partie, testaments et codicilles de la défunte." In her will, Duras named the buyer of the Habitation des Anglais as Monsieur Desgrottes, and noted *une somme de 200,000–300,000 francs des colonies qui me sont encore dus*. See Inventaire après le décès de Madame la Duchesse de Duras, 23 April 1828, MC / ET / I / 831, AN.

80 Henriette-Lucie de la Tour du Pin, *Journal d'une femme de cinquante ans (1778–1815)* (Paris: Berger-Levrault, 1930), 184.

81 Léontine de Noailles, *Vie de la princesse de Poix, née Beauvau, par la vicomtesse de Noailles* (Paris: Lahure, 1855), 107.

82 Charles Brifaut, *Souvenirs d'un académicien sur la Révolution, le premier Empire, et la Restauration* (Paris: Albin Michel, 1920–1921), 50.

83 References are found in letters to Rosalie de Constant and the Comtesse de Swetchine; Pailhès, *La Duchesse de Duras et Chateaubriand*, 63 (Lespinasse), 93–94 (Deffand), 139 (Dangeau).

84 Madame de Duras, *Mémoires de Sophie suivi de Amélie et Pauline: Romans d'émigration, 1789–1800,* ed. Marie-Bénédicte Diethelm (Paris: Éditions Manucius, 2011), 29.

85 Claire de Duras, *Ourika, Édouard, Oliver ou le secret,* ed. Marie-Bénédicte Diethelm, Folio Classique (Paris: Gallimard, 2007), 327; Duras, "À propos d'une ébauche romanesque de Claire de Duras: *Le Paria,*" *Le Magasin du XIXᵉ siècle,* no. 51 (June 2010): 41.

86 Letter from the Duc de Lévis to Duchesse de Duras, 8 November 1825, cited in Pailhès, *La Duchesse de Duras et Chateaubriand,* 473.

87 On the dowering of the Duc de Lévis's wife, Pauline Charpentier d'Ennery, through a mortgage on her grandparents' slave plantation in Martinique, see Contrat de mariage, 23 May 1784, MC / RS / 1544, AN.

88 Pailhès, *La Duchesse de Duras et Chateaubriand,* 292.

89 Alfred de Falloux, ed., *Lettres de Madame Swetchine,* vol. 1 (Paris: Didier, 1873), 15 April 1821.

90 Charles-Augustin Sainte-Beuve, *Portrait des femmes* (Paris: Garnier frères, 1845), 69.

91 Letter of 13 January 1821, Alexander von Humboldt, *Lettres à Claire de Duras (1814–1828): Correspondance inédite,* ed. Marie-Bénédicte Diethelm et al. (Paris: Manucius, 2016), 178–179. See Anita Rupprecht, "Le voyage des aveugles: Le Havre—la Guadeloupe, 1819," in *Les mondes de l'esclavage: Une histoire comparée,* ed. Paulin Ismard, Benedetta Rossi, and Cécile Vidal (Paris: Seuil, 2021), 277–283.

92 According to the Trans-Atlantic Slave Trade Database (slavevoyages.org), the Chateaubriand brothers deported 2,236 Africans from the region of modern-day Togo and Benin to the New World over a period of two decades (1754 to 1775). See Georges Saint-Mieux, "Les armements de M. de Chateaubriand," *Annales de Bretagne et des pays de l'Ouest* (1919): 1–14; Georges Saint-Mieux, "Monsieur de Chateaubriand, armateur," *Annales de la Société d'histoire et d'archéologie de l'arrondissement de Saint Malo* (1913): 137–164; Barthélemy-Amédée Pocquet du Haut-Jussé, "M. de Chateaubriand père," *Annales de Bretagne et des pays de l'Ouest* (1949): 192–194; Jean Mettas, "Pour une histoire de la traite des Noirs française: Sources et problèmes," *Outre-Mers: Revue d'histoire* (1975): 19–46.

93 Serge Daget, "L'abolition de la traite des Noirs en France de 1814 à 1831," *Cahiers d'études africaines* 11, no. 41 (1971): 14–58; see also Joseph la Hausse de Lalouvière, "A Business Archive of the French Illegal Slave Trade in the Nineteenth Century," *Past & Present* 252, no. 1 (August 2021): 139–177.

94 Letter of 28 September 1822, in Marie-Louis-Jean-André-Charles Demartin du Tyrac, comte de Marcellus, *Souvenirs diplomatiques* (Paris: M. Lévy frères, 1858).

95 Alexandre Humboldt, *Lettres à Claire de Duras* (2016), 179n. See also Ernest Daudet, *La police politique: Chronique des temps de la Restauration d'après les rapports des agents secrets et les papiers du cabinet noir (1815–1830)* (Paris: Librairie Plon, 1912), 300.

224 **Notes to Pages 156–159**

96 See Fonds Panon-Desbassayns et de Villèle (1689–1973), 696 AP 21–23, AN. On the illegal trade to the Mascarenes, see Hubert Gerbeau, "Quelques aspects de la traite illégale des esclaves à l'île Bourbon au XIXe siècle," in *Mouvements de populations dans l'Océan indien* (Paris, 1979), 273–308; Marina Carter and Hubert Gerbeau, "Covert Slaves and Coveted Coolies in the Early Nineteenth-Century Mascareignes," *Slavery and Abolition* (1988): 194–208; Richard Allen, "Licentious and Unbridled Proceedings: The Illegal Slave Trade to Mauritius and the Seychelles during the Early Nineteenth Century," *Journal of African History* 42, no. 1 (2001): 91–116.

97 On Barante, see *Journal de la Société de la morale chrétienne* (1 January 1823): 37. He became involved in slave-trade suppression during the July Monarchy. See V. Dalloz et al., *Jurisprudence Générale*, vol. 12 (Lyon: Bibliothèque municipale de Lyon, 1836), 23–24.

98 Marquis de Noailles, *Le Comte Molé, 1781–1855: Sa vie—ses mémoires*, vol. 3 (Paris: Édouard Champion), 233–238.

99 Duras, *Ourika*, ed. Craveri, 81.

100 Maxim 106 from *Characteristics: In the Manner of Rochefoucault's Maxims* (1823), in William Hazlitt, *Selected Writings*, ed. Jon Cook (Oxford: Oxford University Press, 2009), 203.

101 Robin Mitchell, *Vénus Noir: Black Women and Colonial Fantasies in Nineteenth-Century France* (Athens, GA: University of Georgia Press, 2020), 87.

102 Eusèbe Girault de Saint-Fargeau, *Revue des romans: Recueil d'analyses raisonnées des productions remarquables romanciers français et étrangers* (1839; Geneva: Slatkine Reprints, 1968), 202.

103 Duras's story (in my reading) inverts the pathology described in Franz Fanon, *Black Skin, White Masks*, trans. Charles Lam Markmann (London: Pluto, 1986). I interpret Ourika as a white person with a black body of which she disencumbers herself. For an alternative view, see David O'Connell, "Ourika: Black Face, White Mask," *French Review* 47, no. 6 (1974): 47–56. Yasmine Modestine, in line with O'Connell, credits Duras with illustrating "les effets pervers de l'assimilation." Yasmine Modestine, *Noires mais blanches, blanches mais noires: Les figures féminines noires ou métisses au théâtre de Cléopâtre à Ourika* (Paris: L'Harmattan, 2020), 140.

104 Alexandre Gérard, *Lettres adressés au baron François Gérard, peintre d'histoire, par les artistes et les personnages célères de son temps*, 2nd ed., vol. 2 (Paris: Quantin, 1886), 51, 55–59, 63–64, 69–70, 72, 159–160.

105 On the Johannot engraving, see Salon des artistes français, *Explication des ouvrages de peinture et dessins, sculpture, architecture et gravure des artistes vivans* (Paris: Herissant, 1827), 181; and Bellier de la Chavignerie, *Dictionnaire général des artistes de l'École française jusqu'à nos jours*, vol. 1 (Paris: Librairie Renouard, 1882), 831.

106 "Exposition des manufactures royales," *Gazette national ou le Moniteur universel*, 29 December 1825, 1710.

107 "Exposition des manufactures royales."

108 Humboldt to Duras, undated letter of 1824, in Pailhès, *La Duchesse de Duras et Chateaubriand*, 451.

109 *Le Constitutionnel*, 2 January 1826, 4.

110 *Le Corsaire*, 29 March 1824, 2.

111 On performances at the Théâtre de la Variétés and the Gymnase theater, see *Le Constitutionnel: Journal du commerce politique et littéraire*, 4; *Journal des débats*, 28 March 1824; Eugène-Hyacinthe Lafillard, *Année théâtrale ou répertoire générale des pièces jouées à Paris* (1824). On performances beyond Paris, see Mitchell, *Vénus Noir*, 91–101.

112 *La Pandore*, 23 March 1824, 4.

113 *Journal des débats politiques et littéraires*, 29 March 1824, 7.

114 *Journal des dames et des modes*, 5 May 1824, 195.

115 Paul Bonnefon, "Alexandre Duval: Lettres et documents inédits," *Revue d'histoire littéraire de la France* 19, no. 3 (1912): 588–630.

116 *Journal des Débats*, 5 July 1847, 1–2.

117 On the Black female body in nineteenth-century French culture, see Mitchell, *Vénus Noir*, esp. chap. 2; Sylvie Chalaye, *Du noir au nègre: L'image noir au théâtre (1550–1960)* (Paris: L'Harmattan, 1998); Chalaye, "L'invention théâtrale de la 'Vénus noire': De Saartjie Baartman à Joséphine Baker," in *L'altérité en spectacle*, ed. Isabelle Moindrot and Nathalie Coutelet (Rennes: Presses universitaires de Rennes, 2015), 55–66; Sadiah Qureshi, "Displaying Sarah Bartman, the 'Hottentot Venus,'" *History of Science* 42 (2004): 233–257; Gérard Badou, "Sur les traces de la Vénus Hottentote," *Grandhiva: Revue d'histoire et d'archives d'anthropologie* 27 (2000): 83–87.

118 *"L'art de ne pas monter sa garde," Théâtre du Gand: Comptes rendus et programmes, 1837–1838, découpures*, bound clippings, University of Ghent (digi), https://books.google.fr/books?id=F9INAAAAcAAJ&newbks=1&newbks_redir=0&dq=Ourika%20Theatre%20du%20Gand&hl=fr&pg=PA34-IA1#v=onepage&q&f=false.

119 *Le Charivari*, 27 October 1854; *Bulletin des beaux-arts: Exposition de 1842: Soirées de Neuilly: Esquisses dramatiques* (1828); France, Ministre des travaux publics, de l'agriculture et de commerce, *Stud book français: Registre des chevaux de pur sang nés ou importés en France*, vol. 1 (Paris: Imprimerie royale, 1838), 126, 135 196; France, Ministre de l'Agriculture, *Stud book français: Registre des chevaux de pur sang nés ou importés en France 1875 à 1877*, vol. 5 (Imprimerie Typographique Kugelmann, 1878), 387; ibid., vol. 8 (1887), 688; see Bernth Lindfors, "Le docteur Kahn et les Niams-Niams," in *Zoos humains: Au temps des exhibitions humaines*, ed. Nicolas Bancel et al. (Paris: La Découverte, 2004), 203–220.

120 On race culture in nineteenth-century France, see Carole Reynaud-Paligot, "Circulations et usages sociopolitiques de la notion de race du XIXe siècle aux années 1950," *Communications* 107 (2020): 31–44; Claude-Olivier Doron, *L'homme altéré: Race et dégénérescence* (Clamecy: Champ Vallon, 2016); Jacqueline Duvernay-Bolens, "L'homme zoologique: Race et racisme chez les naturalistes de la

226   *Notes to Pages 163–165*

première moitié du XIXe siècle," *L'Homme* 35, no. 133 (1995): 9–32; Hoffmann, *Le nègre romantique;* Léon Fanoudh-Siefer, *Le mythe du nègre et de l'Afrique dans la littérature française de 1800 à la deuxième guerre mondiale* (Paris: Klincksieck, 1968).

121   Katherine Montwieler, "Embodiment, Agency, and Alienation in 'Frankenstein' and 'Ourika,'" *CEA Critic* 73, no. 3 (2011): 72.

122   David Bindman, "Am I Not a Man and Brother? British Art and Slavery in the Eighteenth Century," *RES: Anthropology and Aesthetics,* no. 26 (1994): 68–82. The medallion recalls the posture slaves were compelled to assume during some New World manumission rites in alleged mimicry of the ancient world. Lucie-Henriette de la Tour du Pin describes the manumission in Albany (circa 1796) of her four slaves, who were obliged to kneel before her husband, who touched their heads "absolutely as in ancient Rome." *Journal d'une femme de cinquante ans,* 2:102–103. In Rome, a judge (not the master) touched the slave with his staff (vindicta); recent historians do not mention kneeling in their depictions of this rite. Later manumission ceremonies included spinning the slave around in circles and a slap (alapa). Henrik Mouritsen, *The Freedman in the Roman World* (Cambridge: Cambridge University Press, 2011), 11; Kyle Harper, *Slavery in the Late Roman World, AD 275–425* (Cambridge: Cambridge University Press, 2011), 468–469.

CONCLUSION

1   Miranda Spieler, "Slave Voice and the Legal Archive: The Case of Freedom Suits before the Paris Admiralty Court," in *Hearing Enslaved Voices: African and Indian Testimony in British and French America, 1700–1848,* ed. Sophie White and Trevor Burnard (New York: Routledge, 2020), 165–187.

2   Muron to LGP, 3 December 1764, AB ms. 12,252, fol. 365.

3   Antoine de Sartine, Rapport au conseil des dépêches par Monsieur de Sartine du Projet de Déclaration sur la police des noirs, 9 August 1777, Recueil des pièces rélatives à la législation sur la police des noirs (Paris 1778), ms. Fr 13357, Department of Manuscripts, Bibliothèque nationale de France (Paris).

4   On political rumor in pre-Revolutionary Paris, see Robert Darnton, "An Early Information Society: News and the Media in Eighteenth-Century Paris," *American Historical Review* 105, no. 1 (2000): 1–35. On Paris as a center for the reception and dissemination of global news and rumor, see Tabetha Leigh Ewing, *Rumor, Diplomacy, and War in Enlightenment Paris* (Liverpool: Liverpool University Press, 2014). On news emanating from Paris into the colonies, see Sarah E. Johnson, "Print Culture and the Empires of Slavery," in *Encyclopédie Noire: The Making of Moreau de Saint-Méry's Intellectual World* (Chapel Hill: University of North Carolina Press, 2023), 87–126. On later problems of information control in France's colonial empire, see Arthur Asseraf, "La société coloniale face à l'actualité internationale: Diffusion, contrôle, usages (1881–1899)," *Revue d'histoire moderne et contemporaine* 63, no. 2 (2016): 110–132. On the subsequent role of Paris in fer-

menting and diffusing anticolonial black politics, see Jennifer Boitin, *Colonial Metropolis: The Urban Grounds of Anti-Imperialism and Feminism in Interwar Paris* (Lincoln: University of Nebraska Press, 2010).

5   On the 1760–1761 Jamaican revolt, see Vincent Brown, *Tacky's Revolt: The Story of an Atlantic Slave War* (Cambridge, MA: Belknap Press of Harvard University Press, 2020); on the revolt in Berbice, begun in 1763, see Marjoleine Kars, *Blood on the River: A Chronicle of Mutiny and Freedom on the Wild Coast* (New York: New Press, 2020); Wim S. M. Hoogbergen, *The Boni Maroon Wars in Surinam* (New York: Brill, 1990); see also Silvia de Groot, "The Boni Maroon War, 1765–1793: Surinam and French Guyana," *Boletín de Estudios Latinoamericanos y Del Caribe*, no. 18 (1975): 30–48.

6   Louis Lézin de Milly, *Discours prononcé le 20 février 1790, par M. de Milly, Américain, citoyen de Paris, avocat en parlement, l'un des commissaires nommés par le district des Filles Saint-Thomas* (Paris: Didot le jeune, 1790), 34.

7   Jean-Paul Cointet, "Le Bataillon des filles Saint-Thomas et le 10 août," *Annales historiques de la Révolution française* 182 (1965): 453.

8   The classic work on this topic remains Gabriel Debien, *Les colons de Saint-Domingue et la Révolution: Essai sur le club Massiac (Aug. 1789–Aug. 1792)* (Paris: Armand Colin, 1953). See also Déborah Liébart, "Un groupe de pression contre-révolutionnaire: Le club Massiac sous la constituante," *Annales historiques de la Révolution française* 354 (2008): 29–50; and Malick W. Ghachem, "The 'Trap' of Representation: Sovereignty, Slavery and the Road to the Haitian Revolution," *Historical Reflections / Réflexions historiques* 29, no. 1 (2003): 123–144.

9   Anon., *Idées justes sur les nègres, sur l'importance des colonies pour toute la France, et sur l'intérêt qu'y doit prendre la Capitale* (Paris: Didot le jeune, n.d.), in *Recueil de pièces imprimées concernant les colonies: Traite des noirs, esclavage, droits des noirs, colonies françaises, 1789–1790*, Bibliothèque de Moreau de Saint-Méry, no. 23, Bibliothèque nationale de France (digi).

10 On the language of sentiment in eighteenth-century France, see William M. Reddy, "Sentimentalism and Its Erasure: The Role of Emotions in the Era of the French Revolution," *Journal of Modern History* 72, no. 1 (2000): 109–152. On the relationship between compassion and self-interest, see Norman S. Fiering, "Irresistible Compassion: An Aspect of Eighteenth-Century Sympathy and Humanitarianism," *Journal of the History of Ideas* 37, no. 2 (1976): 195–218.

11 There were abolitionists in Old Regime France, who included people at the pinnacle of society, but there were few outlets, especially in the world of salons, for expressing those views. On antislavery in Old Regime France, see Jean Ehrard, *L'esclavage colonial et l'opinion publique en France au XVIIIᵉ siècle* (Paris: André Versailles, 2008); Maurice Jackson, *Let This Voice Be Heard: Anthony Benezet, Father of Atlantic Abolitionism* (Philadelphia: University of Pennsylvania Press, 2008); Marie-Jeanne Rossignol, "The Quaker Antislavery Commitment and How It Revolutionized French Antislavery through the Crèvecoeur-Brissot Friendship, 1782–1789," in *Quakers and Abolition,* ed. Brycchan Carey and Geoffrey Plank

228 *Notes to Pages 167–168*

(Chicago: University of Illinois Press, 2014), 180–193; Sunil Agnani, *Hating Empire Properly: The Two Indies and the Limits of Enlightenment Colonialism* (New York: Fordham University Press, 2013); Jeremy Popkin and Richard Popkin, eds., *The Abbé Grégoire and His World* (Dordrecht: Kluwer Academic, 2000). On the abolitionism of Jean-Antoine-Nicolas de Caritat, Marquis de Condorcet, see Richard Popkin, "Condorcet, Abolitionist," in *Condorcet Studies I (History of Philosophy)*, ed. Leonora Cohen Rosenfield (Atlantic Highlands, NJ: Humanities Press, 1984), 35–47. Works on French abolitionism during the French Revolution include Marcel Dorigny and Bernard Gainot, *La Societe des amis des noirs 1788–1799: Contribution à l'histoire de l'abolition de l'esclavage* (Paris: Éditions UNESCO, 1998); Alyssa Goldstein Sepinwall, *The Abbé Grégoire and the French Revolution* (Berkeley: University of California Press, 2008).

12   Alain Robbe-Grillet, *Pour un nouveau roman* (Paris: Minuit), 26–27; Philippe Hamon, "Pour un statut sémiologique du personnage," *Littérature*, no. 6 (1972): 86–110; Jean-Michel Heimonet, "De l'homme dieu à l'homme objet," *Romance Notes* 31, no. 3 (1991): 235–243; Yoseph Milman, "Absurdist Estrangement and the Subversion of Narrativity in 'La Plage,'" *Modern Language Review* 89, no. 1 (January 1994): 50–60; Laura Brignoli, "La technique 'privative' du nouveau roman: L'exemple de Robbe-Grillet," *Francofonia* 43 (2002): 57–76.

13   Richard Cobb, *Promenades* (Oxford: Oxford University Press, 1980), 1–6.

14   The extremely rich historiography on French material culture includes Leora Auslander, *Taste and Power: Furnishing Modern France: Studies on the History of Society and Culture* (Berkeley: University of California Press, 1996); Auslander, "Deploying Material Culture to Write the History of Gender and Sexuality: The Example of Clothing and Textiles," *Clio: Women, Gender, History*, no. 40 (2014): 157–178; Daniel Roche, *Le peuple de Paris: Essai sur la culture populaire au XVIIIe siècle* (Paris: Aubier Montaigne, 1981); Roche, *La culture des apparences: Une histoire du vêtement (XVIIe–XVIIIe siècle)* (Paris: Fayard, 1989); Roche, *Histoire des choses banales: Naissance de la consommation dans les sociétés traditionnelles (XVIIe–XIXe siècle)* (Paris: Fayard, 1997); and Michel de Certeau, *Invention du quotidien*, 2 vols. (Paris: Gallimard, 1980). On colonial material culture, see Ashli White, *Revolutionary Things: Material Culture and Politics in the Late Eighteenth-Century Atlantic World* (New Haven, CT: Yale University Press, 2011); Sophie White, *Wild Frenchmen and Frenchified Indians: Culture and Race in Colonial Louisiana* (Philadelphia: University of Pennsylvania Press, 2012).

15   Walter Johnson, "On Agency," *Journal of Social History* 37, no. 1 (2003): 113–124.

ACKNOWLEDGMENTS

I THANK MEMBERS of my family for tolerating abstractness of mind, irregularity of habit, failure to visit, and general negligence toward household duties. My daughter Althea has been a source of light since the instant of her birth. Her forgiving nature made this book possible. Christopher Schmidt-Nowara, Althea's father, died during the research phase of this project, yet shaped it in innumerable ways. He is always with us.

Phyllis Friedberg, my mother, to whom I dedicate this book, was one of the few people who thought there could be a book about slaves in Paris. I am grateful to the brilliant Abigail Mauldin, my sister, who spent late nights editing drafts and created both maps in this book. My father, Paul Spieler, shuttled back and forth across the Atlantic Ocean to make possible research trips to distant archives. I am indebted to my sister Cassie Spieler for holding me up in the worst of times and for everything she taught me about architecture, movement, and space years ago, which made me a different historian. My brother, Benjamin Spieler, classicist-philologist-doctor-officer, the world's last humanist, has been immensely encouraging during the whole of my career as a historian. I thank Dorothy Friedberg, my aunt, for instilling in me a love of urban exploration. My aunt and uncle Emily Spieler and Gregory Wagner have gone out of their way to support this project to the point of risking their health during the outbreak of COVID.

I could not have embarked on this book without the enthusiasm of Kathleen McDermott at Harvard University Press. David Armitage, Lauren Benton, and Simon Schama were early to see the potential of the project. Laurie's understanding of jurisdictional complexity helped me to develop the book's legal framework, while David fired my interest in globalizing the history of Europe. Simon has been a dazzling, avuncular, and forgiving

230   **Acknowledgments**

mentor since the days I called him from gas station pay phones (Cayenne, Roxbury) and wandered around campus with my dog. Stephen Sawyer, Brian Schiff, and other colleagues at the American University of Paris helped me during the writing process by creating a regular forum for the presentation of chapter drafts. Heartfelt thanks to participants from outside AUP in those discussions—Jennifer Boitin, Joshua Cole, Judith Surkis, Thomas Dodman, and Joseph la Hausse de la Louvière—for their invaluable suggestions. My former colleagues Albert Wu and Michelle Kuo, the readers I always wanted, provided astute editorial comments throughout the writing of this book.

I am blessed with friends who are extraordinary French historians. Gillian Weiss stirred my interest years ago by voicing skepticism about the free-soil doctrine and has followed this project to the very end. Cécile Vidal has been shoulder-to-shoulder with me for almost a decade. As ally, friend, teacher, and sounding board, she helped me to develop an approach rooted in social history, sharpened my argument, and led me through an astonishing array of sprawling historiographies. Christy Pichichero has helped me to discover new framings for my research, offered acute comments throughout the writing process, and leavened the sadness of what we study through her sheer zest for life.

I thank Marie Houllemare and François-Joseph Ruggiu for inviting me to their Sorbonne seminar on two occasions, where I sketched ideas that have ripened into this book. Through them, I learned to think on different levels of scale, nourished by their wide-angle approaches to imperial history. François-Joseph eventually helped to take this book over the finish line by correcting a penultimate version of the manuscript. I am indebted to Marie and her husband, Stephane Jettot, for their many quiet acts of neighborly kindness since I moved to France.

During my residential fellowship at the Stanford Humanities Center (2017–2018), I joined a remarkable group of scholars who became my family for ten months. I thank Caroline Winterer, director, and Andrea Rees Davies, associate director, for curating a magical place. At Stanford, I had the opportunity to soak up the creativity and learnedness of scholars around me, including Kristen Mann, Philippa Levine, Kate Van Orden, Londa Schiebinger, and Giovanna Cesarani. Melanie Lamotte, Daniel Ohayon, Elizabeth Marcus, and Daniel Lee brought joy and warmth to a year of new beginnings.

Acknowledgments   231

I have been lucky to present sections of the manuscript at many workshops in France, in the United States, and in the ether of the internet. I began thinking about slaves in Paris long ago, while preparing papers for conferences in 2012—the first, on sovereignty, at NYU and organized by Stefanos Geroulanos, Zvi Ben-Dor Benite, and Nicole Jerr; the second, on law and the French Atlantic, organized by Richard Ross at the Newberry Library. I am grateful to Richard and Stefanos for helping me to embark on this journey. The 2017 Notre Dame–London conference about biographical narratives of enslaved people, organized by Sophie White and the late Trevor Burnard, brought a new perspective to my reading of legal documents.

Under the leadership of Rebecca Spang, my friend for thirty years, the eighteenth-century workshop in Bloomington, Indiana, in 2018 helped me to develop an accessible approach to eighteenth-century law. Sincere thanks to Ashli White for inviting me in 2019 to workshop portions of the book at the University of Miami. I will never repay my debt to Kendra Field for her steadiness while hosting me at Tufts during a descending global lockdown. I thank Jeff Horn, David Troyansky, and participants in the New York History Group for their thoughtful remarks on chapter drafts. Clément Thibaud, Nathan Perl-Rosenthal, Julie Hardwick, Jennifer Heuer, and others who attended the Age of Revolutions e-seminar helped me to work through knots in my Julien chapter during an illuminating discussion of race and rights. I further thank Shandiva Banerjee, Ian Coller, Vincent Denis, Lorelle Semley, Sue Peabody, and other participants in the "Policing Black Presences" working group for commenting on an early version of Chapter 2. Pierre Boulle was generous in volunteering to read and meticulously comment on my unpublished "Black Presences" workshop paper; revised portions of that essay have since found their way into this book. I am also grateful to Alessandro Stanziani for his illuminating remarks on domestic labor and his editorial comments as I revised the introduction.

With the sponsorship of the University of Southern California, Nathan Perl-Rosenthal enabled an online workshop of the whole manuscript in April 2023 with the participation of Michelle McKinley, legal historian of Latin America, and Colin Jones, cultural historian of all things French. They came at the manuscript from different disciplinary angles, and their contrasting perspectives improved the book immeasurably. Even before that event, Colin had come to the aid of this book by swooping in to share long

232 *Acknowledgments*

and incisive written comments on drafts and lead me toward a richer and higher knowledge of just about everything including, of course, Paris.

I have incurred many debts to friends in Paris, near Paris, and on other continents. To Jean Hébrard and Martha Jones, for their kindness and solidarity during our mourning. To Regine Féline and Ambroise Voundi for their graciousness as hosts during my research trip with Althea to Martinique. To Noga Arika, Victoria de Grazia, Elizabeth Foster, Michelle Hoffman, Silyane Larcher, Natasha Lehrer, Vanessa Lincoln, Joy de Menil—whom I cherish for their conversation and because they are themselves.

Finally, I wish to thank the whole team at Harvard University Press, especially Joseph Pomp, for their generosity as interlocutors, and Brian Ostrander of Westchester Publishing Services for his careful work on the manuscript.

INDEX

The letter *f* or *t* following a page number denotes a figure or table, respectively.

Abbey Saint-Martin-des-Champs, 79, 80, 89, 91f, 92–94, 101–102

abduction. *See* kidnapping

abolitionism: colonies not enacting, 125, 128, 147–148; freedom not tied to, 164; Hérault de Séchelles and, 124–125; Julien and, 128–129; medallion on, 162f, 163, 226n122; Ourika's story and, 130, 136–137, 144, 145, 147–148, 152, 155–156, 163; Parisian opposition to, 165–166; Pauline and, 72–73; silence on, 11; societal outlets for expressions of, 227n11

Aché, Anne-Antoine, Vice-Admiral, Comte de, 122

Adonis. *See* Jean, alleged slave of Coustard

Almanzor, Charles-Louis, 122

Amat, Jean-Joseph, 80, 81, 82

Anson, Louis-Joseph, 117–118

archives: anonymous people in, 54; of the Bastille, 3, 7, 8, 17, 41; ego documents in, 166–167; of French colonial empire, 10–12; invisibility and silence on slaves in, 10–14, 131, 166, 167; Jean in, 8, 17–18; Julien in, 8, 106–107, 110, 128–129; of Kersaint, 8–9, 10; Lucidor in, 8, 79–82, 88–89, 94–95; of masters and their households, 10, 11, 14, 20; Ourika in, 8, 130–132; of Paris Court of Admiralty, 7–10, 17, 27, 98, 164–165; Pauline in, 9, 49, 51–53, 55–56

arrests and imprisonment: colonial laws and, 9–10, 29; of Jean, 18, 36, 43; of Julien, 103, 106, 108, 123; lettres de cachet as order for (*see* lettres de cachet); of Lucidor, 83–88; of Mailly de Nesle, 43, 186–187n91; military service vs., 18, 34–40, 88; of Pauline, 9, 49, 62–64, 75–76; research from records of, 2, 3, 7–11 (*see also* archives); return to masters following, 1, 8–9, 18; slave hunts leading to (*see* slave hunts); violence with, 18, 32–33

Asante, 82–83

Azanda, 82

Babette Elizabeth ("Pélagie"), 81

Balthazar, Victor, alleged slave of Archer, 1

Balthazar ("Favory"), alleged slave of Dudresnay Desroches, 2

baptism: freedom maxim tied to, 172n3; interracial family ties and, 116–117; of Jean, 42, 44; names and, 54–55, 116–117; of Pauline, 54–55; registration listing, 79–81; slave ownership and, 33, 42, 53–55

Baptiste, 88

Barante, Amable-Guillaume-Prosper Brugière de, 156, 224n97

Bardin, Pierre, 94–95

Barth, Fredrik, 15–16

233

234 *Index*

Bastille: Archives of, 3, 7, 8, 17, 41; view of, 86f

Baudelle, Julien. *See* Julien, alleged slave of Baudelle

Baudelle, Julien Rose, 105–106, 115–116

Baudelle, Reine. *See* Ruste de Rezeville, Reine (née Baudelle)

Beaumarchais, Pierre-Augustin Caron de, 24–26, 174n17, 181n26. *See also* Lucas, Ambroise

Beauvau, Anne-Louise de, 145–146, 216n3, 222n81. *See also* Poix, Philippe-Louis de Noailles, Prince de

Beauvau, Charles-Juste de, Prince de, 130, 136, 138, 144, 145, 152, 166

Beauvau, Princesse de. *See* Rohan-Chabot, Marie-Charlotte de, Princesse de Beauvau

Bedout, Jacques, 140–141

benevolence, 47, 132, 156, 166

Bernard, Samuel, 67, 96, 204n18, 208n62

Biron, Amélie de (née de Boufflers), 71, 199n97

Biron, Armand-Louis de Gontaut, Duc de, 71

birth certificates, 117–118

Blancheton, Catherine de (née de Salins), 83–84, 87, 96–98, 100, 203–204n16

Blancheton, Pierre-Philibert de, 77, 80, 83–84, 97–98, 203–204n16

Blot, Marie-Cécile-Pauline, Comtesse de (née Ennery), 135, 153–154

Bonaparte, Napoleon, 140, 146–148, 152

Boucaux, alleged slave of Verdelin, 5

Boufflers, Stanislas, Chevalier (later Marquis) de: background of, 137–140; opera-ballet inspired by, 218n18; *Ourika* and, 130, 132, 136–137, 140, 141–144, 153, 166, 216n1; slave trade and, 130, 132–133, 135–137, 138–144; special objects or love tokens of, 141, 142–144, 166; Theleman and, 8, 137, 175n25

Boulle, Pierre, 175nn22,24, 204n21, 231

bounties, 29, 61

Bourbon, Island of. *See* Réunion

Bourval, François, 8, 88–89, 205n32

Bouvet de Lozier, Jean-Baptiste-Charles: background of, 52–53, 58–59, 61, 149, 189n4; Pauline and, 48–59, 61–65, 67, 72–76, 164

Bouvet de Lozier, Pauline (née David), 54–55, 56, 58, 189nn4,6

Brancas, Louis-Paul, Marquis de, 20, 71–72, 85

Brissot, Jacques-Pierre, 124–125, 130

Buffon, Georges-Louis Leclerc, Comte de, 113, 115

business: Boufflers's views of, 138, 139, 142–144; by slaves, 49, 51–52, 55–58, 61–62, 72–74; slave trade as (*see* slave trade)

Capolin, household of Pajot de Villers, 84–85

Castellane-Esparron, Gaspard-Constantin-Boniface, Vicomte de, 67, 68–71

Castellane-Esparron, Marguerite-Renée de (née Fournier de Varennes), 6, 67–71, 73, 76, 174n18

Castries, Maréchal de, 107, 132, 136

Catholicism, 37, 53–54, 80, 192n27

Celse, Jean-Balthazar, 67–68

Chambord, Château de, 35, 35f

charivari, 92–93

Chateaubriand, François-René de, 155, 156–157, 159, 223n92

Chemitz, chaudronnier, and spouse, 102

Chenon, Pierre, Commissaire, 103–105

Chenonceau, Château de, 97, 97f

Chépy, Nicolas, 127

children: birth certificates of, 117–118; enslaved, exhibits of, 113, 114f, 115; gifting of, 83, 84–85, 130, 132–137, 141–142, 144, 149, 153–154; military service of, 36; mixed-race, 105, 111, 115–118, 121 (*see also* Julien, alleged slave of Baudelle); plantation inheritances of, 31; slave trade in, 10, 22–23, 29, 55, 82, 130–137. *See also by name*

Choiseul, Louise-Honorine, Duchesse de (née Crozat), 71–72

Choiseul-Stainville, Etienne-Francais, Duc de Choiseul, 50, 76, 119, 138, 180n15, 186n87, 190n14

clothing and accoutrements: collars and, 25f, 26; for Jean, 29; livery as, 24–26, 25f, 28–29, 104; national color of, 109, 110; prisoners making, 64; sale of, 28–29, 30f, 104; slaves making, 56–57

Code Noir, 29, 31, 50–53, 56, 59–60, 61–62, 115–117, 192n27

Colabeau, Charles, 76. *See also* French Company of the Indies

collars, slave, 25f, 26

colonial empire. *See* French colonial empire

Conan, Armille, 121

Corinne, alleged slave of Marchand-Dumée, 5, 209n68; arrest with household, 40–41, 100

corporate affiliations, 78. *See also* guilds

Coustard, Guy: Jean and, 17–18, 33–34, 41–45; in Paris, 19–20; violence of, 33–34, 42, 43

Coustard, Jean-Jacques, 18

Crispin, Louis-Camille, 26

Crozat, Antoine, 21, 67, 71

Crozat, Pierre, 21

Curran, Andrew, 113, 115

David, Antoine Lélio, 58

David, Pierre-Félix-Barthélemy, 58, 71, 189n5, 199n97

Declaration of the Rights of Man and Citizen, 67, 108, 157

degeneration theory, 113, 115

Delaval, Jean-Pierre-Louis, 106, 108–110, 123

Desperrières, Marie-Françoise Boisgautier, 19–21

Diderot, Denis, 12–13, 72, 90

Diethelm, Marie-Bénédicte, 154

Dorigny, Marcel, 15

dress. *See* clothing and accoutrements

Ducluzeau, Marie-Adélaïde, 159, 161

dueling/dueling masters, 77–78, 87, 88–95, 168, 206n38

Dupin, Claude, 96–97

Dupin, Louise, 96, 97

Dupin de Francueil, Louis-Claude, 77–78, 95–98

Dupin de Francueil, Marie-Aurore (née de Saxe), 96

Dupleix, Jeanne Albert, 62

Dupleix, Joseph-François, 62

Duras, Claire de (née de Kersaint): family and status of, 147–153; notebook of, 153–154; *Ourika* by, 131–132, 144–145, 146–163, 166–167; salons by, 131, 149, 153, 154–157, 161; self reflected in *Ourika*, 144, 148–149, 166–167

Duras, Amédée-Bretagne-Malo de Durfort, Duc de, 147–148, 151–152, 153, 161

Durouzeau, Denis, 51, 73

Épinay, Louis-Denis Lalive de Bellegarde d', 71–72

Épinay, Louise-Florence-Pétronille, Marquise de (née Tardieu d'Esclavelles), 71–72, 96

Esther, alleged slave of Mallecot, 24

Estoupan de Laval, Jean-Baptiste, 58

Estoupan de Saint-Jean, Blaise, 58

Estoupan de Saint-Jean, Charles-Antoine, 58

Estoupan de Saint-Jean, Pierre, 58

Farge, Arlette, 4, 7, 27

Faubourg Sainte-Antoine, 79, 86f, 202n8, 208n54

Faubourg Saint-Honoré, 93; rue du, 145

ferrailleurs, 90–92, 168

236   *Index*

feudalism, 43–45

Figueret, alleged slave of Noronha, 27–28

Fontenelle, Charles-François-Antoine Saillenfest de, 117–118

Foucault, Michel, 4, 7, 26

France: attempted nonwhite expulsion from, 50, 147, 186n87, 190n14; banning of nonwhites from, 120, 123, 132, 147; colonial empire of (*see* French colonial empire); demographics of 18th century, 2–3, 175n24; freedom maxim of (*see* freedom maxim); slaves in (*see* slaves in Paris)

France, Isle de. *See* Mauritius

Francisque, alleged slave of Brignan, 5–6, 109, 120

François, alleged slave of Saige, 76, 100

freedom maxim (*"there are no slaves in France"*): auction of naval prisoners and, 37–38; historian narratives based on, 4–7; invalidity of, 9, 106–107; legal cases citing, 5–6, 50–51, 73, 108, 164–165; Paris as imagined refuge due to, 1–2, 9; text of, 172n3

free people of color: arrests and imprisonment of, generally, 6–8, 100, 104–105; attempted expulsion of from France, 50, 147, 186n87, 190n14; impressment of into military, 37; insecure status of, 50, 77–79, 98–102, 115–116, 125, 128–129; Julien as, 106–108, 110–113, 123, 124–125, 127–129, 164; kidnapping of (*see* kidnapping); Lucidor as, 77, 80, 81–82, 98, 164; Ourika as, 164; Pauline as, 9, 51–52, 55, 58, 61–62, 65, 75, 164; purchase of slaves by for freedom, 57–58; registration of, 79–81, 98–100; self-purchase by slaves to become, 51–52, 58, 61–62, 72, 190–191n18; slave hunts for, 6, 7, 99–100

French colonial empire: abolition not in effect in, 125, 128, 147–148; archives from, 10–12; business and money of slaves in, 49, 55–58, 61–62, 73–74; Code Noir of, 29, 31, 50–53, 56, 59–60, 61–62, 115–117, 192n27; development of, 15; French Revolution reforms not applied to, 125, 128; kidnapping to send to (*see* kidnapping); marriage into Parisian society in, 19–21, 68; military service and, 34–40; Paris society and, 9–10, 14–16, 19–26, 31, 49, 68–73, 76, 165–166; Seven Years War effects on, 49; slave hunts in, 29, 59–61; slave trade and (*see* slave trade); violence in, 9–10, 33–34, 38–39, 50–51, 59–61, 195n53. *See also* Martinique; Mauritius; Réunion; Saint-Domingue

French Company of the Indies: Bouvet and, 58–59; headquarters of, 2, 14, 21; police ties to, 76; records of, 14, 22–23; slave trade by, 52–53, 56, 82–83

French Revolution: Declaration of the Rights of Man and Citizen in, 67, 108, 157; Julien's case and, 108, 123–128; Ourika's experience and portrayal affected by, 145–146, 152, 157; people of color in, 67; reform limits exposed by, 70, 108, 124–128

Fusée-Aublet, Jean-Baptiste-Christian, 121

Genlis, Stephanie Félicité du Crest, Comtesse de, 135, 157

Gérard, François, 159

gifting of slaves, 83, 84–85, 130, 132–137, 141–142, 144, 149, 153–154

Giraud de Crézol, Marie-Catherine Elisabeth, 45–47

Godwin, William, 37

Gontaut, Antoinette-Eustachie, Duchesse de (née Crozat du Châtel), 71

Gratia, alleged slave of Courcel, 7–8

Grouchet, Claire dit Calalou (aka Marie-Elisabeth Bonne), 118
Grouchet, Pierre-Philippe de, 118
Gruel, Marie-Geneviève, 57
guilds, 77–78, 89–94
Guinea Company, 21, 72, 96, 199n97
Guyot de Mongeot, Louis, 33–34

Hall, Gwendolyn Midlo, 17
Hazard, Louis-Pierre, 28, 104
Hélène, alleged slave of Ronseray, 76, 118–119, 120
Hérault de Séchelles, Marie-Jean, Advocate-General, 107, 110–112, 123–125
Hinduism, 53–54, 62
Hôtel de Toulouse, 65–68, 69f, 73–75, 201n110
Hôtel Lambert, 98, 99f
Houdetot, Elisabeth-Sophie-Françoise, Comtesse de (née Lalive de Belle-garde), 71
Humboldt, Alexander, 155, 156
Hume, David, 47
Hurson, Charles-Marin, 116–117

imprisonment. See arrests and imprisonment
interracial marriage, 5, 88–89, 100, 115, 119, 121–122, 147, 172n6
invisibility: in archives, 10–14, 166, 167; of Ourika, 159, 161, 163; slaves' societal role despite, 3, 20
Islam, 53–54, 62
Isle de France. See Mauritius

Jean, alleged slave of Coustard, 17–47; as Adonis, 17, 42, 44, 187–188n100; in archives, 8, 17–18; arrest and imprisonment of, 18, 36, 43; baptism of, 42, 44; colonial-Parisian society context for, 19–26, 31; Coustard and, 17–18, 33–34, 41–45; lettre de cachet

for, 18, 36, 40–42; Mailly de Nesle and, 18, 19, 29, 33, 42–47, 187–188n100; military service and, 18, 34–40; overview of, 17–19; policing and judicial system context for, 18, 23–24, 26–29, 31–34, 40–41; racial epithets and, 41–42; registration of, 34, 45; on slave ship, 131; violence toward, 18–19, 33, 42, 43, 167
Jean-Baptiste, alleged slave of La Prise-Héligon, 6
Johannot, Henri-Alfred, 159, 160f
Joly de Fleury, Omer, 6, 31, 67, 121
judges: colonial slave laws and, 18, 29, 31–32, 50–52, 103–104, 107–109
Julien, alleged slave of Baudelle, 103–129; in archives, 8, 106–107, 110, 128–129; arrest and imprisonment of, 103, 106, 108, 123; escape and concealment of, 106; familial relations and, 105–106, 115–118, 120–121, 128; freedom maxim and, 106–107, 108; freedom of, 106–108, 110–113, 123, 124–125, 127–129, 164; French Revolution and, 108, 123–128; interracial marriage and, 115, 119, 121–122; kidnapping of, 103–105, 106–107, 108–109, 123; legal case of, 105, 106–112, 123–124, 127–128; lettres de cachet for, 108, 112, 123; names and, 105, 108, 117–118, 120–121, 128; race laws and, 111, 119–123; racial identity and, 105, 107–123, 114f

Kersaint, Armand-Guy de Coëtnempren de, Vice-Amiral (father of the Duchesse de Duras), 8–9, 10, 148–149, 150
Kersaint, Claire de. See Duras, Claire de (née de Kersaint)
Kersaint, Guy-François de Coëtnempren de, Vice-Amiral (grandfather of the Duchesse de Duras), 149–150

238 *Index*

kidnapping: of Ambroise Lucas, 6, 24–25; of François, 100; of Julien, 103–105, 106–107, 108–109, 123; of Ourika, 130, 131; of Pauline (attempted), 65, 74–75; in slave trade, 131
Kingston, Duchess of, 44

Lafleur, Antoine, alleged slave of Linsens, 1
Landolphe, Jean-François, 125–126
Laperle, Marie-François, 68
La Tête Noire, 28, 30f
La Tour du Pin, Henriette-Lucie Gouvernet de (née Dillon), 152, 153, 226n122
Lavater, Johan-Casper, 112
Law, John, 67
Law, Robin, 17
Le Cat, Claude-Nicolas, 110
Leclerc, Charles Victor Emmanuel, 147
Le Douceur, alleged slave of Amat, 80, 81
L'Empereur, alleged slave of Bouvet, 48, 63, 188n1
Léogane, 19
Lespinasse, Julie de, 71, 153
Lestobec family, 83
lettres de cachet: for arrests and imprisonment, generally, 3–7, 18, 32, 104–105; attacks on use of, 112–113; colonial slave hunts vs., 29; for Hélène, 119; for Jean, 18, 36, 40–42; for Julien, 108, 112, 123; for Lucidor, 85; military and, 5–7, 34, 36–38, 40–41, 50, 108, 189n8; for Pauline, 49, 64, 75, 189n8; police authority to issue, 26, 64; violence and, 18, 32–33
Lévis, Pierre-Marc-Gaston, Duc de, 153
libertinage, 63–64
Lilti, Antoine, 70–71, 73, 200n103
Lircot, Louis, 8, 89–90, 100, 205n35
livery, 24–26, 25f, 28–29, 104

Loff, Crispin, alleged slave of Kersaint, 8–9, 10, 150
Lorient, Pierre, 36
Louis-Joseph, 89
Lucas, Ambroise, 6, 24–25, 174n17. *See also* Beaumarchais, Pierre-Augustin Caron de
Luce Diancra / Diancourt, 6, 67–68, 74, 174n18
Lucidor, André, 77–102; abuse and violence toward family of, 101–102; in archives, 8, 79–82, 88–89, 94–95; arrest and imprisonment of, 83–88; attempted deportation of, 84, 87, 98, 100; background of, 77, 79–80, 82–90, 100; as dueling master / master of arms, 77–78, 87, 88–95, 168; freedom of, 77, 80, 81–82, 98, 164; homes of, 77, 78–79, 91–96, 98, 101–102, 168; insecurity of freedom and, 77–79, 98–102; labor laws and practices affecting, 77–79, 89–94; lettre de cachet for, 85; marriage of children of, 121; patron of, 95–98; registration practices and, 79–82, 98–100; on slave ship, 85, 131; socioeconomic status of, 93–96, 98; sodomy charges against, 85–88
Lucidor, Louis, 89
Lucidor, Louise, 101–102, 121
Lucidor, Marie-Thérèse, 88, 121
Lucidor, Thérèse-Charlotte (née Richard), 88–89, 95, 101

Mailly de Nesle, Charlotte de, Princesse de Nassau-Siegen: feudalism of, 43–45; Jean and, 18, 19, 29, 33, 42–47, 187–188n100; notoriety of, 43, 186–187n91
Malesherbes, Guillaume-Chrétien de Lamoignon de, 121–122
Malézieux, 50
Mallecot, la Dame, 24

Index 239

Malouet, Pierre-Victor, 70, 76

Manufacture royale d'acier d'Amboise, 126–127

Marat, Jean-Paul, 146

Marie-Thérèse, alleged slave of Giraud de Crézol, 45–47

Marion-Dufresne, Marc-Joseph, 55

marriage: colonial-Parisian, 19–21, 68; of Duras, 147–148, 151–152; interracial, 5, 88–89, 100, 115, 119, 121–122, 147, 172n6; of Julien, 128; of Lucidor, 77, 88–89, 100, 205n32; of Lucidor's children, 121; non-Catholic, 53, 192n27

Martinique: abolition not in effect in, 128, 147–148; interracial marriage in, 115; Julien in/removal to, 105, 106, 108, 120, 128–129 (*see also* Julien, alleged slave of Baudelle); Lucidor in, 88; racial identity in, 111, 116–117; removal to, 6, 9, 106, 108, 150; Seven Years War and, 49; Treaty of Amiens on, 147–148

Marville, Claude-Henri Feydeau de, 32–33

Mascarene Islands. *See* Mauritius; Réunion

Maupertuis, Pierre-Louis, 115

Maurepas, Jean-Frédéric Phélypeaux, Comte de, 31, 36–40

Maurice, Maréchal de Saxe, 34–40, 122

Mauritius: Bouvet family and, 58–59, 61–62; business and money of slaves on, 49, 56–58, 61–62; colonial laws and norms on, 52–55, 59–62; Pauline on, 9, 48–49, 52, 54–58, 59, 61–62; religion on, 53–55; slaves sent to, 100

Médor, Jacques, alleged slave of Goupil de Fontenay, 5–6, 173n13

Memoirs of Sophie, The (Duras), 153

Ménilmontant, 93–94, 96, 207n53

Merger, Jean-Baptiste, 19–21

mestif, 105. *See also* mixed-race people

Michel, Gabriel, 21. *See also* French Company of the Indies

military service: of black men and slaves, 18, 34–40, 88–89, 184n62; of Jean, 18, 34, 39–40; of Lucidor, 88–89; of prisoners, 37–38, 88. *See also* navy

mina slaves, 17

mixed marriage. *See* interracial marriage

mixed-race people, 105, 111, 115–118, 121. *See also* Julien, alleged slave of Baudelle; racial identity

Molé, Mathieu de, 156

Montaran, Jacques-Marie-Jérôme, Michau de, 21

Montmartel, Jean, Pâris de, 21. *See also* French Company of the Indies

Moreau de Saint-Méry, Médéric-Louis-Elie, 111

Muron, Jean-Baptiste, Inspector, 41–42, 52, 63, 65, 67, 74–76

names: baptism and, 54–55, 116–117; familial, 117–118, 120–121, 128; of Jean, 17, 42, 44, 187–188n100; of Julien, 105, 108, 120–121, 128; of Ourika, 130, 136, 142, 216n1; of Pauline, 54–55

Nassau-Siegen, Emmanuel-Ignace, Prince de, 43

Nassau-Siegen, Maximilian-Guillaume-Adolphe, Prince de, 43

Nassau-Siegen, Princesse de. *See* Mailly de Nesle, Charlotte de, Princesse de Nassau-Siegen

navy: auction of prisoners by, 37; colonial governance by, 12, 14; fees for non-white admission to France by, 120; lettres de cachet by, 5–7, 34, 40–41, 50, 108, 189n8; manumission opposition by, 116; racial epithets by, 42; slave trade and, 139–141

Négresse, La, slave ship, 125–126

Noailles, Adrien-Maurice, Duc de, 45–47, 166

Noronha, Bishop of, 27–28

240 *Index*

Olive, alleged slave of Aubry, 120

Orléans, Louise-Marie-Adélaïde, Duchesse d' (née Bourbon-Penthièvre), 141–142

Orléans, Louis-Philippe-Joseph, Duc d', 112, 127, 135

Ourika, 130–163; allowances of, 216n3; in archives, 8, 130–132; background of, 130–132; Beauvau family and, 130–131, 136, 144, 145–146, 152–154, 157, 216n3; Boufflers and, 130, 132, 136–137, 140, 141–144, 153, 166, 216n1 (*see also* Boufflers, Stanislas, Chevalier (later Marquis) de); death of, 130–131, 146–147, 148–149, 153, 167; freedom of, 164; gifting of children and, 130, 132–137, 141–142, 144, 149, 153–154; as literary figure, 131–132, 144–145, 146–163, 166–167; name of, 130, 136, 142, 216n1; plays about, 161–162; racial identity and, 158–159, 160f, 161–163, 224n103; as special object or love token, 141, 142–144, 166; visual images of, 159, 160f, 161

Ourika (Duras), 131–132, 144–145, 146–163, 166–167

Ozenne, Pierre, 106, 107–108, 123–127

Palais Royal, 112–113, 114f, 135

Paris: attempted nonwhite expulsion from, 50, 147, 186n87, 190n14; colonial society and, 9–10, 14–16, 19–26, 31, 49, 68–73, 76, 165–166 (*see also* French colonial empire); as imagined refuge for slaves, 1–2, 7, 9; as imperial city, 4, 14–16; police and judicial system in (*see* arrests and imprisonment; judges; police); slaves in (*see* slaves in Paris)

Pauline, alleged slave of Bouvet, 48–76; in archives, 9, 49, 51–53, 55–56; arrest and imprisonment of, 9, 49, 62–64, 75–76; attempted kidnapping of, 65, 74–75; background of, 48–49, 52–55,

58; Bouvet and, 48–59, 61–65, 67, 72–76, 164; business and money of, 49, 51–52, 56–58, 61–62, 72–74; colonial laws and norms as context for, 50–56, 59–62, 73–74; complaint filed against, 63, 164; escape and concealment of, 9, 49–52, 65–68, 70, 72–76, 165; freedom of, 9, 51–52, 55, 58, 61–62, 65, 75, 164; legal case of, 9, 50–52, 55–56, 72–76; lettres de cachet for, 49, 64, 75, 189n8; name of, 54–55; threats and violence toward, 50–51, 59, 61

Peabody, Sue, 4–5

Pèdre, alleged slave of Guer, 41–42, 76

Penthièvre, Louis-Jean-Marie de Bourbon, Duc de, 34, 65, 67, 70, 75

Pharaon, Jean-Louis, 89, 100

Pierre, alleged slave of Bouvet, 48, 63, 188nn1–2

Place des Victoires, 65–67, 66f, 70, 74–75, 165

Poisson, Charles-Gabriel, Inspector, 103–104

Poix, Philippe-Louis de Noailles, Prince de, 145, 151–152

Poix, Princesse de. *See* Beauvau, Anne-Louise de

police: arrests and imprisonment by (*see* arrests and imprisonment); authority and role of, 26–29, 64; batons of, 103–104; race laws on methods of, 119–120, 122–123; racialized culture of, 99–100; slave hunts by (*see* slave hunts); violence reported to, 33–34, 102

Polidor, alleged slave of Famin, 28, 33

Poncet de la Grave, Guillaume, 41, 119

Pont Neuf, 103, 104f, 105, 106

Portal, Pierre-Barthélemy, Baron, 155

Porte Sainte-Antoine, 86f

pregnancy, declarations of, 117

Prévost de la Croix family, 83

privileged places, 78–79, 202n8, 208n54. *See also* Abbey Saint-Martin-des-Champs

Index 241

Quenaut, Guillaume, 80–82, 90, 92, 100

racial epithets, 41–42, 105, 121, 135, 172n6
racial identity, 105, 107–123, 114f,
    158–159, 160f, 161–163, 224n103
Raimond, Julien, 111
Rama, alleged slave of Estaing and
    Brancas, 84–85
registration of slaves / nonwhites, 5, 7,
    31–32, 34, 45–46, 79–82, 98–100
religion. *See* Abbey Saint-Martin-des-
    Champs; baptism; *specific sects*
Repentigny, Louis, Le Gardeur de, 139
research: archives informing (*see*
    archives); contiguous worlds of slaves
    informing, 13–14, 167–168; history
    and methodology for, 2–16; invisi-
    bility and silence effects on, 10–14,
    166, 167; prior historians and, 4–7,
    12–13, 15–16
Réunion, 48–50, 52, 56–63, 149, 156
Robbe-Grillet, Alain, 167
Rohan-Chabot, Marie-Charlotte de,
    Princesse de Beauvau, 130–131, 146,
    152–154, 157, 221n62
Rouillé, Antoine-Louis de, Comte de
    Jouy, 17, 39, 41, 46
Rousseau, Jean-Jacques, 72, 73, 79, 96
royal writs. *See* lettres de cachet
Rue de Richelieu, 21, 165
Rue du Faubourg Saint-Honoré, 145
Rue Saint-Louis, 98, 99f
Ruste de Rezeville, Henri-Jacques-
    Claude, 108, 128, 150
Ruste de Rezeville, Reine (née Baudelle),
    105–108, 115, 120–121, 124, 127–128

Sabran, Eléonore de, 135, 136, 139–143, 166
Saint-Domingue: grant of land in, 46;
    Haiti formed from, 129, 147; Jean
    enslaved in, 17, 41, 45 (*see also* Jean,
    alleged slave of Coustard); Lucidor
    and, 89; Paris society ties to, 15, 18,
    19–21, 31, 46, 68–73, 76; racial iden-

tity in, 111; settlement of, 19; slave
    hunts in, 29; slavery restored in, 147;
    slaves sent to, 5–8, 18, 31, 76, 82, 112,
    139–141, 150; violence in, 33–34, 195n53
Saint-Pierre, Jacques-Henri, Bernardin
    de, 60
Salaberry, Charles de, 72
Salaberry, Charles-Victoire-François de,
    72, 75
Salins, Catherine de. *See* Blancheton,
    Catherine de (née de Salins)
Salins, Hugues de, 83, 96–97
salons, 71, 73, 131, 135, 149, 153, 154–157,
    161, 200n103
Salpêtrière prison, 64
Sambo, household of the Duchess of
    Kingston, 44
Sand, George, 96, 97
Sartine, Antoine de, 7, 63, 67, 74–76,
    119, 121–122, 165, 174n17, 190n14
Saxe, Maurice, Maréchal de, 34–40, 122
Scipio, in Orléans household, 135–136
Ségur, Louis-Philippe, Comte de, 20,
    139–141
Ségur, Philippe-Henri, Marquis de, 20, 140
self-purchase by slaves, 51–52, 58, 61–62,
    72, 190–191n18
serfdom, 44
Serval, Hyacinthe, 91
Seven Years War, 49–50, 59, 100–101, 102
silence: of archives, 11–14, 131, 166, 167;
    of naming without baptism, 54; of
    Ourika, 132, 141; of Pauline, 51
slave hunts: bounties from, 29, 61;
    colonial, 29, 59–61; free people of
    color as targets of, 6, 7, 99–100; for
    Hélène, 118–119; for Jean, 18; in
    Paris, 23–24, 27–28, 45–46, 49–50,
    75–76, 118–119; for Pauline, 9, 49, 52
slaves in Paris: arrests and imprisonment
    of (*see* arrests and imprisonment);
    colonial influences on (*see* French
    colonial empire); demographics of,
    2–3, 10, 175n24; freedom maxim

242 **Index**

slaves in Paris (*continued*)
encouraging (*see* freedom maxim); hunts for (*see* slave hunts); registration of (*see* registration of slaves / nonwhites); research on (*see* research); self-purchase by (*see* self-purchase by slaves). *See also by name*
slave trade: African context for, 82–83, 126, 132–133, 138–139, 141; Boufflers in, 130, 132–133, 135–137, 138–144; bounties in, 29, 61; changes in, 83; children as victims of, 10, 22–23, 29, 55, 82, 130–137; colonial empire built on (*see* French colonial empire); Duras's family ties to, 149–151, 156; French Company of the Indies in (*see* French Company of the Indies); growth in, 15, 19, 82, 100, 133–134, 133t–134t; love tokens transported via, 143; Middle Passage in, 10, 126, 131, 140; Ozenne in, 106, 108, 123, 125–126; Paris society and, 14–16, 19, 21–22, 71–72; race and, 100, 107–108; revival of, 147; start of French, 15, 52; statistics on, 133–134, 133t–134t; value of slaves and, 22–23, 57–58, 60–61, 84–85
Society for the Abolition of Slavery medallion, 162f, 163, 226n122
Society of the Friends of the Blacks, 73, 124, 130, 136, 163
Stuart, Marguerite, 64

Talleyrand-Périgord, Georges-Julie, Vicomte de, 20
Tassime, Antoine, 122
Télémaque, household of Trudaine de Montigny, 32
theft: of Pauline's money, 49, 51; by slaves, 28–29, 104
Theleman, Joseph, 8, 137, 175n25
Traité de la couleur de la peau humaine, La (Treatise on the color of human skin) (Le Cat), 109–110

Trudaine, Daniel-Charles, 32
Trudaine de Montigny, Jean-Charles-Philibert, 32
Turgot, Étienne-François, 134–135

Ussé, Château d', 151, 151f, 159

value: of currencies, 57; of slaves, 22–23, 57–58, 60–61, 84–85; of special objects or love tokens, 143–144, 166
Vaudreuil, Joseph de Rigaud, Marquis de, 20
Vaudreuil, Louis-Philippe, de Rigaud de, 20
Vaudreuil, Marie-Claire-Françoise, Marquise de (née Guyot de Lamirande), 20, 22
Vaudreuil, Pierre, de Rigaud de, 20
Vendredi, gift of Boufflers, 135–136, 216n1
Villèle, Joseph de, 156
violence: colonial, 9–10, 33–34, 38–39, 50–51, 59–61, 195n53; Jean experiencing, 18–19, 33, 42, 43, 167; lettres de cachet enabling, 18, 32–33; Lucidor family suffering abuse and, 101–102; Marie-Thérèse experiencing, 46; Ourika's story and, 132, 163; Pauline threatened with, 50–51, 59, 61
Voltaire, 72, 73, 130

Walsh, Antoine, 21
weapons: of Boufflers, 137–138; for dueling or dueling masters, 77–78, 87, 88–95, 168, 206n38; restrictions on, 77–78
Widows of Paradise (Paradise-Whydahs), 65
Wilberforce, William, 155

Zimeo, gift of Boufflers, 135–136, 154, 216n1